Temples, Tithes, and Taxes

Temples, Tithes, and Taxes

The Temple and the Economic Life of Ancient Israel

MARTY E. STEVENS

HENDRICKSON PUBLISHERS

Temples, Tithes, and Taxes:
The Temple and the Economic Life of Ancient Israel
© 2006 by Hendrickson Publishers, Inc.
P. O. Box 3473
Peabody, Massachusetts 01961-3473

ISBN 978-1-56563-934-8

Printed in the United States of America

First Printing — November 2006

Cover Art: The cover artwork shows a scale model the temple compound of the Second Temple in Jerusalem at the time of King Herod the Great (ca. 20 B.C.E.). Location: Holy Land Hotel, Jerusalem, Israel. Photo Credit: Eric Lessing / Art Resource, N.Y. Image reference: ART47964. Used with permission.

Library of Congress Cataloging-in-Publication Data

Stevens, Marty E., 1953–
    Temples, tithes, and taxes : the temple and the economic life of ancient Israel / Marty E. Stevens.
      p. cm.
    Includes bibliographical references and indexes.
    ISBN-13: 978-1-56563-934-8 (alk. paper)
    1. Temple of Jerusalem (Jerusalem) 2. Temple of Jerusalem (Jerusalem)—Finance. 3. Temples—Iraq—Finance. 4. Jews—History—953–586 B.C. 5. Jews—History—586 B.C.–70 A.D. 6. Tithes (Jewish law)—History—To 1500. 7. Taxation—Palestine—History—To 1500. I. Title.
    DS109.3.S84 2006
    330.933′03—dc22
                  2006014961

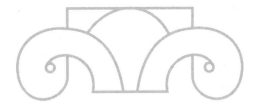

Table of Contents

115350

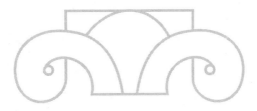

Acknowledgements

This constructive work of scholarship is a product of all my life experiences to date: academy, church, business, and family. First and foremost, I owe a debt of sincere gratitude to my mentors and advisors in graduate school at Union Theological Seminary, William P. Brown and S. Dean McBride Jr. With patient grace, both showed unflagging commitment to developing my scholarly potential and each appreciated the economic perspective I brought to the ancient texts. My professors at Lutheran Theological Southern Seminary initially recognized my potential for scholarship and were strong advocates on my behalf.

My business experience as a Certified Public Accountant and financial management executive was valuable in learning the ways of the world. The adventure of reading ancient texts with financial expertise was undertaken with a commitment to serve the church through biblical scholarship. Three church families in North Carolina formed me into a person of faith: Starmount Presbyterian, Christ Lutheran, and St. John's Lutheran. Finally, and perhaps most importantly, the unfailing love and support of my parents gave me the confidence to follow my vocation.

Any worthwhile contribution is the result of all of these influences, while any errors in fact or judgment are completely my own.

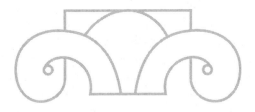

Abbreviations

General

c.	century
ca.	circa
LXX	Septuagint
m.	Mishnah
MT	Masoretic Text

Primary Sources

Ant.	Josephus. *Jewish Antiquities*. Translated by H. St. J. Thackeray and Ralph Marcus. LCL
Geogr.	Strabo. *Geographica*. Translated by Horace L. Jones. LCL
Hist.	Herodotus. *Historae*. Translated by A. D. Godley. LCL
J.W.	Josephus. *Jewish War*. Translated by H. St. J. Thackeray. LCL
Šeqal.	*Šeqalim*
Spec. Laws	Philo. *On the Special Laws*. Translated by F. H. Colson. LCL

Secondary Sources

AASOR	Annual of the American Schools of Oriental Research
AB	Anchor Bible
ABD	*Anchor Bible Dictionary*. Edited by D. N. Freedman. 6 vols. New York, 1992

AJSL	*American Journal of Semitic Languages and Literature*
AnBib	Analecta biblica
BA	*Biblical Archaeologist*
BAR	*Biblical Archaeology Review*
BASOR	*Bulletin of the American Schools of Oriental Research*
BDAG	Bauer, W., F. W. Danker, W. F. Arndt, and F. W. Gingrich. *Greek-English Lexicon of the New Testament and Other Early Christian Literature.* 3d ed. Chicago, 1999
BDB	Brown, F., S. R. Driver, and C. A. Briggs. *A Hebrew and English Lexicon of the Old Testament.* Oxford, 1907
CAD	*The Assyrian Dictionary of the Oriental Institute of the University of Chicago.* Chicago, 1956–
CAH	*Cambridge Ancient History*
CANE	*Civilizations of the Ancient Near East.* Edited by J. Sasson. 4 vols. New York, 1995
CBQ	*Catholic Biblical Quarterly*
ConBOT	Coniectanea biblica: Old Testament Series
CH	Code of Hammurabi from *Law Collections from Mesopotamia and Asia Minor.* 2d ed. Martha T. Roth. SBLWAW 6. Atlanta: Scholars Press, 1997
CHJ	*Cambridge History of Judaism.* Ed. W. D. Davies and Louis Finkelstein. Cambridge, 1984–
EncJud	*Encylcopedia Judaica.* 16 vols. Jerusalem, 1972
HSM	Harvard Semitic Monographs
HSS	Harvard Semitic Series
HUCA	*Hebrew Union College Annual*
IEJ	*Israel Exploration Journal*
JAOS	*Journal of the American Oriental Society*
JBL	*Journal of Biblical Literature*
JBR	*Journal of Bible and Religion*
JCS	*Journal of Cuneiform Studies*
JJS	*Journal of Jewish Studies*
JNES	*Journal of Near Eastern Studies*
JQR	*Jewish Quarterly Review*
JRS	*Journal of Roman Studies*
JSJ	*Journal for the Study of Judaism in the Persian, Hellenistic, and Roman Periods*
JSOTSup	Journal for the Study of the Old Testament: Supplement Series
JSS	*Journal of Semitic Studies*
JTS	*Journal of Theological Studies*

LCL	Loeb Classical Library. Cambridge, Mass.: Harvard University Press, 1900–
NBAD	*Neo-Babylonian Business and Administrative Documents.* Ellen W. Moore. Ann Arbor, 1935
OBO	Orbis biblicus et orientalis
OIP	Oriental Institute Publications
OLA	Orientalia lovaniensia analecta
OTL	Old Testament Library
RCAE	*Royal Correspondence of the Assyrian Empire.* Leroy Waterman. Ann Arbor, 1930–1936
SBLDS	Society of Biblical Literature Dissertation Series
SBLMS	Society of Biblical Literature Monograph Series
SBLSP	*Society of Biblical Literature Seminar Papers*
SBLSymS	Society of Biblical Literature Symposium Series
SBLWAW	Society of Biblical Literature Writings from the Ancient World
TZ	*Theologische Zeitschrift*
UF	*Ugarit-Forschungen*
USQR	*Union Seminary Quarterly Review*
VT	*Vetus Testamentum*
VTSup	Vetus Testamentum Supplements
WUNT	Wissenschaftliche Untersuchungen zum Neuen Testament
YOS	Yale Oriental Series
ZAW	*Zeitschrift für die alttestamentliche Wissenschaft*

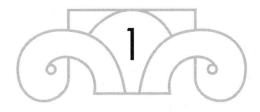

Introductory Matters

This book is about the temple in Jerusalem in its role as the central religious and socioeconomic institution in ancient Israelite society. As the central sanctuary from the time of King Solomon through the time of Jesus, the Jerusalem temple played an important economic role in the community. But why would one even suspect that the Jerusalem temple has anything to do with economics? The cynic may answer, "*Everything* has to do with economics, even religion!" Certainly, there is some truth in that remark, since religious institutions must manage economic resources in their efforts to serve the community. In fact, some would say the major problem with religious institutions today is that they do not pay enough attention to their role as economic enterprises. But the connection between the Jerusalem temple and economics lies not in the overarching role of economics in society, but in the overarching role of the temple in society.

For most of Israel's history, the political and religious authorities cooperated to govern the community in all spheres of life. The temple, therefore, functioned in ancient Israelite society as a central and centralizing institution. Concerned with matters far beyond the modern notion of "religion," the Jerusalem temple played an important role in the economic life of the people and the nation. Yet very little attention has been paid to the economic role of the Jerusalem temple. Most scholarly discussion of the temple has focused on the development of Israelite religion and its relationship to neighboring cultures. Even if scholarship has acknowledged some impact of the temple on economic life, there has been no sustained attention to the question of how the temple functioned economically in ancient Israelite society. I intend to step into this gap.

Basic Terminology

It may be helpful to begin with a brief exploration of some basic terminology regarding ancient societies.[1]

Israel and Judah. The term "Israel" is fraught with multiple meanings—
a person, a small geographic area in the eastern Mediterranean, an even
smaller geographic area, a self-identified religious group. Likewise, "Judah" is
both a person and a geographic area. According to the narrative in Genesis,
the patriarch Abraham began his relationship with YHWH[2] when he was
asked to leave his home and kindred and embark on a journey to "the land
that I will show you" (Gen 12:1).[3] After a detour to Egypt, Abraham and
Sarah settled in the land of Canaan and bore the miracle-baby they named
Isaac ("laughter"). Isaac and Rebekah bore twins, Esau ("hairy") and Jacob
("grabby"). As a grown man who had lived out his "grabby" character in
Canaan and in Haran with his uncle Laban, Jacob wrestled with an angel-
man one night at the River Jabbok. The lasting result, besides a permanent
limp, was that his name was changed to Israel, which may mean "he strives
with God" (Gen 32:28). Later narratives and prophetic oracles used the
name Israel to refer to the person of Jacob, the ancestor of the traditional
twelve tribes, and to the tribal family that descended from the patriarch. The
two names often appear in poetic parallelism: for example: "He (God) declares his words to Jacob, his statutes and ordinances to Israel" (Ps 147:19).

Geographically speaking, Israel was the name designating the entire area
from Dan in the north to Beer-sheba in the south under the united monarchy of King David and his son, King Solomon. This is roughly the territory
of the modern state of Israel. After the death of King Solomon, the united
kingdom split into two kingdoms. The northern kingdom, from just north
of Jerusalem to Dan, took the name Israel for its territory. When the northern kingdom was defeated and assimilated by Assyria in the eighth century,
the remaining southern kingdom appropriated the name Israel, since they
were the remaining on-site heirs to the Israelite identity. More broadly, Israel
was the term used to refer to a religious community that came out of Egypt
under the leadership of Moses and understood themselves to worship

---

[1]For those readers unfamiliar with the transliteration of foreign words, please
see the section "Guide to foreign words" on p. 25 at the end of this chapter.

[2]YHWH is the tetragrammaton ("four letters") representing God's personal
name. The precise vocalization is unknown, although it is often represented as "Yahweh." Out of respect for the Jewish desire to leave the name of God unpronounced,
I will use the four consonants without any vowels to represent God's personal name.

[3]All translations of biblical texts are the author's.

YHWH. This religio-ideological self-designation could be used regardless of geographic location or patriarchal genealogy. Even those who lived in the Diaspora (dispersion) could claim to be members of Israel.

Judah was the name of the southern kingdom formed after the death of King Solomon, from which the term "Jew" later derived. Judah was also the name of a person in the Old Testament, the fourth son of Jacob/Israel, who lent his name to the largest of the traditional twelve tribes.

Ancient Near East (ANE). The ANE is a broad descriptive title for the territories variously inhabited and controlled by the Medes, Persians, Babylonians, Assyrians, Hittites, Arameans, Elamites, Ammonites, Edomites, Moabites, Israelites, and others. Generally speaking, the ANE covers what has traditionally been known as Mesopotamia (modern Iran and southern Iraq), Assyria (northern Iraq and parts of Syria), and Syria-Palestine (modern Syria, Lebanon, Israel, and the Palestinian Authority). Sometimes the term Ancient Near East also includes all the ancient societies of the eastern Mediterranean basin, incorporating Greece and Egypt.

Time. Chronology is divided into two broad eras before and after a point called zero. There is no year zero, however. Previous convention designated these eras as B.C. (Before Christ) and A.D. (*Anno Domini;* Year of the Lord). Sensitivity to non-Christian populations in the world has led to the more recent designations of B.C.E. (Before the Common Era) and C.E. (Common Era). Of course, B.C.E. years count down toward zero, while C.E. years count up from zero. 1 B.C.E. immediately precedes 1 C.E. The numbering of centuries is always ahead of the actual date in years; for example, the sixth century encompasses the years 600–501 B.C.E. or 501–600 C.E.

In this study of the economic role of the Jerusalem temple we are mostly concerned with years B.C.E., since the First Temple was first constructed around 960 B.C.E. and was destroyed permanently in 70 C.E. Although the institution lasted for roughly a millennium, multiple structures served as the Jerusalem temple, and we even speak of time periods in reference to the various buildings. Thus the "First Temple," constructed in the reign of Solomon in the tenth century B.C.E., was destroyed by the Babylonians in 587/6. These centuries are called the First Temple period. The "Second Temple" was (re)built beginning in 520 B.C.E., dedicated in 515 B.C.E., and finally destroyed in 70 C.E. by the Romans. Hence these centuries are the Second Temple period. King Herod undertook a major (re)building effort in the closing years of the first century B.C.E., resulting in what could legitimately be called the "Third Temple," although it is usually included in the Second Temple period.

The years B.C.E. are often categorized in scholarship based on archaeological periods, such as the Bronze Age or the Iron Age. Sometimes it is more

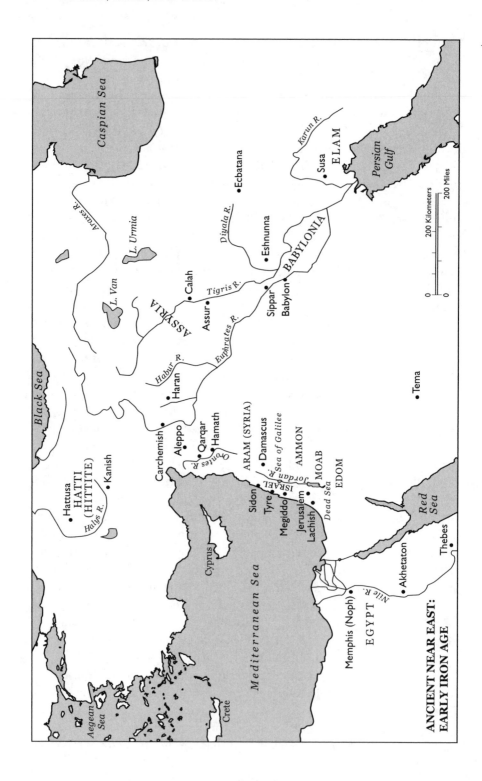

**ANCIENT NEAR EAST:
EARLY IRON AGE**

useful to categorize the centuries based on the dominant empires of the ANE, so we talk about the Neo-Babylonian period or the Persian period. The names of dynasties within these imperial reigns describe smaller segments of time, for example, the Achaemenid dynasty of the Persians or the 25th Egyptian dynasty. For ancient Israel, chronology was punctuated by the Exile, the devastating event of Babylonian deportation and destruction in 587/6 B.C.E. that lasted until the return of the exiles under King Cyrus of Persia in the 530s. Time periods are frequently designated, therefore, as preexilic (before 587/6), exilic (587/6 to 539), or postexilic (after 539).

Temple. Throughout the ANE, a temple was understood to be a focal point of the deity's presence on earth. The divine dwelling place has many names, which can be rendered in English as house, temple, shrine, tabernacle, sanctuary, nave, and holy place. Despite its prominence in the biblical texts, there is no exclusive term for the Jerusalem temple. One would expect that such an important institution in the life of ancient Israelite society for a millennium would have an exclusive term for its designation, something like Temple with a capital T. No such exclusive term exists. The temple in Jerusalem is regularly called "house." Throughout the ANE, the most common term for a temple was the "house" of the deity, the place of divine residence (Hebrew *bayit* when it stands alone or *bêt* when it is combined with another word to mean "house of"[4]). Biblical texts use the terms "house of YHWH" or the "house of God" (or the "house," for short) to designate legitimate temples in Jerusalem, Bethel, and Shiloh. Perhaps even more surprising, "house" also refers to non-legitimate structures in Ephraim and Samaria. Temples devoted to deities other than YHWH, called "house of [deity name]" in the biblical texts, are located in Shechem, Samaria, Beth Shean, Philistia, Egypt, Assyria, and Babylon. So to call the Jerusalem temple "house of YHWH" or "house of God" used the same language as the temple in Ashdod, the "house of Dagon." That is, the awe-inspiring holiness of the site did not derive from the term "house," but rather from the One who took up residence there, whether YHWH or any other god.

The other generic term for a temple in biblical texts is *hêkāl.* The word probably came into Hebrew under Mesopotamian influence from the Akkadian *ekallu* and the Sumerian É.GAL, "great house." When the resident of the "great house" is divine, it is a temple; when the resident is a king, it is a palace. That is, there are plenty of examples in the biblical texts where the term *hêkāl* refers to a temple, usually the Jerusalem temple, and also refers to a

---

[4]We may note here that some conventions of transliteration would render the spelling of "house of" as *beth;* for example, the familiar place names Beth-el (House of God) and Beth-lehem (House of Bread).

royal palace. Again, there is no inherent holiness in the word *hêkāl;* holiness derives from the resident. When these two common terms appear in close proximity to describe one structure, the "house" (*bayit* or *bêt*) generally refers to the overall structure or complex, while the "temple" (*hêkāl*) refers to a large enclosed space located behind the altar. (See the discussion on the construction of the First Temple in chapter two.)

At this juncture one must note that both ancient Israelites and Mesopotamians conceived of the temple as a metaphorical, not a literal divine residence. Even when statues of the gods were present in temples to be clothed, fed, and bathed by temple personnel, the gods were not understood to be *really* dwelling, eating, and bathing. Rather, the statues were symbols of the god's presence there. Everyone, or at least most people, knew that the deity's *real* dwelling was in heaven.

Of course, the biblical texts go a step further than other ancient thinkers by mandating that "You shall never make for yourselves an idol, any likeness that is in the heavens above or that is on the earth beneath, or that is in the waters under the earth. You shall never bow down to them and you shall never serve them" (Exod 20:4–5a; Deut 5:8–9a). In biblical terms, the Jerusalem temple was the place where God caused the divine Name to dwell, thus guaranteeing the divine presence. The divine presence of the Holy One sanctified the space. Accordingly, the Jerusalem temple is also designated as the "holy place" (*miqdāš*), as are sanctuaries in Shechem, Bethel, and Tyre. The wilderness Tabernacle is known as the *miqdāš* and the *miškān,* "indwelling place" in Exodus. In addition to the central "orthodox" temple in Jerusalem, three Jewish temples existed outside of Judah during the Second Temple period: the Temple of YHW in the Jewish mercenary colony on Elephantine Island in southern Egypt; the Temple of Onias in Leontopolis in northern Egypt; and the Samaritan temple on Mount Gerizim, still an object of religious controversy into the first century C.E. (see John 4:20).

The overarching term for worship and its ritual practices, personnel, and accoutrements is "cult," from the Latin *cultus* ("care"). Ancient cults were mainstream demonstrations of devotion to the divine presence involved in all aspects of life. In a complete reversal from its use in discussions about ancient societies, the word has been hijacked in modern parlance to mean something unorthodox and inappropriate.

Offerings. The "tithe" was a cultic ritual throughout the ANE, a mandatory contribution from agriculture and animals, or the equivalent payment in precious metals. Evidence suggests that the compulsory tithe probably amounted to one-tenth of the yearly production or income. These regularized payments were made to local shrines as well as to major temples. A worshiper could also present "gifts" and "offerings"—spontaneous, voluntary

contributions—over and above the amount of the annual tithe in apprecia-
tion for benevolent acts of the deity or to compensate for sinful acts. "Taxes"
were regularized payments owed to the governing political authority, often
charged as a percentage of income or as a specified activity fee; in other
words, taxes were the secular version of tithes. Analogous to sacred gifts and
offerings to the temple, "tribute" was an occasional contribution to the political authority, typically offered by a lesser political authority to avert military
action. The following chart summarizes the distinction in these terms.

	Religious	*Political*
Compulsory	Tithes	Taxes
Voluntary	Gifts & Offerings	Tribute

But the actual usage of these terms in excavated administrative documents is not as neat as presented here. Ancient texts tell us that taxes were
due to the temple, tithes were presented to the palace, gifts were owed to the
king, predetermined amounts of tribute were paid annually, the state appropriated gifts to the temple, and the temple made use of gifts destined for the
crown. In a close reading of biblical texts, we will see tithes and taxes associated with the temple, yet managed by the crown. (See a full discussion in
chapter four.)

Sources of Information

The sources of information for the Jerusalem temple are material artifacts and literary texts, both biblical and extrabiblical. Excavations at the
Temple Mount, the undisputed site of the central Israelite sanctuary, have
been limited to visible structural features such as the Western Wall, Robin-
son's Arch, and the City of David. As the third holiest site in Islam and the
site of the Dome of the Rock, the location of the ancient Jerusalem temple itself cannot be excavated. However, archaeologists have taken advantage of
full access at other sites in Syria/Palestine to uncover structural remains and
artifacts related to sanctuaries outside Jerusalem. Material remains at sites
such as Megiddo, Arad, Shechem, and Hazor, as well as sites in Syria, have
contributed to an understanding of temple architecture.

Excavations at temple sites in Mesopotamia have yielded treasure beyond structural remains, namely, cuneiform tablets stored in the temple archives. Cuneiform was the ancient writing of Mesopotamia, written by
pressing a stylus with a wedge-shaped tip into wet clay tablets. Such tablets
from major temples in Sippar, Nippur, and Uruk, as well as from smaller

temple sites, have revealed temple operations concerned with far more than worship. These temple archives contained varied judicial documents and a wide range of economic records: inventories, land leases, loan documents, transfer of liens, and trade contracts. Excavations at temple sites in Greece and Asia Minor demonstrate the role of temples in commercial lending, safeguarding personal wealth, and issuing letters of credit. Egyptian temple archives also indicate involvement in lending to the community.

Unfortunately, no extensive archives from the Jerusalem temple have yet come to light. Although some material artifacts give hints about economic activities in Israel, the biblical texts must serve as the primary source for information about the economic role of the Jerusalem temple. But there are some problems inherent in relying on biblical texts for economic information about the temple. First, biblical texts were not specifically written as inventory lists, pay records, real estate transaction registers, and loan documents comparable to archival documents from Mesopotamia. Although some biblical texts contain information of an economic nature, it is second-order information when compared to the first-order theological information. Second, modern scholarship has increasingly discounted biblical texts as accurate witnesses to history. Although some verifiable kernel of historical information may lie underneath and inform the texts, some (but by no means all) scholars assert that historical accuracy is sacrificed on the altar of religious ideology. Third, many biblical texts long postdate the events they record, or have undergone significant editing in a later period, decreasing the historical reliability of the narratives. One example is the book of Ruth, set "in the days when the judges judged" (pre-1000 B.C.E.), but probably a postexilic composition (post-539 B.C.E.). Nevertheless, until economic archives from the Jerusalem temple are excavated and published, the biblical texts must serve as our best source of information about the temple's economic role in society.

The Old Testament provides wide-ranging coverage of the role of the Jerusalem temple in ancient Israel's life. Texts from the Pentateuch (Genesis, Exodus, Leviticus, Numbers, and Deuteronomy), the Historical Books (Joshua, Judges, Samuel, and Kings), the Prophets, and other books are concerned with various aspects of Israel's worship life. Sanctuary designs appear in Exod 25–30 and 35–39, 1 Kgs 6–8 (and the parallel in 2 Chr 2–4), and Ezek 40–48. The book of Leviticus details rituals of sacrifice and holiness essential to worship. Hymnic psalms suggest liturgies for use at the temple. The prophet Haggai exhorts the postexilic community to rebuild the temple in Jerusalem as a prelude to inestimable prosperity, and the prophet Amos rails against ritual (in sanctuaries at Bethel and Gilgal) without accompanying justice and righteousness. Nonbiblical texts from writers such as Josephus and Philo comment on the Jerusalem temple and its operations. From these and other texts of multiple genres, differing historical periods, and various theological perspectives, we will attempt to construct a picture of the economic role of the Jerusalem temple.

Ancient Record-Keeping

If we are to rely on archaeological artifacts and ancient literary texts to reconstruct the economic role of the Jerusalem temple, we must ask, how reliable are these sources? To what degree did ancient people give attention to the modern notions of generally accepted accounting principles and historical accuracy?

Here the evidence is mixed. On the one hand, careful economic record-keeping began at least as far back as the fourth millennium B.C.E. At that time, clay tokens could be sealed in a clay pouch to indicate, for example, the number of animals for which a herdsman was accountable. In time, persons drew pictures to indicate the number and kind of the items being recorded. Later, pictographs of the particular animals under care developed into cuneiform (wedge-shaped symbols), a much more efficient system of drawing/writing.

Economic activity seems to have been the impetus to the widespread use of writing. All kinds of accounting texts proved useful in the course of daily life. Summation texts counted and totaled items in inventory. Production quantity texts included, for example, a recipe for how much of what grain to produce a certain quantity and quality of beer. Allocation and distribution texts included work in progress reports and ration lists. Balancing texts compared receipts to disbursements, something like an ancient income statement, as well as comparing theoretical vs. actual production. At the administrative center of Nuzi in Mesopotamia, an ingenious system accounted for animals on hand in the mid-second millennium B.C.E. Accountants could move stones representing categories of animals among different receptacles to track the movements of the animals between pasture, fold, shearing shed, and slaughterhouse. Written instructions often accompanied the transferred stones. As writing became more widespread and reliable, symbolic stones dropped out of use.[5]

The Sumerians generally receive credit for the development of writing in the early fourth millennium, although the western Semitic innovation of the alphabet sometime in the second millennium B.C.E. revolutionized writing by

---

[5]A. Leo Oppenheim, "On an Operational Device in Mesopotamian Bureaucracy," *JNES* 18 (1959): 121–28.

reducing hundreds of symbols to fewer than thirty alphabetic letters. But even with the advent of simplified alphabetic writing, literacy remained the domain of the elite of society, and written texts reflected their views of the world.

The uses of writing expanded from economic record-keeping to celebrating royal endeavors and documenting priestly rituals and epic myths, whatever the script used. Although ancient Near Easterners wrote chronicles and in other ways preserved records of the past, the self-consciousness that reflects a truly critical approach to history began in Greece in the fifth century B.C.E. For his role in initiating historiography ("history-writing") as a genre of literature, Herodotus, active during the fifth century B.C.E. in Greece, is often called the "Father of History." As he states in his own words, "What Herodotus the Halicarnassian has learnt by inquiry is here set forth: in order that so the memory of the past may not be blotted out from among men by time, and that great and marvelous deeds done by Greeks and foreigners and especially the reason why they warred against each other may not lack renown" (Herodotus *Hist.* 1.1). By modern standards, his work would not be seen as historically "accurate," since it contains obvious factual errors and is told primarily from the Greek perspective. Historiography as practiced by Herodotus was an interpretive endeavor, a way of analyzing events and personalities for underlying motives of action. Herodotus was reading from within a particular social location, that is, bringing his own cultural "baggage" and allowing that to influence his writing. Historiography does not claim to be an eagle's eye view of disconnected factoids reported by a nonbiased, disconnected news source, if that is even possible. In fact, that would not be history at all. History is always an interpretive event, performed by a particular culturally-conditioned human who selects events to be recounted in a particular sequence, emphasizing certain connections and ignoring others.

Biblical texts are "historical" texts in that the authors recount events of the past and present. Biblical writing is "historiography" in that the authors interpret the events they are recounting in light of their theological, political, economic, and social location. In other words, the authors exercise considerable influence in the telling of history—which events are recounted and in what order, which characters are highlighted or ignored, what moral values are upheld, or what lessons are to be learned. Likewise, the readers of the biblical texts in every age interpret texts and construct meanings that may or may not be what the author intended. The net result is that multiple constituencies contribute to interpreting the biblical texts: the historical events themselves, the first recorders of those events, the later recorders and editors, and the readers. Moreover, the biblical texts have undergone significant editing in the centuries-long process from underlying event to the written record available today.[6] Even selection and ordering of the texts to be included in the biblical canon of sacred scripture involved interpretive decisions that influence our reading of the overall narrative. The Hebrew Scriptures, ordered as Torah, Prophets, and Writings, ending with the repatriation proclamation by King Cyrus of Persia (2 Chr 36:23) presents a different storyline than the Old Testament, more loosely ordered as Pentateuch, Historical Books, Writings, Prophets, ending with the prophetic admonition by Malachi to recognize Moses and Elijah as forerunners of the upcoming Day of the Lord. The former leads to hope grounded in return to the land; the latter, to hope in a Messiah inaugurating the Kingdom of God (see Assumptions, p. 22).

Ancient Israelite Economy

If we are attempting to examine the role of the Jerusalem temple in the ancient Israelite economy, it would help to look briefly at the economic landscape. A land bridge between the continents of Africa and Asia, the small geographic region bordering the Eastern Mediterranean Sea known as Syria-Palestine or its subregion Israel/Judah enjoyed a moderate climate throughout the coastal plain and hill country. Formed of mountain ranges and related valleys, the area benefited from early rains in October and late rains in April/May. The climate and topography of the region encouraged small-scale farming and herding, in marked contrast to the large-scale agriculture and broad-based animal husbandry in the irrigation-fed valleys of the Nile or the Tigris and Euphrates. The Deuteronomist explained the difference between an irrigation-dependent economy and a rainfall-dependent economy as evidence of God's blessing:

> For the land where you are going to possess is not like the land of Egypt from which you came out, where you sow your seed and water with your feet as a garden of herbage. The land to which you are crossing over to inherit is a land of hills and valleys, which will drink water from the rain of heaven, a land which YHWH your God is overseeing; continually the eyes of YHWH your God are on it, from the beginning of the year until the end of the year. (Deut 11:10–12)

Agriculture and animal grazing permitted subsistence-level living, with little surplus accumulation to hedge the risks of unfavorable climatic conditions, pestilence, or war, and to support the institutional entities of palace and temple. Israel/Judah's strategic location along well-established trading

---

[6]The literature on the historicity of biblical texts is extensive. For an excellent discussion of the state of the issue, see the appendix by William P. Brown in John Bright, *A History of Israel* (4th ed.; Louisville: Westminster John Knox, 2000), 465–85.

routes, with reasonable access to ports and harbors, promoted limited trade and handicraft production to supplement the output of farms and flocks. In addition to cereals, fruits, and textiles for export, the region could export minerals from the Dead Sea, and it enjoyed a monopoly on the balsam tree. As in the rest of the ANE, profits accumulated by the merchant class were heavily reinvested in land, since there were few other opportunities for capital investment.

Climate and topography combined to limit the development of urban centers, so that village life centered around the cycles of the various agricultural and animal husbandry tasks. Archaeological excavations attest to the transformation of Israel/Judah from dispersed villages to a nation-state in the tenth century B.C.E. or a little later, characterized by fortified governmental centers (e.g., Hazor, Megiddo, Lachish, Gezer), dynastic leadership, and a state-sponsored temple in Jerusalem. Despite a national bureaucracy, the family remained the primary producer and consumer in Israel/Judah, without widespread redistribution throughout the economy. Although products of field, vineyard, and orchard were certainly subject to tithes and taxes by the cultic and political authorities, the family used the majority of the harvest for subsistence or for barter trade.

Eventually, Samaria and Jerusalem developed as the primary candidates for the label "urban center." Urbanization is usually accompanied by a high degree of specialization and full-time labor in a profession, with corresponding methods to distribute and acquire specialized products. Certainly, the temple personnel were specialists in Jerusalem, and the government administration would have required specialized civil servants. Literate temple personnel would also have provided administrative support in the government. Also, specialized skills were handed down from generation to generation. Thus the genealogy of priests determined their temple service area, and Jerusalem had a bakers' street (Jer 37:21). The city also had a potter's house (Jer 18:3). Solomon hired a worker in bronze (1 Kgs 7:14). Specialized artisans and craftsmen, probably few in number, worked primarily in the temple precincts and in the palace bureaucracy.

The economic picture created of ancient Israel/Judah for most of its history is a subsistence-level, rainfall-based, agricultural, kinship-based society with limited trade opportunities, governed by a petty ruler dominated by neighboring powers, worshiping a national deity in a national temple. To the east, Mesopotamia, a land of large-scale irrigation-based agriculture managed by the two great institutions of palace and temple, was more urbanized and specialized. To the south, Egypt, with its large-scale storage economy, was closely managed by the divine Pharaoh, whose temples served essentially as a branch of the national government. To the west, Greece resembled

Israel/Judah in its rainfall-based agriculture, but was more widely connected to the broader Mediterranean economy through active trade in urban ports and was organized politically into city-states (some of which were democratic after a fashion). Obviously, all these socioeconomic factors influenced the economic role of temples in ancient societies.

Brief History of Israel/Judah

The history of Israel/Judah vis-à-vis the temple and the economy may be categorized in four periods, according to the biblical texts.[7]

I. Early Monarchical Period (1020–722)

Saul	before 1000
David	ca. 1000–960
Solomon	ca. 960–932

Judah/Southern Kingdom		*Israel/Northern Kingdom*	
Rehoboam	931–915	Jeroboam I	932–911
Abijah	915–913	Nadab	911–910
		Baasha	910–887
		Elah	887–886
Asa	913–873	Zimri	886
		Omri	886–875
Jehoshaphat	873–849	Ahab	875–854
Jehoram	849–842	Ahaziah	854–853
Ahaziah	842	Jehoram	853–842
Athaliah	842–837	Jehu	842–815
Joash	836–797	Joahaz	815–799
Amaziah	797–769	Jehoash	799–784
Uzziah	769–741	Jeroboam II	784–744
		Zechariah	744
		Shallum	744
Jotham-Ahaz	741–726	Menahem	744–735
		Pekahiah	735–734
		Pekah	734–731
		Hoshea	731–722
		Fall of Samaria	722

---

[7]Chronology of Israelite kings from Niels Peter Lemche, "The History of Ancient Syria and Palestine: An Overview," in *CANE* (4 vols.; ed. Jack Sasson; New York: Charles Scribner's Sons, 1995), 2:1212.

II. Late Monarchical Period (722–587)

Hezekiah	726–697
Manasseh	697–642
Amon	640
Josiah	640–609
Jehoahaz	609
Jehoiakim	609–598
Jehoiachin	598
Zedekiah	598–587
Babylonian Exile	587

III. Second Commonwealth (539–333)

Edict of Cyrus; repatriation allowed	538
(Re)building of Second Temple	520–515
Nehemiah/Ezra	445–400 ?

IV. Hellenistic (333–63)

Alexander the Great	333–323
Ptolemies and Seleucids	323–165
Judean independence	165–63
Roman control	63

1. Early Monarchical (early tenth to mid-eighth centuries B.C.E.)

According to the biblical narrative, the ark of the covenant was the symbol of YHWH's presence with the people. The wilderness tabernacle was an elaborate tent to house the ark, functioning essentially as a portable temple. (See more about construction of the wilderness tabernacle in chapter two.) As tribal clans settled in the Promised Land, they located the ark of the covenant in a temple at Shiloh in the hill country of Ephraim north of Jerusalem (Josh 18:1). The temple at Shiloh was called the "house of YHWH" (1 Sam 1:24; 3:15) and the "house of God" (Judg 18:31). Significantly, Shiloh is the only shrine outside Jerusalem termed "temple (*hêkāl*) of YHWH" (1 Sam 1:9; 3:3), testifying to Shiloh's importance as a cultic center in the premonarchic period and probably the fact that its traditions moved to Jerusalem. The Danites established a shrine at Dan, the northernmost limit of Israel, after their migration from the southern coastal area (Judg 18:29–31). The biblical text specifically mentions the graven image set up in the temple, cared for by priests from the lineage of Moses, not Aaron (Judg 18:30). Noted as a place of sacrifice in the patriarchal period, the sacred site of Bethel could be termed a temple since God was thought to be resident there (1 Sam 10:3). In fact the place name Bethel means "house (*bêt*) of God (*ʾēl*)." According to Judg 20:26–28, the ark was at Bethel during the conflict with the Benjaminites. Amaziah the priest warns the prophet Amos, "Do not prophesy again at Bethel, for it is the sanctuary (*miqdāš*) of the king and a house (*bêt*) of the kingdom" (Amos 7:13). Sacred places in Gilgal and Mizpah appear in the story of Saul, Israel's first king (e.g., 1 Sam 7:5–11; 11:14).

Foundational to the historical and theological story of Judah in the biblical texts is David's inauguration of a dynasty at the beginning of the tenth century B.C.E. Locating his administrative center in Jerusalem, David transferred the ark of the covenant from Shiloh to a tent-shrine in the new capital (2 Sam 6). The building of a permanent home for the ark would be left to his son Solomon (1 Kgs 5–6, 8). The Chronicler, although acknowledging the construction of the Jerusalem (First) temple in Solomon's reign, attributes all the preparations to David (1 Chr 22–28). Materials for construction came from trade with Tyre and Sidon with their access to the resources of the forests of Lebanon (1 Kgs 5), since Solomon operated fleets of ships for trading missions to Tarshish (probably Spain) and Africa (1 Kgs 9:26–28; 10:22, 28). By divine command, persons offered their tithes at the local "Establishment" sanctuaries, that is, those that the monarchy sponsored. On the basis of architectural design and excavated artifacts, it is possible to locate "Establishment" sanctuaries at Dan in the north, Megiddo and Lachish in the center, and Beer-sheba and Arad in the southern desert. The latter two "reasonably stand out as 'regional' centers of worship [that] coordinate with governmental centers obviously built to extend the influence of the central government into economically important peripheral areas."[8] The biblical narrative gives the impression that the Jerusalem (First) temple was a royal chapel managed by the king for the benefit of the nation, supported by tithes and taxes extracted from the populace. An intimate connection between palace and temple appears in the 1 Kings narrative when it positions the description of the palace (1 Kgs 7:1–12) in the middle of the temple construction account (1 Kgs 5–9). Comments about Assyrian temples also apply to the Judean temple: "The link between the temple and the palace is well motivated: the king could only rule with the divine consent and was obliged to establish the worship . . . On the other hand, the temple was the venue of royal festivities like enthronements and

----

[8]John S. Holladay Jr., "Religion in Israel and Judah Under the Monarchy: An Explicitly Archaeological Approach," in *Ancient Israelite Religion: Essays in Honor of Frank Moore Cross* (ed. Patrick D. Miller, Paul D. Hanson, and S. Dean McBride Jr.; Philadelphia: Fortress, 1987), 271.

triumphs after victorious wars, which made the rituals occasions of the royal manifestations of power."[9]

The united monarchy was unable to survive beyond the tenth century B.C.E. Upon the death of Solomon two separate kingdoms emerged, the northern kingdom (Israel) centered in the hill country north of Jerusalem with Samaria as its eventual capital, and the southern kingdom (Judah) in the hill country immediately surrounding and south of its capital, Jerusalem. The first monarch of the northern kingdom, Jeroboam I (932–911 B.C.E.), renovated the ancient sanctuaries at Bethel and Dan as convenient worship sites for his subjects, perhaps hoping to discourage pilgrimage to Jerusalem and the attendant economic outflow of goods (1 Kgs 12:26–33).

Evidence of economic activity has been unearthed at sacred sites throughout the northern region. Artifacts include a stone mold for figurines and a crushing vat for oil burning lamps in the precincts of the second-millennium sanctuary at Nahariyah, a coastal city between Acco and Tyre; a potter's kiln and potters' workshops near shrines in Hazor in Galilee; a clay mold for figurines and numerous weaving weights and spindle whorls in the tenth-century "Cultic Structure" at Ta'anach south of Megiddo; and a weaving workshop located in the ninth–eighth century fortress-sanctuary in Kuntillet Ajrud in the Sinai.[10] Excavations at Arad in the Negev desert have unearthed potsherds detailing the disbursement of rations to itinerant military personnel, as well as a structure interpreted by most scholars as a temple dedicated to YHWH.

The ninth century saw the political and economic ascension of Israel under the Omride dynasty. Following preparatory work by his father Omri, King Ahab (874–854 B.C.E.) built a new capital at Samaria (1 Kgs 16:24), which would serve as the administrative center of the northern kingdom for a century and a half, until its eventual conquest by Assyria in 721 B.C.E. Frequent territorial advances by King Ben-hadad of Syria prompted Ahab to form an alliance with King Jehoshaphat of Judah (873–849), although Judah was certainly not an equal partner in the relationship. The Chronicler reports the stationing of Levitical personnel by Jehoshaphat throughout the cities of Judah to teach the Torah of YHWH (2 Chr 17:9), though the evidence for this activity is late. The same source reports that Jehoshaphat also "built in Judah fortresses and store-cities, and he had great stores in the cities of

---

[9]Martti Nissinen, "City as Lofty as Heaven: Arbela and Other Cities in Neo-Assyrian Prophecy," in *"Every City Shall Be Forsaken": Urbanism and Prophecy in Ancient Israel and the Near East* (ed. Lester L. Grabbe and Robert D. Haak; JSOTSup 330; Sheffield: Sheffield Academic Press, 2001), 173–74.

[10]Lawrence E. Stager and Samuel Wolff, "Production and Commerce in Temple Courtyards: An Olive Press in the Sacred Precinct at Tel Dan," *BASOR* 243 (1981): 96.

Judah" (2 Chr 17:12). The Levitical temple personnel were logical candidates to serve as administrators for the crown's collection of surplus commodities for royal consumption or for emergency reserves.

In the second half of the ninth century, both kingdoms weakened politically and economically, becoming vassals of Assyria. After a brief revival under King Jeroboam II of Israel and King Uzziah of Judah in the mid-eighth century, the military might of Assyria guaranteed that increasing amounts of tribute exited the Israelite and Judean economies. Within a few decades, Israel had formed an alliance with Syria to march against Judah to organize resistance against Assyria, but to no avail (Isa 7). Following a revolt by Israel and Syria in 722 B.C.E., King Sargon II of Assyria swiftly retaliated and deported the population of the northern kingdom. Samaria was rebuilt as the seat of the Assyrian provincial governor, the sanctuary at Bethel was renovated, and foreigners were resettled into the former Israelite territory who would become the ancestors of the despised Samaritans in the first century C.E.

2. Late Monarchical (mid-eighth to mid-sixth centuries B.C.E.)

The southern kingdom of Judah escaped annexation by Assyria in the final decades of the eighth century when King Ahaz of Judah paid substantial tribute to King Tiglath-pileser III of Assyria with money obtained by dismantling the bronze furniture in the temple precincts (2 Kgs 16:17–18). The southern kingdom enjoyed brief periods of resurgence under King Hezekiah (726–697) and King Josiah (640–609). During Hezekiah's reign, King Sennacherib of Assyria was forced to spend substantial time and energy defending his kingdom from northern and eastern threats. Meanwhile, Egypt had united under Dynasty XXV, and it encouraged Hezekiah to undertake certain reforms in anticipation of greater independence. He strengthened his defensive position by fortifying the walls of Jerusalem (2 Chr 32:5) and by constructing a tunnel to conduct water to a pool inside the city walls (2 Kgs 20:20). Jar handles stamped "belonging to the king" (*lmlk*), marked royal commodities stored to supply military garrisons throughout Judah. A fragment of an inscription from Jerusalem (perhaps) reads "heaps of silver" and may relate to collections made in the seventh year of Hezekiah.[11]

Both 2 Kings and 2 Chronicles concentrate upon the religious reforms implemented by King Hezekiah, especially the centralization of worship at the Jerusalem temple and the related destruction of other shrines (2 Kgs 18:4–6, expanded in 2 Chr 29–31). Although both the Deuteronomistic

---

[11]Frank Moore Cross, "A Fragment of a Monumental Inscription from the City of David," *IEJ* 51 (2001): 44–47.

historian and the Chronicler attribute these reforms to Hezekiah's pure devotion to YHWH, the political and economic ramifications are equally obvious. By centralizing worship in Jerusalem, Hezekiah was able to undercut the power of the priests of the local shrines and to tie the people more effectively to the royal house by means of a national shrine, the Jerusalem temple. By inviting northern refugees to participate in Jerusalem, he advertised his reign as the best hope for reunification of the two kingdoms and for achieving some measure of independence from Assyrian domination. Hezekiah's plans were thwarted by King Sennacherib of Assyria, who refused to allow the region to gain its independence. Not only did Assyria rely on Judean tribute to support the imperial administration, but the trade routes in the region were vital to the imperial economy. Perhaps more importantly, Judah served as a buffer zone between Assyria and the perennial power to the south, Egypt. In 701 B.C.E. Sennacherib swept through the territory, devastating the towns and fields of Judah and threatening Jerusalem (2 Kgs 18–19). Although Hezekiah escaped capture, Sennacherib increased the amount of annual tribute and reduced the size of Judah's territory. When the kingdom passed to Manasseh four years later, Judah was an Assyrian vassal state with little prospect for political or economic power.

The final period of resurgence for Judah came in the reign of Josiah (640–609). With Assyria in decline, Egypt reasserted its influence in Syria-Palestine. The boy king Josiah was able to extend his territory into the former northern kingdom of Israel, since Egypt was not particularly concerned with the internal affairs of the petty kingdom of Judah as long as the trade routes remained accessible. The biblical accounts commend Josiah for extensive religious reforms undertaken in response to the "book of the Torah" discovered during renovations of the Jerusalem temple. Similar to those implemented by Hezekiah almost a century earlier, Josiah centralized worship in Jerusalem by purging the land of other shrines and idols (2 Kgs 23:4–20). Of course, there is no guarantee that his religious reforms effectively established pure Yahwistic worship. Josiah's reforms certainly had the beneficial fiscal effect of collecting royal taxes more efficiently by reducing the number of collection sites. More efficient tax collection meant that a greater percentage of the agricultural harvest was required from peasants, leading to increased demands for credit. In a seventh-century inscription excavated at a town south of Joppa on the Mediterranean coast, a grain-harvester complains to a regional official that his garment was unjustly taken, presumably in pledge for a loan.[12] Legislation promulgated under Josiah regarding debt easement served to appease the peas-

---

[12]J. D. Amusin and Michael Heltzer, "The Inscription from Mesad Hashavyahu: Complaint of a Reaper of the Seventh Century BC," *IEJ* 14 (1964): 148–57.

antry while weakening those who extended credit, his primary rivals for power. The cumulative effect of Josiah's reforms prompted the adulation, "Before him there was no king like him, who turned to YHWH with all his heart and with all his being and with all his strength, according to all the Torah of Moses; nor did any like him arise after him" (2 Kgs 23:25).

But even this exemplary man of God could not survive the turbulent late seventh century. Preferring to be a junior partner of Babylon rather than a puppet state of Egypt, Josiah opposed the Egyptian-Assyrian alliance and was killed by Pharaoh Neco at Megiddo in 609 B.C.E. (2 Kgs 23:29–30). Two decades later the Babylonians under King Nebuchadnezzar marched into Jerusalem, burned the temple, plundered the city, and exiled the leadership to Babylon (2 Kgs 24–25). The independent kingdom of Judah had come to an ignominious end. The temple in Jerusalem was now a memory, resurfacing as a vision in Ezekiel's prophecy (Ezek 40–48).

3. Second Commonwealth (mid-sixth to mid-fourth centuries B.C.E.)

The Neo-Babylonian Empire soon fell prey to the people of the territory north and east of the Fertile Crescent, a mixed tribal group known as the Persians, when Cyrus the Great entered the city of Babylon without a fight in 539 B.C.E. Upon the rise of this Achaemenid dynasty, Judah began a two-century long period as a province of the Persian Empire. Yehud, the name for Judah in this period, was a subregion within the larger Trans-Euphrates satrapy and was subject to imperial authority in all its political and economic manifestations. The Persian government employed strategies to exert and maintain control over annexed territory, including ruralization or the deliberate depopulation of urban centers, increased commercialized trade over long distances, establishment of a military presence in fortified garrisons, and organization of the citizenry into economic units not related to kinship groups.[13] The Persian Empire, unlike its Neo-Assyrian and Neo-Babylonian predecessors, permitted a certain amount of governmental and religious autonomy for its provinces. The administrative reorganization accomplished by Darius I sought to maximize imperial revenues at a minimum cost. The empire's decentralized structure with authority delegated to provincial governors (called "satraps") contributed to strong regional economies, but at the risk of strengthening potential political rivals.

---

[13]Kenneth G. Hoglund, "The Achaemenid Context," in *Second Temple Studies: 1. Persian Period* (ed. Philip R. Davies; JSOTSup 117; Sheffield: Sheffield Academic Press, 1991), 56–65.

Scholars intensely debate the social demographics of Yehud owing to conflicting biblical traditions, methodological disagreements, and fragmentary archaeological evidence. Probably, Persian-period Jerusalem was a small urban center with a relatively low population of 1,500 or less, serving as the capital of the province of Yehud, an area of about 25 km around Jerusalem with a population of around 15,000. The citizenry consisted of returnees and non-exiled Judeans who farmed and herded at a subsistence level. The returning exiles practiced a type of Yahwism in basic conformity with its preexilic antecedents. Only gradually did the leaders of the Second Commonwealth see the need to reshape Yahwistic doctrine and practice. This attempt at identity redefinition produced the biblical texts of Ezra, Nehemiah, and Chronicles.

For the purposes of this study—and perhaps for the restoration community—the most important postexilic event was the rebuilding of the Jerusalem temple. Unfortunately, the biblical texts are confusing and even contradictory regarding the authority and financing of this Second Temple (see further discussion in chapter two). Upon his accession to the throne in 539 B.C.E., Cyrus returned the Jerusalem cult vessels to Sheshbazzar and allowed the repatriation of all willing Judeans, especially the priests and the Levites. When Darius I reorganized the Persian Empire in 520 B.C.E., temple construction in Jerusalem was at a standstill. By financing construction of the Second Temple from the tax receipts of Yehud, King Darius stimulated the construction effort, and the temple was completed and dedicated in 515 B.C.E.

Unlike the First Temple, however, the Second Temple did not serve as a royal chapel. Not surprisingly, since royal financing of a temple translates ideologically to a royal shrine, the biblical traditions do not directly ascribe the financing to Darius. In Yahwistic theology, the new temple, like its predecessor, was YHWH's temple, not Darius's. Presumably, the Second Temple resembled the first one in architectural design, but the rebuilding of the Second Temple likely had more of an immediate impact on the economy than the building of the First Temple. Economically-depressed Jerusalem now needed cultic personnel for religious rituals, civil servants to administer Persian imperial interests in Yehud, and specialized personnel for the temple and city hall. The dedication of the Second Temple was a celebration, not just of the house of God, but of the rebirth of Judah/Israel.

The reconstruction of the Jerusalem temple was important not just for the residents of the province of Yehud, but for the Yahwists outside of the area who lived in the Diaspora. Significant economic support flowed into Jerusalem from the Jews in the Diaspora in the form of pilgrimages for festivals and in the form of the mandatory temple tax. A Yahwistic temple in Elephantine (an island in the Nile near the First Cataract) was already operating when King Cambyses conquered Egypt in 525 B.C.E. The Elephantine correspondence includes a letter in which the Jews appealed to their brethren in Jerusalem to intercede on their behalf with the Persian authorities to allow the rebuilding of the local temple. (See the excursus on the Elephantine temple in chapter two.)

As the fifth century dawned, Persian attention turned westward to the Mediterranean as Greek alliances challenged Persian authority in the area. For the remainder of the fifth century and for most of the fourth, Persia engaged in battles to maintain control of the Mediterranean basin. In this time period the biblical (and deuterocanonical) texts describe the activities of Ezra and Nehemiah in Judah. The problems surrounding the reconstruction of their work are legion, but probably both lived in Jerusalem during the mid-fifth century after the reconstruction of the Second Temple. Information on life in Persian Yehud after Ezra and Nehemiah is sketchy. Apparently, with the Persian armies occupied to the west, the small region of Judah was of little concern as long as the peace was kept and the taxes were paid.

4. Hellenistic (mid-fourth to mid-first centuries B.C.E.)

The Greek alliance was ultimately successful in overthrowing the Persians under the command of Alexander the Great in 333 B.C.E. In the closing centuries of the era, Hellenism would influence all the cultures of the Mediterranean basin and the Near East. The major economic legacy of the Greeks was the widespread acceptance of money as a means of exchange, gradually replacing the barter economy and setting the stage for increased commercial trade and the flowering of credit arrangements. After Alexander's untimely death in 323 B.C.E., the various provinces intermittently engaged in military struggles for independence until the Roman and Parthian Empires took control in the first century B.C.E. Judah's history in the Hellenistic period is one of interfamilial infighting, as various members of the priestly line schemed to gain power in the temple hierarchy, and, therefore, in the province.

In addition to the temple in Jerusalem, the Hellenistic period spawned the construction of three other Yahwistic temples. The closest to Jerusalem was the Samaritan temple on Mt. Gerizim, modeled after the Jerusalem temple according to Josephus (Josephus, *Ant.* 11.310). A temple at 'Araq el-Emir, southwest of Amman, was apparently connected with the Tobiad family that interfered with Nehemiah's work in Jerusalem. The most distant Yahwistic Hellenistic temple was at Leontopolis in northern Egypt, built by Onias IV around 150 B.C.E., perhaps to serve Yahwists in the Delta region. (See the excursus in chapter two.) Perhaps these three temples were Hellenistic alternatives to the Jerusalem temple for those at a distance, either geographically or doctrinally.

Assumptions

As discussed above authors have considerable influence in the construction of a narrative, selecting which incidents to include and exclude, which items to emphasize or ignore, and what connections to highlight or obscure. Every author, modern no less than ancient, operates from a particular social location. At this point, therefore, I want to identify several assumptions that undergird the work of this book.

First, I do not believe the biblical texts are inerrant or scientifically verifiable with respect to every factoid of information. Nevertheless, I will treat them as reliable witnesses to historical circumstances underlying the theological interpretation by the authors and editors. In an article about the mission of Ezra and a letter from King Artaxerxes, David Janzen has given a helpful distinction between "authentic" and "reliable": "If the letter as we have it is *authentic,* then it is the same document, or virtually so, as the one that Ezra received; if *reliable,* then the document has been edited or perhaps been composed whole cloth by a later editor, but reflects the actual commands and disposition of the Persian monarch."[14] This is particularly relevant to the work of the Chronicler. Writing about the First Temple period based on a first-hand knowledge of the Second Temple period, the Chronicler's work is heavily influenced by a theological agenda to elevate the status of King David and provide an etiology for temple operations in his own day.

I often explain this phenomenon to classes with the following anecdote: Imagine yourself at an annual family reunion at which great-uncle Fred is absent for the first year anyone can remember, having died the previous spring. As folks settle in around the picnic tables to enjoy fried chicken and potato salad, the conversation drifts from this to that and back again. Before you know it, someone is telling a story about great-uncle Fred that he remembers from childhood. Soon, other relatives chime in, reminiscing about the way great-uncle Fred played semipro baseball as a young man or loved chocolate-covered cherries or always tinkered with his Ford truck or played pranks on the neighbors. Whether Fred actually did any of these things exactly the way the story is told is beside the point; rather, the story tells exactly the way Fred would have performed at baseball as it was played in the early part of the twentieth century or would have tinkered with an old Ford truck put up on blocks in the garage. The oral historiography reflects accurate historical circumstances interpreted through the lens of selective memory to give insight into a person's character and motivation for living.

---

[14]David Janzen, "The 'Mission' of Ezra and the Persian-Period Temple Community." *JBL* 119 (2000): 623, my emphasis.

Second, since the biblical texts are interpretive historical texts, they are not economic and administrative records of the sort unearthed in Mesopotamian temple archives. Caution is warranted in gleaning economic information from theological-ideological texts. Nevertheless, since the biblical texts are concerned with the whole of life before God, they *are* concerned with economic matters, even if that concern is not primary. Careful reading can discover economic concerns in the texts.

Third, I am concerned with the economic role of the Jerusalem temple as an institution in Israelite society. I am less concerned, therefore, with strictly differentiating between the First and Second Temples. I intend to present a synchronic view, commingling information from different time periods to develop a composite paradigm of how the Jerusalem temple as an institution functioned in the ancient Israelite economy in the first millennium B.C.E. I am not claiming that, were we able to be transported back to a particular decade, the Jerusalem temple actually functioned according to all aspects of my composite, synchronic paradigm. For example, we know that temples in the ANE were active in lending grain and silver to persons in the community, and biblical texts hint at such practices in the Jerusalem temple, but that is not to say that every generation of priests in Jerusalem made loans.

Fourth, Israel was an heir to, and participant in, the wider ANE culture, meaning that the Jerusalem temple did not function in isolation from its broader context. In art, architecture, literature, law, and religion, we can see the footprints of Egyptians, Assyrians, Babylonians, Persians, and Greeks in Israelite society. It is reasonable to assume that similar footprints were left in the soil in which Israelite economic life flourished. Furthermore, both the ancient agrarian economy and the temple institution were relatively stable throughout the first millennium B.C.E., despite changing imperial politics. Twentieth-century scholarship has been fascinated with analyzing the religious, political, and socioeconomic dimensions of various ANE cultures, leading to the phenomenon of "parallelomania." Recent study has resulted in "finding small differences between Israel and its neighbors but emphasizing that much of what was thought to be uniquely Israelite was shared between Israel and its neighbors."[15] Since few economic records are directly available for ancient Israel, I shall rely on information from its closest neighbors.

Fifth, with respect to the economic role of the Jerusalem temple, Israel's most influential neighbor was Mesopotamia during the seventh to fifth centuries B.C.E., and life in Mesopotamian temples then is well documented. The

---

[15]Marc Zvi Brettler, "The Many Faces of God in Exodus 19," in *Jews, Christians, and the Theology of the Hebrew Scriptures* (ed. Alice Ogden Bellis and Joel S. Kaminsky; SBLSymS 8; Atlanta: SBL, 2000), 359 n. 25.

vast majority of Mesopotamian temple archives document activity precisely during these centuries, so there is a large quantity of data upon which to draw. Given the extensive influence of Mesopotamia upon Judah during the Neo-Babylonian (7th c.) and Persian (6th–4th c.) periods and the fact that the leaders of the postexilic Judean community were exiles under the Neo-Babylonian regime, we should expect heavy Mesopotamian influence on Judean conceptions of the temple. Judah was part of the administrative province encompassing Babylonia, Syria, and Palestine for over fifty years of the early Persian Empire. The biblical texts became stabilized during the exilic and postexilic periods when Judah was under Neo-Babylonian and Persian control. The Second Temple was reconstructed and functioned under the imperial authority of the Persians. Based on these factors, it is reasonable to assume the Jerusalem temple functioned in an economic role similar to Mesopotamian temples of the seventh to fifth centuries B.C.E.

Purposes of Study

My purposes for writing this book are twofold. First, I propose to raise the consciousness that the temple in ancient Israel was not *just* for worship. Most folks correlate the ancient temple with their local sanctuary. They picture ancient worshipers coming regularly on the Sabbath for prayer and praise, led by priests in elaborate vestments. They know some sort of comprehensive sacrificial system was operative, and imagine the people bringing lambs to slaughter on an altar. Certainly, the temple was a place for sacrifice and worship, but such actions were only a small part of the functions of the ancient temple. The temple was the central socioeconomic-religious institution in ancient Israel, combining the modern-day IRS, Supreme Court, National Cathedral, Congress, and CitiBank. One scholar suggests the multiple functions of the temple can be best illustrated

> . . . by imagining that we are staging a play in modern dress about the Second Temple. How would we costume the chief priests? Besides bishops' or cardinals' robes and hats, we would need butchers' aprons, bankers' (and high level bureaucrats', such as tax-collectors') three-piece suits, Supreme Court judges' robes, and some insignia of executive political office. The set, moreover, would have to indicate that the scene is the capital of a tiny third-world country with the client rulers for an imperial regime in charge.[16]

---

[16]Richard Horsley, "Empire, Temple and Community—but No Bourgeoisie!" in *Second Temple Studies: 1. Persian Period* (ed. Philip R. Davies; JSOTSup 117; Sheffield: Sheffield Academic Press, 1991), 164 n. 1.

While the temple is primarily concerned about religion, it is also concerned about economics.

My second purpose derives from the first, namely to demonstrate that worship is not disconnected from politics, economics, or sociology. If one central institution served multiple functions in ancient Israelite society, then society understood those functions to be integrated in life. Western democratic separation of church and state has artificially divided life into arenas of sacred and secular, divorcing economics from religion. I do not advocate a return to a theocracy, a political system ruled by religion. I do suggest that the life of discipleship is not to be divided into sacred and secular, as is our modern tendency. The biblical prophets precede me in this regard, announcing that worship without economic justice and societal righteousness is an abomination to the One we worship. I hope that understanding the economic role of the Jerusalem temple may help us recapture something of the integrative, holistic character of life that our ancestors in the faith experienced and that the Divine desires for all creation.

Guide to Foreign Words

Since this book concerns the economic role of the temple institution in the Ancient Near East, by necessity we are dealing with source material written in ancient languages. For my own work, I have chosen to transliterate the ancient Hebrew, Greek, or Akkadian using the academic style and to note the transliterated word in italics. Scholars will easily recognize the underlying foreign word; nonreaders of the ancient languages may simply ignore the extraneous marks and imagine a pronunciation roughly similar to the English letters. For example, the chief sun-god in Mesopotamia was named Šamaš. The diacritical mark "ᵛ" over the "s" indicates the sibilant consonant pronounced "sh" in English. But readers unfamiliar with academic diacritical markings may just as easily understand the name as Samas.

Citations of translations of ancient cuneiform texts are a different and far more complicated matter. I have quoted the translation exactly as it appears in the source, even though this means that my readers must deal with differing conventions used by various translators and transcribers of the text. Some translators maintain the diacritical marks (e.g., Šamaš) and some do not (e.g., Shamash). Also, we must note that Akkadian, the ancient language of Mesopotamia, was written in cuneiform, wedge-shaped signs impressed into clay or carved into stone. Akkadian as written in cuneiform was sometimes comprised of signs representing words, called logograms, inherited from the Sumerians. Translators indicate these logograms with the word in

small capital letters. More often, signs representing syllables were combined into words as in the example of the five cuneiform signs as drawn above taken from the beginning of Law Forty-four of the Code of Hammurabi. These signs represent the the five sounds, "šum," "ma," "a," "wi," and "lum," which when sounded out are two Akkadian words, *šumma awīlum,* meaning "If [a] man . . ." . Translators indicate these syllables with lower case letters. For example, the Sumerian ancient measure of volume, the "*gur*" (about 300 liters) was written in Sumerian with a logogram we know as GUR. The word was borrowed and came into the Akkadian language as *kurru.* It was usually written with two signs, a "kur" and a "ru," to sound/spell out the Akkadian *kurru.* But sometimes the Akkadian writers used the single logogram GUR as a kind of shorthand. Thus in a given text one may find the Akkadian word *kurru* represented by the logogram GUR or we may find two syllable signs, "kur" and "ru." Some translators preserve the logogram in their translation (5 GUR of barley); some use the shortened Akkadian translation (5 *kur* of barley); some represent the logogram as if it were an Akkadian word (5 *gur* of barley). Another common example of such varied ways of writing a word are the logogram and syllable signs to designate the idea, "king." Sometimes the Akkadian word *šarru* is represented by the Sumerian logogram used for their word for king, LUGAL, while other times the actual Akkadian word for "king," *šarru,* is spelled out in cuneiform syllables, e.g., "šar" and "ru." The observant reader will even note that some words are composed of combinations of syllables and logograms.

The following conventions are widely used in the translation and transliteration of texts.

( )	underlying foreign words or explanatory comments
[ ]	reconstruction of a corrupted or broken text
italics	additional words needed for the sake of English grammar
PN	Personal Name (PN2 second personal name; PN3 third personal name, etc.)
MN	Month Name
RN	Royal Name
DN	Divine Name

Pictograph form (ca. 3100 BCE)	Early cuneiform representation (ca. 2400 BCE)	Late Assyrian form (ca. 650 BCE)	Sumerian equivalent and meaning
			MUŠEN bird
			GU$_4$ ox
			SAG head
			GIN/GUB walk/stand
			ÁB cow
			A water
			KU$_6$ fish

Sumerian-Akkadian syllabic sign evolution. (Courtesy of Greenwood.)

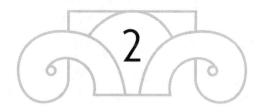

Temple Construction

From the earliest days of civilization in the ANE, one of the most important duties of the king was building a temple for the deity. Throughout the ANE, including Israel, kings demonstrated the divine basis of their authority by dedicating sanctuaries to the deities who had chosen them as rulers. On stone or metal commemorative items placed in building foundations and in prologues to law codes, kings proudly proclaimed their fulfillment of the sacred royal duty to provide a dwelling place for the god. Even if temples were in good repair, the king's piety often led him to demolish the existing structure and reconstruct it more grandly. The biblical texts describe three major sanctuaries built for Israel's God: the wilderness tabernacle, the First Temple, and the Second Temple.

The Wilderness Tabernacle

According to the biblical narrative, the first shrine devoted to YHWH and built by divine direction was the tabernacle constructed in the wilderness of Sinai. Until that time, patriarchs had built altars for burnt offerings and set up sacred memorial pillars in recognition of the divine presence in their lives. For example, "Noah built an altar to YHWH" and burned sacrifices, the soothing scent of which evoked a divine promise never to destroy every living creature again (Gen 8:20–21). Abram built an altar to YHWH at "the oaks of Mamre, which are at Hebron" (Gen 13:18), while his son Isaac built an altar to YHWH at Beer-sheba upon hearing the ancestral covenant repeated by God (Gen 26:23–25). Isaac's son Jacob memorialized the divine presence four times, each with a name: "Now this stone that I set up as a memorial pillar will be 'the House of God' (bêt-ʾĕlōhîm)" (Gen 28:22); "And he

Model of the wilderness tabernacle Holy Place and Holy of Holies.

stationed there an altar, and he named it 'God, God of Israel' (*'ēl 'ĕlōhê yiśrāēl*)" (Gen 33:20); "And he built there an altar, and he named the place 'God of the House of God' (*'ēl bêt-'ēl*)" (Gen 35:7); "And Jacob stationed a memorial pillar in the place where he had spoken with him, a pillar of stone . . . And Jacob named the place . . . 'House of God' (*bêt-'ēl*)" (Gen 35:14–15). The narrative of Joseph's rise to power in Egypt (Gen 37–50) does not indicate that Joseph built an altar to YHWH, although certainly the narrator believes in Joseph's favor in God's eyes. We simply do not know the ritual locations that may have been operative during the Israelite sojourn in the land of Goshen in Egypt.

When Moses encounters the divine in the burning bush, he is instructed to go to Pharaoh and say, "YHWH, God of the Hebrews, met with us; now, let us go a three-day journey in the wilderness so we may sacrifice to YHWH our God" (Exod 3:18b). Of course, the king of Egypt has no intention of letting his slave labor force walk into the desert for three days (one way) to build an altar and hold a festival to their god. Only after suffering the ravages of ten plagues does Pharaoh permit the Israelites to escape the bondage of Egyptian slavery and journey to Mt. Sinai (also called Mt. Horeb in the biblical texts). The divine command to build a tabernacle comes to Moses while he is engulfed by the cloud on the top of Mt. Sinai:

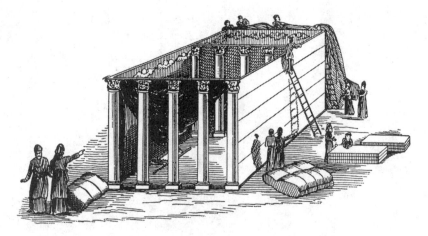

Schematic drawing of a reconstruction of the wilderness tabernacle.

YHWH spoke to Moses: Speak to the children of Israel, so that they may take for me an offering; from every person whose heart is stirred you shall receive my offering. And this is the offering you shall receive from them: gold, silver, and bronze; violet, purple, and scarlet threads, linen, and goat's hair; tanned hides of rams and leather; acacia wood; oil for the lampstand, spices for the anointing oil, and incense of spices; onyx stones and stones for setting in the ephod and breast-piece. They will make for me a sanctuary (*miqdāš*) so that I may dwell in their midst. According to all that I am showing you–the pattern (*tabnît*) of the Tabernacle (*miškān*), the pattern of all its furnishings–thus you shall make. (Exod 25:1–9)

The range of gifts specified—precious metals, textiles, wood, oil, stone— makes it immediately obvious that this is a shrine of a far different character than an altar or pillar erected by the patriarchs. This will be a *miqdāš*, a holy place (from the Hebrew root q-d-š "to be holy"), a place appropriate for the presence of the Holy One. This will be a *miškān,* a dwelling place (from the Hebrew root š-k-n "to dwell"), a place where the divine presence resides. This will be constructed from precious materials of great extravagance, worthy of the divine presence. Israel should construct the building according to the *tabnît* ("pattern/image") that God reveals. This will be God's holy sanctuary and tabernacle, the guaranteed place of God's dwelling.

Despite what the narrative says about the Israelites plundering the Egyptians (Exod 12:35–36), it is virtually impossible that the freed slaves would have had access to these specified materials in the wilderness of the Arabian Peninsula. Scholars, therefore, agree the description of the elaborate Tabernacle in Exodus is a based on a later structure, either the tent shrine for the ark in Shiloh or the First Temple. The rationale of the biblical authors and editors might have gone something like this: "We don't have any living witnesses to what the wilderness tabernacle looked like, but it must have been a grand structure. After all, our Israelite ancestors were celebrating their liberation from generations of slavery and would have contributed their most precious materials to the construction effort. Besides, we know that the tabernacle was divinely designed—every deity designs his own temple—and a divinely designed worship space must have been glorious in every respect." This is not to say that some type of portable tent structure for the ark of the covenant did not exist in the wilderness, only that Exodus exaggerates its opulence.

For five chapters, YHWH gives Moses the explicit patterns for the tabernacle and its furnishings in excruciating detail: the ark containing the testimony (25:10–22); the table for the bread of the Presence (25:23–30); the seven-branched lampstand (25:31–40); curtains, frames, veil, and screen for the tabernacle (26:1–6, 15–37); curtains for the tent over the tabernacle[1] (27:7–14); altar and utensils for burnt offerings (27:1–8); court enclosure hangings (27:9–19); lamp (27:20–21); priestly vestments (28:1–43); ordination rituals (29:1–37); daily burnt offerings (29:38–46); incense altar (30:1–10); ransom rituals (30:11–16); laver (30:17–21); and anointing rituals (30:22–38). Moving from the innermost space to the outer courtyard, from the most sacred furnishing to the most accessible, the blueprint specifies a portable sanctuary. Unlike the stone pillars that the patriarchs erected in Canaan to mark God's presence in one place, this tabernacle provides the means for God to dwell with the people while they are on the move. The portable wilderness tabernacle means that God can never lose God's people, no matter how far they stray.

Exodus interrupts the account of tabernacle construction with three chapters wherein the covenant just articulated is broken by the people and then reinstituted by God. According to this ancient narrative, rather than make a freewill offering of their gold for the construction of a divine dwelling place, the people offer their gold to Aaron to fashion a golden calf as their deity. Anger and punishment are the results of their rebellious actions. The sons of Levi visit the wrath of Moses on the people, but they are spared the wrath of YHWH by Moses' passionate intercession, followed by divine recommitment to this people.

When Moses returns from Mt. Sinai the second time, he assembles the congregation and repeats virtually word for word the command to bring offerings to YHWH (Exod 35:4–9 equals 25:2–9). The narrator next recounts

---

[1]The term "tent of meeting" (*'ōhel mô'ēd*) is often used in biblical texts interchangeably with the term "tabernacle" (*miškān*).

a detailed inventory of the offerings. Then Moses informs the people that YHWH has appointed Bezalel as the chief artisan or foreman for the tabernacle construction (35:30–36:1). "So Moses called Bezalel and Oholiab and every man with ability to whom YHWH gave wisdom, every one whose heart was stirred to draw near to do the work. And they received in the presence of Moses every offering that the children of Israel brought to do the work of the service of the holy place (haq-qōdeš)" (Exod 36:2–3). Then, for five chapters the narrator recounts in excruciating detail how the construction of the tabernacle and its furnishings are made according to the patterns that YHWH revealed to Moses. When the work on the tabernacle is completed, the Priestly tradition accounts for all of the precious metals received by the craftsmen by detailing their use in the finished sanctuary (Exod 38:24–31). The comprehensive accounting is introduced as follows: "These are the things produced for the tabernacle, the tabernacle of the testimony, which were produced on the command of Moses, for the work of the Levites, at the disposal of (běyad) Ithamar, son of Aaron the priest" (Exod 38:21). The things produced (and about to be listed in detail) are (1) for the tabernacle, (2) authorized by Moses, (3) for the Levites to use in their work at the tabernacle, (4) and held accountable to Ithamar, an Aaronide who is the head of the Levites.

Why would the biblical writers include so much detail about the construction of the wilderness tabernacle? If God revealed the plans to Moses on the mountain (Exod 25–30), could the reader not assume that Moses would carry out the divine plan and construct the tabernacle just so? Would a summary sentence not be sufficient, something like "And Moses did just as the Lord commanded; he built the tabernacle according to the pattern revealed by YHWH"? This type of summary sentence is common, appearing for example, in the divine instructions for the Passover in Egypt: "So the children of Israel went and did; just as YHWH commanded Moses and Aaron, thus they did" (Exod 12:28). Why, then, does the biblical account of the wilderness tabernacle recount not only the details of the divine blueprint but also the details of the construction itself?

We noted earlier that the repetition of the tabernacle blueprint details and completion details brackets the Golden Calf narrative. In ch. 32–34 the covenant is broken and then re-documented. The Priestly source is surely making the theological point that, despite the people's unfaithfulness, God faithfully continues to be present among the people by means of the completed tabernacle. But from an economic perspective, the double reporting of the plan for precious materials and the use of said materials is well documented in the Mesopotamian temple archives. Excavated texts record a comprehensive inventory accounting procedure using the Akkadian term iškaru.

Materials termed *iškaru* are dispensed to a worker, who is held accountable for these working materials. For example, one text records, "PN is responsible to the palace for all the gold (he holds) as working material, he and the god Šamaš guarantee as partners" (*CAD* I–J:246). The texts describe the materials as disbursed *ina pāni,* "at the disposal of a person." This phrase emphasized the seriousness of the worker's obligation to safeguard the precious goods disbursed to him by the temple. To modern ears, the phrase "at the disposal of" sounds like the recipient of the goods has the personal authority to utilize the materials in whatever way seems appropriate, with little or no accountability. In ancient ears of the first millennium, however, the phrase echoed the same one used in debt agreements. Ancient loan documents recorded the item being lent as "at the disposal of" (*ina pāni*), with repayment strictly mandated. With the value at stake in materials entrusted to craftsmen, strict accountability for the use of precious stocks was economically prudent. Using language adopted from debt agreements underscored the imperative accounting for the materials issued from the temple storehouses to the various craftsmen.

In fact, the texts in the Mesopotamian temple archives use the same word, *iškaru,* for the materials or supplies issued to workmen *and* for the finished products returned to the storehouses by the workmen. That is, by using the same technical term for both raw materials and finished product, the temple administrators underscored the accountability of the craftsmen and the legal obligation to return the appropriate quantity of finished product. Texts mandating delivery of the *iškaru* finished product are composed as commands with a penalty for non-performance. For example, "whoever delivers less than (his) *i.* [= *iškaru]* commits a crime against god and king" (*CAD* 7:247). In one Mesopotamian text, a temple storehouse overseer accused of stealing precious materials declares his innocence. Not satisfied with his assertion, the supervisor questions three doorkeepers of the temple storehouse, and then brings the doorkeepers into the assembly of the gods to swear to the overseer's innocence (*NBAD,* #170).

How does the Mesopotamian *iškaru* system of inventory accountability apply to the biblical account of the construction of the wilderness tabernacle? I suggest that the detailed narratives in Exodus perform a similar function as the *iškaru* texts. On a macroeconomic level, the plan of the tabernacle revealed to Moses in Exod 25–31 functions as the record of raw materials dispensed as *iškaru* by the ruler of the temple (YHWH) to the chief administrator (Moses), who then turns the work over to the appointed artisans (Bezalel and Oholiab). This "disbursement of materials" *iškaru* section ends with the admonition from YHWH to Moses, "According to all that I have commanded you, they shall do" (Exod 31:11). The account of the completion of

the tabernacle in Exod 36–39 functions as the record of the return of the finished product to the chief administrator (Moses), who double-checks the
work against the work order in Exod 25–31 and accepts the work on behalf
of the ruler of the temple (YHWH). Recall the introduction to the final accounting: "These are the things produced for the Tabernacle, the Tabernacle
of the testimony, which were produced on the command of Moses, for the
work of the Levites, at the disposal of (*bĕyad*) Ithamar, son of Aaron the
priest" (Exod 38:21). The Akkadian phrase *ina pāni*, "at the disposal of,"
corresponds to Hebrew *bĕyad* in the biblical text. The "finished product"
iškaru section concludes, "According to all that YHWH commanded Moses,
thus the children of Israel did all the work. And Moses saw all the work that
they had done; just as YHWH commanded, thus they did. So Moses blessed
them" (Exod 39:42).

The details of the construction of the wilderness tabernacle and its furnishings yield several nuggets of economic information. First, YHWH has
good taste! The divine dwelling place is a space filled with splendor—gold
and silver, exquisite carvings, graceful sculptures, colorful woven fabrics, aro-
matic spices, and flickering luminaries. This is no earthen altar or standing
stone set up as a memorial to a personal experience of God. This is sacred
space, filled with the finest products of the land.

Second, the design of the tabernacle is divinely ordained, making Moses
accountable for following the revealed pattern and for using the right materials in the construction. Upon completion, all raw materials are accounted
for in the finished product. An audit of the work confirms the accuracy of the
design, "so Moses blessed them" (Exod 39:42).

Third, all the people give generously to the building fund for the tabernacle. Repeatedly, the biblical narrative exhorts "every one whose heart is
stirred" to give to the project. As the workmen exclaim, "The people are
bringing in abundance, more than enough to do the work that YHWH commanded" (Exod 36:5). So Moses has to constrain any further contributions.
In the context of the canonical narrative, the abundance of the people's resources in the midst of the wilderness of Sinai is unbelievable, attributable
solely to the extraordinary providence of God. The implication is that if the
people donate their wealth for the use of the sanctuary and its rituals, God
will continue to meet their needs in the future. That is, the generosity of the
people in the wilderness, with no immediate prospects of replacement goods,
implies a divine economy of abundance. There is no need to operate on a
principle of scarcity, assuming there are limited resources to be allocated
among all the necessary functions of society. Rather, Israel should give resources over to the cult with the expectation that replacement resources (and
more?) will be available in the future. The prophet Haggai also employs this

economic vision when he exhorts the returned exiles to spend their scarce resources on rebuilding the temple so that "all the treasures of the nations shall come in" (Hag 2:7).

Fourth, even as there are gradations of holiness in the tabernacle area, there are persons specially made holy for service at the tabernacle. By divinely prescribed ritual, Moses consecrates Aaron and his sons with holy blood for service in the holy space. Part of the divine instructions obligate the people to support the priests economically. Their offerings are to provide clothing and food for all who serve in the cult. "Aaron and his sons will have a perpetual portion from the children of Israel, for it is an offering, and the offering will be from the children of Israel from their peace sacrifices, their offering to YHWH" (Exod 29:28). Later, when the monarchy bears construction costs for the sanctuary, the people still must support the priests.

The wilderness tabernacle served the people well as they journeyed through the desert from Sinai to Zion. Whenever the cloud of glory descended on the tabernacle, the people were confident of God's presence in that place. "The cloud covered the Tent of Meeting and the glory of YHWH filled the tabernacle" (Exod 40:35). The tabernacle is rightly named in Hebrew *miškān,* "dwelling place," since it was here that the God of Israel chose to call home. The biblical wilderness tradition, however, also includes the recurrent promise of the gift of productive land as the dwelling place for God's chosen people, along with the accompanying admonition to worship YHWH in the new land. According to the Deuteronomist,

> You will cross over the Jordan and dwell in the land that YHWH your God causes you to inherit, and he will give you rest from all your enemies round about you, and you will dwell in safety, and there will be a place that YHWH your God will choose to establish his name. There you will bring all that I am commanding you: your whole burnt offerings and your sacrificial offerings, your tithes and the contribution of your hand, and the choicest of your vows that you vowed to YHWH. (Deut 12:10–11)

In time, Jerusalem would be that place that "YHWH your God will choose to establish his name." Until then, the ark of the covenant would be stationed at Shiloh in the hill country of Ephraim, between Bethel and Shechem (Josh 18:1).

The Deuteronomist, or his sources, does not, however, envision this as the exclusive "residence" of YHWH. Rather, the ark of the covenant traveled with the people of Israel into battle as tangible evidence of the presence of God in their midst (1 Sam 4:4; 14:18). Shrines continued to function on the high places (*bāmôt*), and pillars marked places of encounter with the divine. Saul became king over Israel with the timeless acclamation "Long live the king!" when "Samuel called all the people to YHWH at Mizpah" (1 Sam 10:17). Saul's successor, David the son of Jesse, would transfer the ark from Shiloh to his new royal capital of Jerusalem: "And they brought the ark of YHWH and stationed it in its place in the middle of the tent that David had pitched for it, and David offered up burnt offerings and peace offerings before YHWH" (2 Sam 6:17).

The Jerusalem First Temple

Every king in the ANE needed three things to maintain his kingdom and the attendant economic benefits of royal rule: secure borders, secure lineage, and secure divine presence. Secure borders insured that enemies could not plunder the nation's assets. Secure lineage insured control of the throne and the attendant taxes, tribute, and provisions due to the royal household. Secure divine presence insured subordinate loyalty, economic prosperity, and the safety to enjoy it.

When King David brought the ark of the covenant to its new resting place in the royal capital of Jerusalem, two of the three necessities were in place. After years of skirmishes with the Philistines under the military leadership of King Saul, David "smote the Philistines from Geba all the way to Gezer" (2 Sam 5:25), a twenty-mile swath of Benjaminite territory from just north of Jerusalem westward almost to the Mediterranean coast. Beyond this specific rout of the coastal enemy, the narrative in 2 Sam 7 emphasizes that the kingdom ruled by King David is secure from all enemies: "YHWH had given him rest from all his enemies round about" (v. 1); "I (YHWH) was with you wherever you went and I cut off all your enemies from before you" (v. 9); "my people Israel . . . will not be agitated again, and unjust men will not afflict them any more, as formerly" (v. 10); "I will give rest to you from all your enemies" (v. 11). The narrative leaves the reader with the impression that the kingdom of Israel/Judah has, and will continue to have, secure borders.

The second thing every king needs is a secure lineage so that potential rivals remain out of power and the throne remains under dynastic control. The Bible reports that David sired six sons by six different wives as king over Judah at the royal capital in Hebron (2 Sam 3:2–5). Throughout the ANE, however, the principle of dynastic primogeniture was not well established, leading to contenders for the throne both inside and outside the royal family. But just as God promised to secure the borders, God promised to provide a secure lineage:

For your days will be fulfilled and you will lie down with your fathers, and I will raise up your offspring after you who comes forth from your loins, and I will establish his kingdom. . . . I will establish the throne of his kingdom forever. I will become a father to him, and he will become a son to me, so that when he commits iniquity, I will rebuke him with the staff of men and with strokes of mortal men. But my steadfast love will not depart from him as I removed it from Saul, whom I removed from before you. Your house and your kingdom will be made steadfast forever before you; your throne will be established forever. (2 Sam 7:12–16)

The story culminating in 1 Kgs 1–2 describes the succession of Solomon as the divinely sanctioned heir.

With secure borders and a secure lineage, it was time for David to turn his attention to the third necessity: secure divine presence. Just as a king needs a palace, a god needs a temple as a permanent place to call home. One night David muses to the prophet Nathan about the inequity of the king living in a house of cedars, and God not living in a house at all. The solution is obvious to the king: he will build a house for God, i.e., a temple. The prophet Nathan agrees with the king's plan at first, but, after divine revelation, tells David that God does not need a house. "Moreover, YHWH declares to you that YHWH will build a house for you" (2 Sam 7:11b). Now since David already has a fine house made out of the cedars of Lebanon constructed by Phoenician carpenters, he must realize that God is not talking about a house per se, but about a household. And since David also has sons and a household, he must further realize that God is not even talking about a household per se, but about a multi-generational household, that is, a dynasty. God declares that a member of this Davidic dynasty will build a house for God, a temple, in Jerusalem.

Through the political machinations of the prophet Nathan and David's wife Bathsheba, Solomon is acclaimed king over Israel/Judah at the Gihon spring outside Jerusalem around 960 B.C.E. King Solomon appropriated for himself the divine revelation to his father David: "Now, YHWH my God has given me rest from those round about; there is no adversary nor evil occurrence. Therefore I propose to build a house for the name of YHWH my God, just as YHWH spoke to my father David, saying, 'Your son whom I will set on your throne in place of you—he will build the house for my name'" (1 Kgs 5:18–19 [Eng 4–5]). Although the divine revelation through Nathan recounted earlier had not specified *which* son would ascend the throne and build the divine house, Solomon claims to be the fulfillment of the prophecy. So he undertakes to build a temple in Jerusalem at great economic cost. The timber to construct the temple needed be harvested from Lebanon, floated down the coast of the Mediterranean 90 miles from Tyre to

Joppa, and then hauled overland to Jerusalem, 35 miles away and 2,500 feet above sea level. To accomplish this, "King Solomon raised a labor-gang from all Israel, a labor-gang of 30,000 men. And he sent them to Lebanon, 10,000 men per month in relays: one month they were in Lebanon and two months at home" (1 Kgs 5:27–28 [13–14]; the parallel version of the story in 2 Chr 2 indicates that King Hiram was to provide the work force). In addition to supplying the labor, Solomon paid King Hiram wheat and fine oil for the timber, although different versions of the story specify differing quantities, as shown below.

	Wheat	Barley	Oil	Wine
1 Kgs 5:25 [11]: MT	20,000 kors			20 kors
1 Kgs 5:25 [11]: LXX	20,000 kors			20,000 baths
2 Chr 2:9 [10]: MT & LXX	20,000 kors	20,000 kors	20,000 baths	20,000 baths

Typically, one *kor* held about 6.5 bushels of grain, so 20,000 *kors* of wheat and barley would be approximately 130,000 bushels or 3,900 tons of grain. At an average consumption rate of 350 pounds per year, 20,000 *kors* of wheat would supply the needs of over 22,000 people per year! Without engaging in mathematical wizardry, we see that the payment of fine oil and/or wine was just as lavish. We may interpret these fantastic quantities as the ancient way of acknowledging that no price was too extravagant for the house of God. Especially since the royal palace complex would be constructed of and furnished with the finest materials in the ANE, the divine temple complex deserved no less. The limestone for the foundation of the temple could be quarried from the central highlands, Galilee, and the Shephelah. "Solomon had 70,000 burden-bearers and 80,000 stone-hewers in the hill country. . . . The king commanded and they quarried out great stones—precious stones—to lay the foundation of the house with hewn stones" (1 Kgs 5:29, 31 [15, 17]).

The construction of the First Temple takes up two chapters in the book of 1 Kings. (The parallel version in 2 Chr 3–4 recounts the same basic information, with helpful additional information in a couple of places). In contrast to the tabernacle narratives, Kings does not conceive of the temple as following a divine blueprint. The Chronicler, however, attributes all temple plans and preparations to King David, as revealed by YHWH to him. "David gave to Solomon his son the pattern [*tabnît*] of the porch (of the temple) and its houses, treasuries, roof chambers, and inner chambers, and the house of the mercy seat–the pattern of all that was in his mind" (1 Chr 28:11–12a). This account deliberately echoes Exod 25's account of the revelation of the *tabnît* of the wilderness tabernacle.

In any case, Solomon constructed a temple like others of the area, a rectangular structure divided into three sections, with side chambers on three sides for storage. "The lowest story was five cubits in width, the middle was six cubits in width, and the third was seven cubits in width, for he set ledges in the walls of the house all around the outside, so as not to intrude in the walls of the house" (1 Kgs 6:6). That is, the walls of the storage chambers were thickest on bottom, allowing for larger spaces on the higher floors.

The "Holy of Holies" was at the back:

> He built 20 cubits at the back of the house with planks of cedar, from the floor up the walls, and he built this part of the house for an inner sanctuary [děbîr], for the Holy of Holies. Forty cubits was the house [bayit]-that is, the temple [hêkāl]—before it. . . . Now he established the inner sanctuary in the midst of the house to put the ark of the covenant of YHWH there. The inner sanctuary was 20 cubits long and 20 cubits wide and 20 cubits high, and he overlaid it with reserved gold and he overlaid an altar with cedar. (1 Kgs 6:16–20)

A scale model of a reconstruction of the Second Temple in the time of Jesus, built by Herod the Great and thought to reflect the basic structure of the Solomonic Temple.

The Kings account of the construction consists of several major blocks as follows, indicated by the paragraph markers in the Hebrew text: General information about the construction (6:1–10); interpretive theological commentary (6:11–13); construction of inner sanctuary (6:14–37); [construction of Solomon's palace (7:1–12)]; construction of bronze pillars and sea (7:13–26), bases (7:27–37), and basins (7:38–39); summary of use of bronze and gold (7:40–50); summary and dedication (7:51—8:11). The account begins auspiciously: "Four hundred eighty years after the children of Israel came out of the land of Egypt, in the fourth year, in the month of Ziv (it is the second month [of the year]), in the reign of Solomon over Israel, he built the house for YHWH" (1 Kgs 6:1). The parallel opening verse in the Chronicler's version clarifies that in his fourth regnal year, Solomon "began to build" the house of YHWH. Further, Chronicles specifies the location: "in Jerusalem on the mountain of Moriah where he (YHWH) appeared to David his father at the place that David established, at the threshing floor of Ornan the Jebusite" (2 Chr 3:1). This additional information demonstrates the Chronicler's consistent tendency to portray David as one who accomplished all tasks related to building the temple except the actual construction.

Measuring 60 cubits long and 20 cubits wide (approximately 90 feet by 30 feet), the structure was built on the threshing floor of Araunah (Ornan) purchased by David (2 Sam 24:18–25). The temple structure consisted of hewn stone "finished at the quarry so neither hammers nor axe nor any iron tool was heard at the house when it was being built" (1 Kgs 6:7).

According to the biblical description, the house for YHWH was paneled inside from floor to ceiling with cedar from Lebanon, while the floor was paneled in cypress, also imported from the north. The cedar paneling was carved with cherubim and palm flowers and then covered with gold leaf. In fact, in the biblical account of the temple, every surface was covered with expensive imported wood or hammered gold. Utensils and temple accoutrements were worked from bronze or gold. In typical narrative exaggeration, "the weight of bronze could not be found out" (1 Kgs 7:47). Again, the reader is to understand that Israel spared no expense in imported timber, quarried stone, bronze, gold, craftsmen, laborers, and provisions for the men and animals in building the temple.

Who paid for such extravagance? The literal answer is King Solomon, but, of course, the king accumulated his wealth from tribute and taxes paid into the royal treasury. The text confirms the accumulation of royal wealth: "Solomon brought the holy things of David his father—the silver and gold and vessels he put in the treasuries of the house of YHWH" (1 Kgs 7:51). The text is clear—the temple functioned as the treasury for the accumulation of wealth by the royal family. Temple storehouses contained all manner of precious metals and provisions for the benefit of the king and the royal household (see chapter four). The three levels of storage chambers surrounding the temple housed silver and gold, vessels used in worship, wine, oil, wood, "devoted" and "sacred" things, and, more generally, tithes, contributions, and stores.

At the temple dedication ceremony, "King Solomon and all the congregation of Israel, who were assembled around him, were with him before the ark, sacrificing sheep and oxen that could not be counted or numbered from their abundance" (1 Kgs 8:5). When "the priests brought the ark of the covenant of YHWH to its place, to the inner sanctuary [*děbîr*] of the house [*bayit*], to the Holy of Holies, beneath the wings of the cherubim, . . . a cloud filled the house of YHWH, so that the priests could not stand to minister because of the cloud; for the glory of YHWH filled the house of YHWH" (1 Kgs 8:6, 10–11). Divine approval greeted the magnificent temple, securing divine sanction for the monarchy.

Or so they thought. Time would prove that the temple in Jerusalem was indeed vulnerable to the invading Babylonian army:

> In the fifth month, on the seventh day of the month—it was the nineteenth year of King Nebuchadnezzar, king of Babylon—Nebuzaradan, chief of the bodyguard, servant of the king of Babylon, came to Jerusalem. He burned the house of YHWH, the house of the king, and all the houses of Jerusalem; every great house he burned with fire. . . . The bronze pillars that were in the house of YHWH and the bases and the bronze sea that was in the house of YHWH the Chaldeans shattered, and they took their bronze pieces to Babylon. . . . The chief of the bodyguard took the gold for gold and the silver for silver. (2 Kgs 25:8–9, 13, 15)

Forty-eight years would pass before the spoils of war would be returned to Jerusalem from Babylon.

The Jerusalem Second Temple

When Nebuchadnezzar plundered the "treasures of the house of YHWH and the treasures of the house of the king" (2 Kgs 24:13), he was following in the well-established traditions of conquering armies. To the victor go the spoils! But there may be more to the removal of sacred treasure than mere greed. When King Jehoiachin of Judah surrendered to King Nebuchadnezzar of Babylon on March 16, 597 B.C.E., the accompanying understanding was that YHWH had lost to Marduk, the chief god of Babylonia. With the exception of Israel, which banned graven images, ANE cultures usually represented gods by cult statues. These statues were fashioned from the most precious stone or metals and attended to by priestly personnel as if they were living gods. Offerings of "food" and "drink" were presented several times daily. The statues were regularly bathed and clothed in fine garments. The accession of a king, the anniversary of a king, or a military victory were celebratory occasions on which priests clothed the cult statue in fine ritual garments and carried it in procession by boat or by portable litter outside of the inner sanctuary as throngs of people gathered in adoration. Sometimes the cult statues of defeated nations were brought to the victorious capital city to illustrate the submission of the defeated deity.

Since the temple in Jerusalem had no cult statue of YHWH per se, perhaps the plundering of the cult vessels—"the pots, the shovels, the snuffers, the dishes for incense, and all the bronze vessels used in the temple service, as well as the firepans and basins" (2 Kgs 25:14–15a)—somehow symbolized the defeat of the god of Israel. It is interesting that the biblical witness takes pains to note the transfer of the temple vessels to Babylon.

Another possibility is that Nebuchadnezzar brought the vessels of the Jerusalem temple as symbols of YHWH to Babylon as an additional measure of divine protection for the Babylonian capital. Even though Marduk had defeated YHWH in the battle for Jerusalem, YHWH still possessed divine strength that could be useful in the Babylonian Empire. Evidence of similar actions exists from the end of the reign of Nabonidus, the last king of Babylon (555–539 B.C.E.). As Cyrus was gathering his Persian troops for invasion, Nabonidus ordered the movement of the cult statues resident in the great Eanna temple in Uruk and other surrounding temples to Babylon, along with cultic personnel and quantities of food and drink for the regular offerings. Apparently, Nabonidus was "ensuring the continued substantial presence of the deities at his side."[2] His efforts at divine retrenchment failed, for Cyrus, the leader of a mixed tribal group known as the Persians, entered the city of Babylon without so much as a fight in 539 B.C.E. and ushered in the Achaemenid dynasty.

Upon his accession to the throne, one of the first regnal acts of Cyrus was to repatriate the cult statues and personnel that Nabonidus had gathered to Babylon. Whereas the Babylonian imperial strategy had been to centralize the population of the empire by deporting people from the edges and resettling them in the center in order to increase agricultural production and tribute, Cyrus implemented a strategy of gradually strengthening the boundaries of the empire by allowing exiles to go home. The Cyrus Cylinder, a cuneiform document from 538 B.C.E., describes the selection of Cyrus by the god Marduk as the ruler over Babylon. According to the cylinder, Cyrus assumed the throne and then demonstrated the wisdom of Marduk's choice by abolishing the system of forced labor, returning the images of the gods to their local sanctuaries, and allowing deportees to return to their homelands. The Cyrus Cylinder parallels other ANE proclamations of freedom that establish justice by allowing exiles to return home, by restoring towns and cities, by pardoning prisoners, and by canceling debts. Throughout the period of

---

[2]Paul-Alain Beaulieu, "An Episode in the Fall of Babylon to the Persians," *JNES* 52 (1993): 257.

Persian imperialism, the monarchy employed the strategy of promoting local customs in the conquered lands, thereby promoting peace and stability at the borders of the empire. The empire encouraged the return of cult statues to their native temples and the worship of parochial deities. The rebuilding of temples stimulated job growth in the local economies, satisfied the administrators of the temples, and made the religious folk appreciate the benevolence of Cyrus. All of this increased the local populations' loyalty and submission to the Persian Empire. So, Ezra reports in the opening chapter that in the first year of his reign, King Cyrus has published a decree: "All the kingdoms of the earth YHWH, the God of heaven, has given to me. He has charged me to build for him a house in Jerusalem, which is in Judah. Whoever among you from all his people—may his God be with him!—he may go up to Jerusalem, which is in Judah, and he may build the house of YHWH, the God of Israel; he is the god who is in Jerusalem" (Ezra 1:2–3). In fact, Cyrus did not want a mass exodus out of the center of the empire to the provincial edges, because the infrastructure was not yet in place to support large numbers of people. Cyrus encouraged slow and steady returns, gradually incorporating the returnees into the life of their homelands. Although the biblical narrative reports the total number of returnees at over 42,000 in Ezra 2:64–67, this number is certainly exaggerated. Berquist estimates that the number of returning exiles did not equal the number of nonexiled Judeans until the end of the reign of Cambyses in 522 B.C.E.,[3] though we cannot be sure even of this.

The biblical witness emphasizes that King Cyrus of Persia grants permission for the Jewish exiles in Babylon to return to Jerusalem and rebuild the temple, but there is confusion in the texts regarding the authority for and the financing of the construction of the Second Temple.[4]

The First Attempt

As tangible evidence of his goodwill offer of repatriation and permission for rebuilding the temple in Jerusalem, "King Cyrus brought out the vessels of the house of YHWH that Nebuchadnezzar brought from Jerusalem and deposited in the house of his god(s)" (Ezra 1:7). Over fifty years had passed,

---

[3]Jon L. Berquist, *Judaism in Persia's Shadow: A Social and Historical Approach* (Minneapolis: Fortress, 1995), 27.

[4]For a summary of the problems, see Sara Japhet, "The Temple in the Restoration Period: Reality and Ideology," *USQR* 44 (1991): 195–251; idem, "Composition and Chronology in the Book of Ezra-Nehemiah," in *Second Temple Studies 2: Temple and Community in the Persian Period* (ed. Tamara C. Eskenazi and Kent H. Richards; JSOTSup 175; Sheffield: Sheffield Academic Press 1994), 189–216.

and the cult vessels from Jerusalem were still identifiable in the temple of Marduk in Babylon! Did they have separate storage chambers labeled with the names of the conquered temples: Jerusalem, Damascus, Ashur, Nineveh, or Uruk? Why had they not melted down the gold and silver utensils from Jerusalem and fashioned replacement utensils for Marduk? In fact, we read that Cyrus specifically "left alone" the vessels from Jerusalem when he began to destroy Babylon (1 Esd 4:44). If the biblical witness is to be believed, the cult vessels from Jerusalem must have represented far more than simple worship implements in the minds of the Marduk priests; somehow YHWH, the god of Israel, still had jurisdiction over those particular pots and shovels and firepans.

These vessels belonging to YHWH "King Cyrus brought out at the disposal of (*ʿal yad*) Mithredath, the treasurer (*ḥag-gizbār*), and he counted them to Sheshbazzar, the leader of Judah" (Ezra 1:8). We saw in the Exodus account of the wilderness tabernacle, "the things produced for the Tabernacle, the tabernacle of the testimony, which were produced on the command of Moses, for the work of the Levites, at the disposal of (*bĕyad*) Ithamar, son of Aaron the priest" (Exod 38:21). Hebrew *bĕyad* (lit. "in the hand of") and *ʿal yad* (lit. "on the hand of") are the equivalent of the Akkadian *ina pāni,* (lit. "in the face of"), connoting "at the disposal of." All three expressions mean that the items are placed under the responsibility of another who must strictly account for those items when handing them over at the final destination. So, in Ezra's narrative, an inventory of the temple vessels follows in verses 9–11. Ironically, despite the need for strict accountability, the parallel account in 1 Esd 2:13–14 lists different quantities.

	Ezra 1:9–11	1 Esd 2:13–14
Gold basins/cups	30	1000
Silver basins/cups	1000	1000
Knives(?)/Silver censers	29	29
Gold bowls	30	30
Other silver bowls	410	2410
Other vessels	1000	1000
Total gold and silver vessels	5400	5469

The vessels are counted out to Mithredath, called the "treasurer" using a loan-word from Persian. In Ezra and Nehemiah, this same Persian word is combined with the Greek word for "prison" to form a compound word to describe the storage chambers surrounding the temple area (lit. "treasure-prison"). Mithredath was probably the chief accountant of the Marduk temple, or at least the person in charge of the storage of cult vessels from conquered temples. He did what any responsible Persian accountant would do—he counted out the vessels to Sheshbazzar and, by so doing, transferred accountability to him. On the way back to Judah, camped by the river Ahava, Ezra selected leading men to go to Iddo, the leader in Casiphia (*Kāsipyāʾ*) in order to ask Iddo and his associates for "ministers for the house of our God" (Ezra 8:17). To these men, Ezra "weighed out in their disposal (*ʿal yadām*)" silver talents and vessels of gold, silver, and bronze (8:26), admonishing them, "Be watchful and guard (them) until you weigh (them) out . . . in Jerusalem" (8:29). Upon arrival in Jerusalem, "we weighed the silver and the gold and the vessels in the house of our God in the disposal of (*ʿal yad*) Meremoth, son of Uriah, the priest and [list of names]. With number, with weight for all, so all the weight was recorded at that time" (8:33–34).

In the parallel account in 1 Esdr 8:41–64, while encamped at the river Theras, Ezra selected leaders to go to "Iddo, the leader, the one at the place of the treasury" (*gazophylakiou;* lit. "treasure-prison") in order to ask Iddo and "the treasurers at that place" to send men to be accountable for the silver and the vessels. The implication here is that the ones accountable for the precious cargo from Babylon to Jerusalem were associated with the Babylonian treasury accounting system. Apparently, the Greek translators understood Casiphia (*Kāsipyāʾ*) to be a place for storing silver (*kesep*).

The Ezra narrative contains three accounts of the decree of Cyrus and the role of Sheshbazzar in the rebuilding of the temple. The first account we have already seen in chapter one. The second account appears in the fifth chapter. Tattenai, the governor of the province Beyond the River, which included Judah, wrote a letter to King Darius in which he described the answer given by Jewish workers when he questioned their reconstruction efforts. The workers related that King Cyrus had decreed their repatriation and given permission for the rebuilding of the temple. In addition, they brought out the gold and silver vessels plundered from the Jerusalem temple and delivered them to Sheshbazzar. "Then this Sheshbazzar came and laid the foundations of the house of God which is in Jerusalem, and from then until now it was being built, but it is not completed yet" (Ezra 5:16). The third account appears in the sixth chapter, where King Darius, in response to the letter from Tattenai, searches the official government archives for Cyrus's decree. Interestingly, the text notes that at first Darius thought the decree would be found in the archives in Babylon, probably in the Marduk temple. Instead, the decree was located in Ecbatana, the former capital of the Medes. He quotes the decree in a reply to Tattenai, recorded in Aramaic:

> As for the house of God in Jerusalem, let the house be built as a place where sacrifices are sacrificed, and let its foundations be raised, with its height 60 cubits, its width 60 cubits, with 3 rows of quarried stone and one row of wood. Let the outflow be given from the house of the king. Further, as for the vessels of the

house of God made of gold and silver that Nebuchadnezzar brought out from the temple (*hêkāl*) in Jerusalem and brought to Babylon, let them be returned and brought to the temple in Jerusalem to their rightful place; you will deposit them in the house of God. (Ezra 6:3–5 = 1 Esd 6:24–26)

This third account offers new information regarding the decree of Cyrus, although its accuracy is not a foregone conclusion. First, it explicitly describes the temple in Jerusalem as a place for sacrifice. Second, it specifies the structure's height and width, along with the construction materials and technique. Although we can easily understand a royal decree that permits repatriation and temple rebuilding, as indicated in the first two accounts, it is hard to imagine why the Persian king would care about the dimensions and construction materials of the temple in Jerusalem, a rural outpost of the empire more than 700 miles away.

For our purposes, the most interesting new information is that the "outflow" comes from the house of the king. Exactly what is the "outflow," (*nipqâ* in Aramaic) that is to be provided by the king? Most English translations give the translation as "cost" or "expenditure." Further investigation of the word *nipqâ* suggests an alternative. The Greek version of Ezra 6:4 uses the word *dapanē* and 1 Esd 6:25 uses the word *dapanēma* to translate the Aramaic *nipqâ*. These two Greek words come from the same root verb that means "to use up or pay out material or physical resources."[5] The Aramaic word *nipqâ* comes from the verbal root *n-p-q*, "to go or come out."[6] In the Aramaic section of the book of Daniel, the subject of this verb is "he," "a decree," "men," and "fingers." In Ezra 5:14, this same verb describes what Nebuchadnezzar did to the gold and silver vessels from the temple in Jerusalem, and what Cyrus then did when the vessels were in the temple in Babylon. Again, in Ezra 6:5, Nebuchadnezzar "brought out" the vessels from the temple in Jerusalem. So the noun *nipqâ* would be something like, "that which is brought out, that which goes out." In Ezra's narrative the "thing which is brought out" that is the subject of so much attention is the pile of gold and silver vessels transferred from the Jerusalem temple to the Babylon temple. Since the king has authority over the precious items stored in the temple, the king orders that these items be "brought out" from the house of the king, that is, under his authority. The traditional translation of *nipqâ* as "cost" would mean that Cyrus provided the *funds* to rebuild the temple. Other than this word in Ezra 6:4, there is no indication in the biblical texts that Cyrus financed the construction of the Second Temple in Jerusalem. Moreover, if Cyrus had done so, the people should have rebuilt the temple

---

[5] *BDAG*, 212.
[6] BDB, 1103.

immediately upon returning from Babylon. Instead, in the initial account of the decree of Cyrus in the first chapter of Ezra, we find a financing plan that does *not* involve the royal treasury:

> And every one remaining from all places, wherever he resides, let the men of his place assist him with silver and with gold and with portable property and with beasts, with freewill offerings for the house of God that is in Jerusalem. So the heads of the ancestors of Judah and Benjamin and the priests and the Levites—everyone whose spirit God aroused—arose to go up to build the house of YHWH that is in Jerusalem. And all those around them strengthened them with their hands, with vessels of silver, with gold, with personal property, and with beasts, and with choice things, besides all that was freely offered. (Ezra 6:4–6)

After an extensive genealogy, the narrative continues:

> When they came to the house of YHWH that is in Jerusalem, some of the heads of the ancestors made freewill offerings for the house of God to erect it on its site. According to their resources, they gave to the treasury for the work 61,000 gold darics, 5,000 minas of silver, and 100 priestly garments. (Ezra 2:68–69)

The text obviously exhibits confusion at this juncture because the folks making the initial return from Babylon under King Cyrus could not possibly have been carrying gold *darics*, since *darics* were first minted under the reign of King Darius at least two decades after Cyrus. At any rate, the text makes the point that the returning exiles footed the cost of the temple project. As we have seen, whatever construction efforts Sheshbazzar and the exiles started, they did not successfully rebuild the temple.

The Second Attempt

The book of Ezra credits the second attempt to rebuild the Jerusalem temple to Jeshua, son of Jozadak, and Zerubbabel, son of Shealtiel (3:2). Haggai adds that Jeshua was the high priest and Zerubbabel the governor of Judah (1:1). The chronology of the biblical texts becomes confusing, since three successive chapters of Ezra indicate three different Persian kings reigning at the time of the rebuilding project: Cyrus (539–530) in Chapter 3; Ahasuerus/Artaxerxes (464–424) in Chapter 4; and Darius (521–486) in Chapter 5. Clearly the reign of Ahasuerus/Artaxerxes is out of order; some other tradition of interaction between the officials of Judah and the Persian king has intruded into the story at this point. Careful reading of the chapter reveals that, in fact, the rebuilding project under Ahasuerus/Artaxerxes does not involve the temple, but rather the walls and foundations of Jerusalem. The likely explanation is that this incident is to be associated with Nehemiah and the reconstruction of the walls of Jerusalem in approximately 450 B.C.E. rather than with Jeshua's and Zerubbabel's attempt to rebuild the temple.

To return to the narrative in Ezra 3, Jeshua and Zerubbabel "built the altar of the God of Israel to offer up on it whole burnt offerings as it was written in the Law of Moses" (3:2). The text takes pains to describe the people's strict obedience to the prescribed daily and festival offerings, presumably grain, sheep, and incense proffered by the returning exiles. In verse 6, the narrative specifically states, "But the temple (*hêkāl*) of YHWH was not founded (yet)." That is, the altar in front of the temple was functional, so that the people could observe the Mosaic commandments regarding sacrifices and festival celebrations, but the temple, including the Holy of Holies, was not yet rebuilt. "So they gave silver to the masons and craftsmen, food and drink and oil to the Sidonians and Tyrians to bring cedar trees from Lebanon to the sea, to Joppa, according to the permission of Cyrus, King of Persia, given to them" (Ezra 3:7). The Hebrew word I have translated "permission" is *rišyôn,* and it appears only here in the Old Testament. The verbal root is assumed to be *r-š-h,* although it never appears in the Old Testament. In other cognate Semitic languages, however, the root *r-š-h* means "to permit, to have power over, to cause, to allow."[7] In past scholarship, this word has been interpreted as "grant," as if Cyrus paid for the supplies and laborers needed for the temple in Jerusalem. (See the discussion above regarding Ezra 6:4 and the "outlay" from the house of the king.)

I suggest that this verse supports the interpretation that Cyrus *permitted* the repatriation of the exiles and *allowed* the rebuilding of the temple, provided that the Jews could pay for the project. Jeshua and Zerubbabel pulled together enough resources to bring quarried stones and timbers to the temple site in Jerusalem. Then "the builders laid the foundation of the temple (*hêkāl*) of YHWH" to the celebratory music of the priests and Levites (Ezra 3:10). "All the people shouted a great shout in praising YHWH because the house of YHWH was founded. But many of the priests, the Levites, and the heads of ancestors—elders who saw the first house (of YHWH) when it was established, were weeping aloud when they saw that this was the house (of YHWH); but many (others) raised a sound with a shout and with joy" (Ezra 3:11).

This verse is often quoted as an indicator that the Second Temple was by no means the magnificent structure that was the First Temple. But the text is clearly concerned not with the aesthetic grandeur of the finished structure, but, rather, with the emotional import of laying the foundations of the Second Temple on the same site as the First Temple. After everything these ex-

---

[7]Ibid., 957.

iles had suffered—the siege of Jerusalem, the burning of the First Temple, the apparent defeat of YHWH by Marduk, the captivity in Babylon, the return to a devastated capital city—the laying of the temple foundations must have been quite an emotional event. It is completely understandable that in such a situation, both weeping and shouting with joy were appropriate emotional responses.

The text then recounts a conflict that halted the rebuilding project so earnestly begun by the returning exiles.

> The adversaries of Judah and Benjamin heard that the exiles were building a temple (*hêkāl*) to YHWH, the God of Israel. So they approached Zerubbabel and the head of the ancestors and said to them, "Let us build with you, because, like you, we seek your God and to him we have been sacrificing since the days of Esarhaddon, King of Assyria, who brought us here." But Zerubbabel, Jeshua, and the rest of the heads of the ancestral families for Israel said to them, "Not you, but *we* will build a house (*bayit*) for our God because we alone will build (a house) for YHWH, the God of Israel, just as King Cyrus, King of Persia, commanded us." Then the people of the land (*ʿam hā-ʾāreṣ*) disheartened the people of Judah and discouraged them from building, and hiring advisors against them to frustrate their plan all the days of Cyrus, King of Persia, until the reign of Darius, King of Persia. (Ezra 4:1–5)

Who are these "adversaries of Judah and Benjamin?" The text says they are worshipers of YHWH, converted to Yahwistic religion after being resettled into the area by the King Esarhaddon of Assyria (680–669 B.C.E.).

Even after more than a century had passed, animosity was fierce between the returning exiles and the descendants of the immigrants from eastern lands. These immigrants were not purebred Israelites; they were not part of the ancestral families; they did not share the common salvation story of the Exodus from Egypt; they were not orthodox Yahwists. But then the text mentions "the people of the land, the *ʿam hā-ʾāreṣ*," as the ones who discouraged the exiles and frustrated the building project. "The people of the land" were those remaining in Judah after the Babylonian deportations. In the first siege of Jerusalem in 597, Nebuchadnezzar "exiled all Jerusalem, all the leaders, all the warriors (ten thousand exiles) all the craftsmen and the smiths; no one remained, except the poorest people of the land (*ʿam hā-ʾāreṣ*)" (2 Kgs 24:14). Ten years later, after the second siege, "the rest of the people, the remnant who were in the city and the fallen who had fallen under the king of Babylon, the rest of the crowd, Nebuzaradan the chief of the bodyguard exiled" (2 Kgs 25:11). This verse, in conjunction with the prophetic announcements of the complete destruction and depopulation of Judah and the postexilic biblical texts that concentrate on the returning exiles reclaiming the land, prompted the "myth of the empty land" among scholars for years.

But clearly, there were "people of the land" remaining in the villages of Judah after the devastation by the Babylonians. Jeremiah even mentions ongoing worship of YHWH at the temple site: "On the second day of the murder of Gedaliah, when no one knew, eighty men came from Shechem and Shiloh and Samaria, with shaven beards, torn garments, and cut bodies, with a grain offering and incense in their hands to bring to the house of YHWH" (Jer 41:4–5). For fifty years the people of the land had lived up to their name, eking out a living in the hill country of Judah with subsistence farming and petty trade. The natives were sure to contest the property claims of the returnees. Those who had presided over the community's worship life after the destruction of the temple would have resented the returning priests' assumption of power. When the exiled elite returned and set about to rebuild the temple using precious resources of silver, food, drink, and oil, no wonder the people of the land opposed the project. If the returning exiles were wealthy enough or resourceful enough to build a grand temple, surely they were resourceful enough to help their fellow Israelites who had been holding down the fort and continuing to pray to YHWH for half a century! Apparently, the priority of the elite was to erect a great house for YHWH because they believed the outdoor worship by the people of the land insufficient for the God of Israel. Politically, the natives were probably indifferent to the reigning overlord—life was a struggle to feed one's family and support the imperial administration under the Assyrians, the Babylonians, and now the Persians. But the returning exiles had a certain loyalty to the Persian administration since their position and power in society depended on the benevolence of the Persian regime. Perhaps more importantly, there would have been continuing conflict over the theological interpretation and implications of the exile.[8] The people of the land caused enough disruption that the leaders abandoned their plan to build the temple until the prophetic encouragement of Haggai and Zechariah in the second year of King Darius of Persia, that is, 520 B.C.E.

The Third Attempt

The prophets Haggai and Zechariah enter the Ezra narrative in chapter five when they "prophesied to the Jews who were in Judah (Yehud) and in Jerusalem in the name of the God of Israel who was over them. Then Zerubbabel, son of Shealtiel, and Jeshua, son of Jozadak, arose, and they began to

---

[8]Most scholars see the writings of Third Isaiah (Chapters 56–66) as evidence of the growing conflict in postexilic Judah. Scholars, however, differ over the identities of the conflicting parties: visionaries vs. hierocrats; Yahwists vs. syncretists; or priestly immigrants vs. political immigrants vs. natives.

build the house of God that is in Jerusalem, and with them were the prophets of God, supporting them" (Ezra 5:1–2). Since Ezra does not record the words of the prophecy, we turn to the books of Haggai and Zechariah. Between these two prophets, there are six prophecies dated to the second year of King Darius.

(1) Year 2, Month 6, Day 1 (Hag 1:1–14). The people have resisted the use of scarce resources for building the temple in Jerusalem, saying, "The right time has not come to build the house of YHWH" (1:2). But YHWH indicts the people using their own words: "Is it the right time for you to live in your finished houses when this house is desolate?" (1:4). Reconstruction of personal houses had begun after the return from exile, but the divine house still lay in ruins, presumably with a functioning altar and laid foundations, but nothing else. Then YHWH makes a causal connection between the economic prosperity of the people and the state of the divine residence.

> Go up to the hill country, bring wood, and build the house (i.e., the temple) so that I may be pleased with it and I may be honored, says YHWH. Turning toward abundance, yet only a little you brought to (your) house and I blew (even) it away. Why? An oracle of YHWH of hosts. Because my house—it is desolate! But you are running to your own houses. On account of this, the heavens above you have refrained from the dew and the earth has refrained from its produce. And I have summoned a drought over the earth, the hills, the grain, the new wine, the oil, and over all that the soil brings forth, and over human and beast and every labor. (Hag 1:8–11)

As long as the divine house lies in ruins, the economy will lie in ruins as well! Conversely, reconstructing the temple will reconstruct the orderly ways of nature that drive the agricultural economy. The ancient world well understood this tit for tat behavior between the gods and humans. In fact, the *raison d'être* of the temple complex in the ANE was to meet the needs of the deity in anticipation that the deity would meet the needs of the king and the people. To quote an ancient aphorism, "Reverence begets favor; sacrifice prolongs life" (*CAD* N/2:258). A letter from an Assyrian to King Ashurbanipal (669–627 B.C.E.) explicitly addresses the reciprocal relationship:

> Shamash and Adad, through their steadfast regard for the king my lord (and) his dominion of the lands, have established a gracious reign, orderly days, years of righteousness, abundant rains, copious inundations, and acceptable prices. The gods are graciously inclined. The fear of God is strong. The temples cause prosperity. . . . Reproduction is blest. . . . Those who have been sick many days are recovered. The hungry are satisfied. The lean grow fat. The destitute are supplied with clothing. (*RCAE*, #2)

The translator's commentary on this letter is that "the gifts to the gods are a paying investment." It seems that the prophet Haggai would agree with this assessment. Using resources to finance the construction of the divine house will pay off for the community in economic prosperity.

In the prophetic tradition, human actions often have their consequences in the realm of nature. Amos announces that YHWH will send a devouring fire on Judah because the people "have rejected the Torah of YHWH and have not kept his statutes" (Amos 2:4–5). Micah links the destruction of Jerusalem and the temple to the destructive behaviors of its leaders: "Its leaders judge for a bribe, its priests teach for a price, and its prophets practice divination for silver. Yet they lean on YHWH saying, 'YHWH is in our midst, isn't he? Evil will not come upon us!' Therefore on account of you, Zion will be plowed as a field, Jerusalem will become a heap of ruins, and the mountain of the house like high places of the forest"(Mic 3:11–12). Haggai directly links the forces of nature with the economic condition of the people, and blames their poverty on their neglect of the temple of YHWH. His prophecy inspired the leaders and the people: "They came and did work on the house of YHWH of hosts, their God" (1:14).

(2) [Year 2] Month 6, Day 24 (Hag 1:15; 2:15–19). According to the Hebrew text, Hag 1:14 ends the paragraph. Most scholars believe that Hag 1:15 should be understood as the dating for the prophecy in 2:15–19 and transpose those verses there. The date in 2:18, "Day 24 of the ninth" is probably a gloss to the text. The precise resolution of the textual confusion is difficult. Whether delivered in month 6 or month 9, the point is much the same as the preceding prophecy, whether three weeks or three months earlier.

> And now, set your heart from this day forward: before a stone was set to stone in the temple of YHWH, how was it going? One came to a pile of 20, but there were only 10; one came to the wine vat to draw off 50 measures from the wine press, but there were only 20. I smote you and all your labors with blight, mildew, and hail, yet you would not belong to me, an oracle of YHWH. . . . From the day that the temple of YHWH was founded, set your heart, is there still seed in the storehouse? Do the vine, fig tree, pomegranate, and olive tree still not bear (fruit)? From this day I will bless (you). (2:15–19)

Laying the foundation and commencing the reconstruction of the temple will reverse the economic fortunes of the people. The prophet Malachi would later promise a blessing for the people if they would worship YHWH with their tithes and offerings as prescribed by the law:

> Bring all the tithe to the treasure-house in order that there may be food in my house and in this prove me, says YHWH of Hosts, whether I will open for you the windows of heaven and pour down for you an overflowing blessing. (Mal 3:10)

(3) Year 2, Month 7, Day 21 (Hag 2:1–9). If we accept Haggai's chronology, the people had been working on the temple for a little over six weeks.

Perhaps the erstwhile enthusiasm was waning in the face of difficult circumstances, or perhaps working with large stones and timbers was simply arduous. Apparently, some were despairing of ever constructing a temple that would favorably compare to the grand and glorious temple that King Solomon built. YHWH calls upon Haggai to address the leaders and the remnant again.

> Thus says YHWH of Hosts: Once again, in a little bit, I will be shaking the heavens and the earth, the sea and the dry land. I will shake all the nations so that the desirable things of all the nations will come in, and I will fill this house with glory, says YHWH of Hosts. The silver will be mine and the gold will be mine, an oracle of YHWH of Hosts. Greater will be the glory of this latter house than the former, says YHWH of Hosts, and in this place I will give wholeness, an oracle of YHWH of Hosts. (2:6–9)

Haggai's prophecy promises that the construction of the temple will have cosmic implications. Treasure will once again flow into the house of YHWH, to the benefit of all.

(4) Year 2, Month 8 (Zech 1:1–6). We learn from the Ezra narrative that the prophets Haggai and Zechariah, contemporaries in the postexilic period, reinvigorated the temple construction project in Jerusalem. As we have seen already, Haggai criticizes the building of private residences while the temple lies in ruins and links economic disaster with the state of the temple. Zechariah's prophecy, by contrast, is much less explicit. While Haggai mentions the house/temple of YHWH 10 times in 38 verses, Zechariah mentions the house/temple only 7 times in 121 verses (chapters 1–8).[9] Zechariah's oracle of the eighth month of year two of King Darius does not mention the temple at all. Rather, the prophet reminds the people to return to YHWH so that their fate will be different from that of their ancestors. Coupled with Haggai's words, we are to understand this warning as further impetus to honor YHWH by completing the temple.

(5) Year 2, Month 9, Day 24 (Hag 2:10–14, 20–23). Two prophecies are announced to Haggai on Day 24. First, the situation of a priestly teaching is described. In response to the question of law (*tôrâ*), of whether a clean item can transmit cleanness to other items, the priests answer that each item must be made clean by ritual ceremony. However, they continue, anything touched by an unclean item is made unclean. The priests give the interpretation of the Levitical laws regarding holiness. YHWH accepts the priests' teaching and applies it to "this people and all this nation before me—an

---

[9]Scholars have long recognized that Chapters 1–8 belong to the postexilic contemporary of Haggai, whereas Chapters 9–14 were written two to three centuries later in the Hellenistic period and attached to the earlier prophet's work. See the standard commentaries on Zechariah.

oracle of YHWH—and thus every work of their hands and whatever they present there is unclean" (2:14). The connection with rebuilding the temple is obscure. Apparently we are to understand that the people cannot fulfill their call to holiness unless and until they have built a temple for the Holy One. The Greek translation of verse 14 adds specific examples of such mistreatment of others: ". . . because of their unjust gains in the early morning, they will suffer pain from their pains; and you hate whoever shows your fault in the gates." The Greek addition specifically links uncleanness to unjust economic gain.

The remedy for uncleanness in priestly material usually involves the passage of time and priestly atonement. The following is typical: "The priest shall make atonement for him with the ram of guilt offering before YHWH on account of his sin that he sinned. And his sin that he sinned will be pardoned" (Lev 19:22). The lack of a fully functioning temple made the sacrificial system that conveyed divine forgiveness impossible, and thus there would be no way of ridding the community of its uncleanness before YHWH. YHWH is holy and has chosen Israel to be holy, which it can be only through the means of grace found in the divinely ordained sacrificial system. Without the temple, the divine enactment of forgiveness is in jeopardy.

The second prophecy of Haggai on Day 24 repeats language of the earlier prophecy in verse 6: "I will be shaking the heavens and the earth" (2:21). This time the result will not be treasure pouring in, but the overthrow of the political authority and military might of the other nations. "I will overturn the throne of kingdoms; I will destroy the strength of the kingdoms of the nations; I will overturn chariot and its riders; horses and their riders will go down, each by the sword of his kinsman" (2:22). The language of chariots, horses, and riders echoes the victory that YHWH won over the Egyptians at the Sea of Reeds (e.g., Exod 14:26–28; 15:1, 4, 21). Haggai's final prophecy ends with a promise: "On that day—an oracle of YHWH of Hosts—I will take you Zerubbabel, son of Shealtiel, my servant—an oracle of YHWH—and I will set you as a signet ring because I have chosen you—an oracle of YHWH of Hosts" (2:23).

The threefold repetition of "an oracle of YHWH," bracketed by the additional designation "of Hosts," serves to underline the reliability of the promise. Replete with echoes from other biblical messianic texts, this final verse in Haggai holds out hope of the restoration of the Davidic monarchy upon completion of the divine sanctuary since Zerubbabel is the grandson of the last monarch of Judah, Jehoiachin. Just as YHWH had once chosen David as dynastic monarch and Zion as divine dwelling place, YHWH has once again affirmed the Davidic line and the sacred site.

(6) Year 2, Month 11, Day 24 (Zech 1:7–6:15). Here Zechariah describes eight night visions interpreted by a divine messenger. Each vision confirms YHWH's choice of Israel out of all the nations to be in special relationship and Jerusalem as the center of the universe once again. YHWH confirms the success of the temple rebuilding project in two of the visions: "I have returned to Jerusalem in compassion; my house will be built in it—an oracle of YHWH of Hosts—and the measuring line will be stretched out over Jerusalem" (1:16) and "The hands of Zerubbabel have founded this house and his hands will complete it" (4:9). The concluding prophecy in 6:9–15 is similar to the final prophecy of Haggai, except that the text in Zechariah has mistakenly substituted the name Joshua, the high priest, for the name Zerubbabel, the governor, as the one who will sit on the throne.

Two clues allow us to call this substitution mistaken. First, the text names the future ruler "Branch," a messianic term. Zerubbabel, a compound name of Zerub and Babel means "offspring or branch of Babylon," while Joshua, or Jeshua as he is called in Ezra, means "salvation."[10] It makes no linguistic sense to translate Joshua as "Branch." Second, the text says, "A priest will be by his throne, and good counsel will be between the two of them" (6:13b). If Joshua, the high priest, is the ruler on the throne, why would he need a priest beside him? But if Zerubbabel is on the throne, then Joshua is the priest who is standing beside him with good counsel. The one named Branch, that is Zerubbabel, "will build the temple of YHWH; *he* will build the temple of YHWH" (6:12b–13a).

In this diversion from the book of Ezra, we have been examining the prophecies of Haggai and Zechariah in the books named after them. These prophecies span the second half of the second year of the reign of King Darius of Persia and indicate that, although the returning exiles made a good faith effort to start rebuilding the temple, their zeal for the project soon lagged. The prophets continue to encourage them to commit precious resources to the work, promising tangible economic benefits, threatening them with punishment familiar from their ancestral history, and assuring them that rebuilding the temple is indeed congruent with the divine will. Ezra reports that the prophets were "supporting" Zerubbabel and Jeshua as they "began to build the house of God that is in Jerusalem" (Ezra 5:2).

Meanwhile, according to Ezra 5, Tattenai, the governor of the province Beyond the River, questioned the authorization for the rebuilding. We have already been introduced to this letter above in the discussion of Sheshbazzar and the decree of King Cyrus that permitted repatriation and rebuilding. At

---

[10]Of course, the Greek form of this name is Jesus.

this time we are interested in the additional authority granted by King Darius in response to Tattenai's inquiry.

> Now, Tattenai, governor of Beyond the River, Shethar-bozenai, and you, their associates, the officials of Beyond the River, be distant from them [the Jews working on the temple]! Leave them alone for the work of this house of God; as for the governor of the Jews and the elders of the Jews, let them build this house of God on its site. I set a decree as to what you will do for these elders of the Jews to rebuild this house of God: from the property of the king, that is, from the tribute of Beyond the River, diligently the outlay (*nipqĕtâ*) will be given to these men without ceasing. And whatever is needed—young bulls, rams, lambs for whole burnt offerings to the God of heaven, wheat, salt, or oil as the priests in Jerusalem command—let it be given to them day by day without neglect so that they may offer up soothing sacrifices to the God of heaven and they may pray for the life of the king and his sons. . . . (curse for altering the decree) I, Darius, set a decree. Let it be done diligently. (Ezra 6:6–10, 12b)

Once again, as in Ezra 6:4, we encounter the Aramaic word *nipqâ*, translated "outlay." In the previous case, the "outlay" was the temple vessels. In both contexts, the word is associated with the king. In 6:4, the outlay was to be from the house (or authority, status) of the king. Here, it is from the property (or goods, wealth, riches) of the king. More specifically, the outlay comes from the tribute (*mindâ* or *middâ*) that the province Beyond the River owes the royal treasury. According to this new decree, Darius has committed to financing the rest of the construction project and the cost of the daily offerings from the tribute normally paid by the province. This must have been a double blow for Tattenai—not only does he not get a royal decree to stop the reconstruction, but he has to finance the project out of the silver and/or commodities that he is required to remit to the king.

The historical context of the early years of the reign of Darius provides a plausible setting for the decree described in Ezra. When King Cyrus conquered the Babylonians, he understood the political expediency of repatriation of native populations that had been forcibly relocated to the Babylonian heartland. Allowing exiles to return home and worship their local deities would, Cyrus believed, make these peoples more readily accept their foreign overlords. Since he had just come to power by uniting the Medes and the Persians, who lacked an adequate administrative system, Cyrus managed the empire essentially in the same way as the Babylonian Empire before him and the Assyrian Empire before that.

Cyrus' son Cambyses (529–522) was occupied with subduing revolts in the eastern parts of the empire and with the ambitious goal of conquering Egypt. He launched an attack from Tyre by sea, thereby avoiding marching his army through Judah, and captured the capital Memphis in 525 B.C.E.

Upon hearing of the possible usurpation of the throne back home, Cambyses left Egypt, but died before reaching Babylon.

Darius, a military officer and a member of a cadet line of the royal family, took the throne by force in 521 and spent the next two years quelling rebellions and solidifying his hold on the empire. Darius understood that the policy of conquest and consolidation employed by Cyrus and Cambyses would not continue to support the administration of the empire, so he implemented an administrative system that would bring the Persian Empire to its zenith. He organized the empire into twenty provinces and appointed Persian officials loyal to the king, such as Tattenai. Furthermore, he devised a system of variable taxation for each province based on the measurable land acreage and type of native crop. Communication was improved by increasing the safety of the routes, using regular way stations with fresh horses, and requiring regular reporting by officials. Eventually standard coinage came into use on a limited basis. One of the administrative changes that Darius introduced was the requirement that temples pay taxes to the crown. In return, rebuilding and maintenance of temples throughout the empire would be a royal obligation. For example, when Darius returned to Egypt in 519 B.C.E. as king of the Persian Empire, which included Egypt, he commissioned the rebuilding of a local temple with its library and medical school, thereby winning the gratitude and loyalty of the temple administration and religious adherents.

The shift in religious policy proved to be one crucial element in the rebuilding of the Jerusalem temple. No longer did the project depend on claiming a share of the scarce resources of the Jews. Now, the Persian Empire would foot the bill. Another crucial element in the rebuilding of the Jerusalem temple was its role as a collection location for local taxes. Further discussion about the temple's role as a tax collection location will be discussed in chapter four. For now, suffice it to say that in anticipation of increased tax payments as a result of his administrative reorganization of the empire, Darius needed the Jerusalem temple completed in order to serve as a tax collection location. Still another crucial element in its completion was Darius' strategy regarding Egypt, the southern superpower. Whereas Cambyses had launched his conquest of Egypt by sea from Tyre, Darius planned to march his army through the provinces all the way to Egypt, thus displaying his military prowess to all the provinces. Locals were required to provide foodstuffs for the army as it passed through their territory. So, Darius encouraged the rebuilding of the Jerusalem temple beginning in 520 B.C.E. in preparation for his march to Egypt, providing significant funds for the work. He would have wanted Judah to be stable and productive, relatively satisfied with the Persian administration, and ready to supply the army as it came through.

Haggai and Zechariah urged the people to comply with Persian policy, although they couched their prophecies in Yahwistic language. At the same time, the prophets seek to allay any fears about an army marching into Judah, remembering what happened on the last occurrence of such an event in 587 B.C.E.

All of these factors—royal financing, anticipated increased tax receipts, the Egyptian campaign, and prophetic encouragement—combined to spur the Jews to complete the rebuilding of the Second Temple. What the impoverished citizenry could not accomplish during the reigns of Cyrus and Cambyses took place within four years of Darius' decree of financial support. "They completed the building task by the decree of the God of Israel and by the decree of Cyrus and Darius and Artaxerxes, King of Persia. So this house was finished on the third day of the month of Adar in the sixth year of the reign of Darius the King" (Ezra 6:14b–15).

Perhaps the most interesting puzzle of the Second Temple is why the biblical texts do not give any physical description of it. The description of the wilderness tabernacle takes up twelve chapters in Exodus; the description of the First Temple takes two chapters in Kings and two in Chronicles. Even extracanonical texts do not describe the Second Temple with any detail. As scholar and pundit Robert Carroll once said, "This is so strange and surprising a lack in a book over-determined by accounts of temple building, that Sherlock Holmes' 'curious incident of the dog' comes instantly to mind as a fruitful analogy for biblical studies."[11]

Finally, a word must be added about the enlargement of the Second Temple under Herod the Great (37–4 B.C.E.). The historian Flavius Josephus describes Herod's project:

> It was at this time, in the eighteenth year of his reign, after the events mentioned above, that Herod undertook an extraordinary work, (namely) the reconstructing of the temple of God at his own expense, enlarging its precincts and raising it to a more imposing height. (Josephus, *Ant.* 15.380)

According to Josephus, Herod offers to undertake the project, ". . . since, by the will of God, I am now ruler and there continues to be a long period of peace and an abundance of wealth and great revenues, and—what is of most importance—the Romans, who are, so to speak, the masters of the world, are (my) loyal friends . . ." (Josephus, *Ant.* 15.387). There follows a description

---

[11] Robert P. Carroll, "So What Do We *Know* About the Temple? The Temple in the Prophets," in *Second Temple Studies 2: Temple and Community in the Persian Period* (ed. Tamara C. Eskenazi and Kent H. Richards; JSOTSup 175; Sheffield: Sheffield Academic Press, 1994), 34.

of the temple design, including the stonework, the doors, the cloisters and pillars, the gates, and the increasingly discriminating courts for women, men, and priests. "In this (priests' court) was the temple, and before it was an altar, on which we used to sacrifice whole burnt offerings to God" (Josephus, *Ant.* 15.419). Herod's is the temple most familiar to modern readers, because many tourists have seen reconstructed models and actual ancient stones excavated from the Herodian period displayed on the Temple Mount in present-day Jerusalem.

Excursus—Temples to YHWH outside Jerusalem

Within Israel

The closest in proximity to Jerusalem was the Samaritan temple on Mount Gerizim, still a subject of controversy in the first century C.E. (John 4:20). According to Josephus, the temple on Mt. Gerizim was modeled after the Jerusalem temple (Josephus, *Ant.* 11.310).

The sanctuary in Arad in the Negev is interpreted by some as a Yahwistic temple, since it resembles the layout of the Jerusalem temple. Excavations at

A reconstruction of the altar found at Arad.

The temple precinct at Arad. Note the "holy of holies" or inner niche in the
center of the photograph with its four carved upright stones found in loci.
The front two are for incense.

Arad have unearthed inscribed pottery shards detailing the disbursement of
rations to itinerant military personnel and other administrative records related to the sanctuary there. The records' mention of the temple in Jerusalem
and of tithes has led some scholars to wonder about the Jerusalem temple as
the source of the commodities stored and disbursed in Arad.

The ancient sanctuaries at Dan and Bethel were renovated by the first
monarch of the Northern Kingdom, Jeroboam I (932–911 B.C.E.) as convenient worship sites for his subjects, perhaps hoping to discourage pilgrimage to Jerusalem and the attendant economic outflow of goods (1 Kgs
12:26–33). Evidence of economic activity has been unearthed at sacred sites
throughout the region. Excavated examples include a stone mold for figurines and a crushing vat for oil burning lamps in the precincts of the second
millennium sanctuary at Nahariyah, a coastal city between Acco and Tyre; a
potter's kiln and potters' workshops near shrines in Hazor in Galilee; a clay
mold for figurines and numerous weaving weights and whorls in the tenth
century B.C.E. "Cultic Structure" at Ta'anach south of Megiddo.[12] Noted as a
place of sacrifice in the patriarchal period, the sacred site of Bethel could be

---

[12]Stager and Wolff, "Production and Commerce," 96.

termed a temple since God was thought to be resident there (1 Sam 10:3). According to Judg 20:26–28, the ark of the covenant resided at Bethel during the conflict with the Benjaminites. Amaziah the priest warns Amos, "Do not prophesy again at Bethel, for it is the sanctuary of the king (*miqdaš-melek*) and a house of the kingdom (*bêt mamlākâ*)" (Amos 7:3).

The area of the altar at Tel Dan. Note the reconstructed outline of the altar in metal.

In Egypt

In addition to the temples in Jerusalem and Mt. Gerizim, two Yahwistic temples were situated in Egypt. One was at Leontopolis in northern Egypt, built by Onias IV around 150 B.C.E., perhaps to serve Yahwists in the Delta region.

The other is the Temple of YHW at Elephantine at the first cataract of the Nile in Southern Egypt.[13] The origins of the Jewish Elephantine community are lost in history. Many scholars assign the military settlement in Egypt to the reign of Manasseh (697–642), but this remains speculative. According to the second-century B.C.E. text *Letter of Aristeas,* Judeans assisted the Egyptian

---

[13]The divine name in papyri is YHW; in ostraca it is YHH. The vocalized spelling is customarily Yahu.

Psammetichus I against the Ethiopian king in 655 B.C.E., but they may have originally settled in Egypt under the Assyrian king Ashurbanipal a decade earlier. The textual archives from Elephantine illuminate aspects of daily life in a Jewish military garrison of the Persian period established to guard the southern border of Egypt as well as to facilitate river commerce between Egypt and Nubia by protecting transport caravans.

The soldiers stationed at Elephantine were under the control of the king, no doubt under the authority of the provincial governor. Organized into small groups termed *degels*, persons are usually identified in legal contracts according to their *degel* designation, which provided a ready vehicle for partnerships in lending and land ownership. Crown officials disbursed compensation for services in rations and in silver, using weights standardized by the "stones of the king," a measure different from the standard weight in Persia. Although the exact amount of monthly wages remains uncertain, the cost of living in Elephantine was relatively inexpensive compared to Mesopotamia or Greece. Letters written on papyri or pottery shards suggest that soldiers and officials routinely supplemented government salaries by raising sheep and tilling small plots of agricultural land.[14]

In Aramaic documents, the temple is regularly termed ᵓêgôrāᵓ, presumably a loan word from the Sumerian É.KUR, "mountain house," through the Akkadian *ekurru,* "temple."[15] Evidence from Elephantine indicates an overwhelming proportion of names contained the divine element YHW or YHH. Several Aramaic pottery shards from Elephantine contain the oath "by the life of YHH," and other texts document oaths sworn in the name of Egyptian deities. Whether the Jews of Elephantine actually worshiped deities other than the ancestral YHWH or simply conformed to the judicial practices of the day is not known. We do know of extensive social contact between the Jews of Elephantine and their Egyptian neighbors, as well as with their Aramean counterparts stationed at nearby Syene. Egyptian, Aramean, Babylonian, and Jewish shrines honored various deities. Some Jews may have "occasionally expressed devotion to the god(s) of their spouses at the same time that they continued to revere YHW."[16]

One of the few documents from the Elephantine archive relating directly to the temple is the so-called "Collection Account." According to the heading on the columned papyrus, the contributors each donated two shekels of silver to "YHW the God." Despite inaccuracies in the interim and final tallies of contributors and contributions, the allocation of funds is surprising.

---

[14]Ibid., 277.
[15]Ibid., 109.
[16]Ibid., 173.

Designated at the beginning for YHW, the contributions are divided in the end between YHW (126 shekels) and two other deities, Eshembethel (70 shekels), and Anathbethel (120 shekels).[17]

From the archive of Jedaniah ben Gemariah we are able to eavesdrop on the ongoing conversation regarding religious relations between the Jews and the Egyptians. Apparently, the Jewish sacrifice of lambs at the Passover festival insulted the Egyptian priests of the ram-god Khnum, who intervened to prevent the festival. The Jews at Elephantine wrote to the priests at the Jerusalem temple, who interceded with Darius II by way of the provincial governor Arsames. A royal decree permitted the Jews to observe the Passover. The Khnum priests reacted by destroying the Temple of YHW in 410 B.C.E. and plundering the sacred vessels. After petition by the Jews in Elephantine, permission to rebuild was granted, although sacrifice of lambs was no longer allowed. The Jewish community leaders agreed:

> If our lord [sen]d (a letter) and our Temple of YHW the God be rebuilt in Elephantine the fortress as it was former[ly bu]ilt—and sheep, ox and goat are [n]ot made there as burnt offering but [they offer there] (only) incense (and) meal-offering—and should our lord mak[e] a statement [about thus, then] we shall give to the house of our lord si[lver, . . . and even] a thousa[nd] ardabs of barley.[18]

The majority of the texts extant from Elephantine are contracts of various kinds between individuals: documents of sale, gifts, transfer of property, or some other grant. In a document concerning property dated July 6, 451 B.C.E., Ananiah ben Azariah is identified as "*leḥen* of YHW (who is) in Elephantine," the same term used in late Assyrian documents to describe temple officials.[19] The house sold to Ananiah lay across the street from the Temple of YHW and next to the royal treasury. Perhaps the shrine and the royal storehouse sat adjacent to each other not just as an accident of urban sprawl, but as deliberate juxtaposition of collection site (temple) and storage site (storehouse).

---

[17]Bezalel Porten and Ada Yardeni, *Textbook of Aramaic Documents from Ancient Egypt, vol. 3: Literature, Accounts, Lists* (Jerusalem: Hebrew University, 1993), xvii.

[18]Bezalel Porten, *Jews of Elephantine and Arameans of Syene (Fifth Century B.C.E.): Fifty Aramaic Texts* (Jerusalem: Hebrew University, 1976), 100–101.

[19]Bezalel Porten, *Archives from Elephantine: The Life of an Ancient Jewish Military Colony* (Berkeley: University of California Press, 1968), 200.

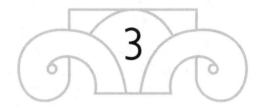

Temple Personnel

We have seen that the cultures of the ANE prescribed a "house" as the residence for the local deity. Just as the king needed a palace to live in, the god needed a temple, known in the texts as "the house of [Divine Name]." The "house" of the god necessitated the "household" of the god—the personnel and material resources needed to care for the god. This was as true in Jerusalem as in the rest of the region. All kinds of skilled personnel were needed to preside over sacrificial rituals, communicate with the divine realm, maintain the temple facilities, oversee the temple administration, and provide needed supplies and repairs. Biblical texts are replete with references to various personnel connected with the temple. One in particular, an incident involving the repair of the First Temple in the reign of King Jehoash of Judah (836–797 B.C.E.), is instructive regarding the roles of temple personnel. The passage is quoted at length, since it serves as the basis for the work of this chapter.

> In the seventh year of Jehu (King of Israel), King Jehoash (began to rule) and for forty years he ruled in Jerusalem; the name of his mother was Zibiah from Beer-sheba. Now Jehoash did what was right in the eyes of YHWH all his days, what Jehoiada the priest (*hak-kōhēn*) taught him. Except, the cultic high places were not put away; the people still made sacrifices and offered incense at the cultic high places. Now Jehoash said to the priests, "All the silver (*kesep*) of the sacred offerings that is brought to the house of YHWH—silver passed on by each as silver for his personal valuation, all the silver that is brought up on account of each one's heart to bring to the house of YHWH—the priests will take from each person, and they will strengthen the weakness of the house wherever is found any weakness."

> But by the twenty-third year of Jehoash, the priests had not strengthened the weakness of the house. So King Jehoash summoned the priest Jehoiada and the other priests and he said to them, "For what reason are you not strengthening the weakness of the house? Now, do not take silver from your neighbors and

give it for the weakness of the house." So the priests agreed not to take silver from the people to strengthen the weakness of the house. So the priest Jehoiada took a chest (*ʾărôn*) and bore a hole in its lid and he set it beside the altar on the right as one entered the house of YHWH; the priests who were keepers of the threshold (*šōmĕrê has-sap*) deposited there all the silver that was brought to the house of YHWH. When they saw the abundance of silver in the chest, the counter (*sōpēr*) of the king and the great priest went up, secured, and counted the silver that was found in the house of YHWH. Then they gave the silver that was measured into the hands (*ʿal yĕdê*) of the ones doing the work who were made overseers in the house of YHWH; then they paid it out to the craftsmen in wood and to the builders who were working on the house of YHWH, to the masons, the stonecutters, to acquire timber and quarried stones, to strengthen the weakness of the house of YHWH, and for all that was needed for the house to strengthen it. But there was not made for the house of YHWH silver basins, snuffers, bowls, trumpets, any vessel of gold or silver from the silver that was brought to the house of YHWH. Rather, to the ones doing the work they gave it, and they strengthened the house of YHWH with it. They did not require an accounting from the men into whose hands (*ʿal yādām*) they gave the silver to give to the ones doing the work, because they were working faithfully. Silver of guilt offerings and silver of sin offerings was not brought into the house of YHWH; it belonged to the priests. (2 Kgs 12.2–17 [1–16])

This passage mentions several categories of personnel associated with the temple: priests, keepers of the threshold, counters, and craftsmen.

Priests

The most familiar category of personnel associated with the temple is the priest, the principal cultic ritualist. The priests received, prepared, and presented agricultural offerings, lighted, trimmed and refilled lamps, slaughtered animals and sacrificed them on the altar, mixed spices for burning as incense, and identified and removed ritual uncleanness. The Hebrew word *kōhēn* is the generic word for "priest," used in combination with the deity being served.[1]

---

[1]The common Jewish name Cohen is the anglicized version of the Hebrew word for priest, *kōhēn*. For example, Melchizedek was the "priest of God Most High" (Gen 14:18); "the priests of Dagon" avoid stepping on the threshold of the temple (1 Sam 5:5); King Jehu of Israel summoned "all the prophets of Baal, all his worshipers, and all his priests" (2 Kgs 10:19); as evidence of divine judgment, Jeremiah announces that "Chemosh (chief god of Moab) shall go out into exile with his priests and his leaders" (Jer 48:7) and that "Milcom (chief god of Ammon) shall go

Priest as Occupation. The overall impression from the biblical texts is that the most sacred ritual duties were the prerogative of the priests, while the Levites carried out nonsacrificial duties. Careful reading of the biblical texts, reflective of multiple traditions over several centuries, shows that the distinction between priests and Levites as well as the unilateral association of priests with the authorized worship of YHWH is a postexilic phenomenon. The development of the roles and responsibilities of the priesthood throughout Israel's history is much more complicated.[2] Briefly put, the priestly function that once belonged to the family patriarch was delegated to a specialist. These ritual specialists were associated with specific sanctuaries: Eli at Shiloh (1 Sam 1:9); Ahimelech at Nob (1 Sam 21:1); Amaziah at Bethel (Amos 7:10). Priestly rivalries flourished, perhaps in evidence in King David's appointment of two priests in charge of worship. "Zadok, son of Ahitub" is a descendant of Aaron, the lineage of the Aaronides or Zadokites; "Ahimelech, son of Abiathar" is a descendant of Moses, the lineage of the Levites (2 Sam 8:17). Apparently the biblical tradition that links Moses and Aaron as brothers does not recognize that fraternal connection in the priestly lineages. Later, Solomon banished the Levite family of Abiathar from the priesthood and retained the Aaronide family of Zadok exclusively as priests.[3] Eventually, the office of "chief priest" developed at the temple. Setting aside the complicated development of the priesthood, our focus in this study is on the economic implications of the priesthood in ancient Israel.

First, we note that the occupation of priest was not a career choice open to everyone. Typically, one was born to the profession, since the biblical texts refer to priests as the "sons of Aaron" or as "Levites," that is, to persons belonging to the tribe of Levi. The poetic Mosaic blessing of the tribes in Deut 33 extols Levi as the tribe who ministers before YHWH and demonstrates faithful loyalty (Deut 33:8–11). The literary center of the book of

---

out into exile with his priests and his leaders" (Jer 49:3). Sometimes, texts identify priests with a geographic area rather than with a deity: Joseph married "Asenath, daughter of Potiphera, priest of On (Heliopolis in Egypt)" (Gen 41:45); the father-in-law of Moses was the "priest of Midian" (Exod 3:1).

[2]For a discussion of priests and Levites in the biblical texts with concomitant proposals for the historical development of cultic personnel, see, e.g., Frank Moore Cross, *Canaanite Myth and Hebrew Epic: Essays in the History of the Religion of Israel* (Cambridge: Harvard University Press, 1973), 195–215; Patrick D. Miller, *The Religion of Ancient Israel* (Louisville: Westminster John Knox, 2000), 162–74, and the bibliographies therein.

[3]The priestly Sadducees in the New Testament are the descendants of the Zadokite line. The translation of the Hebrew word "Zadokite" into Greek recorded the sound of the letters by transforming the Hebrew Z into a Greek S and the Hebrew Q into a Greek K.

Deuteronomy is the declaration of the divine choice of the Levites as priests: "For YHWH your God chose him (Levi) out of all your tribes to stand and minister in the name of YHWH, him and his sons, all the days" (Deut 18:5).

Second, even persons born into a priestly family could be excluded on the basis of inappropriate behavior. For example, fire from YHWH consumed the two sons of Aaron when "they offered up to YHWH strange fire that he had not commanded them (to offer)" (Lev 10:1). The two sons of Eli, the priest at Shiloh, were condemned to death by God because "they treated the offering of YHWH with contempt" (1 Sam 2:17). Likewise, the earth swallowed the Levite Korah and his family after he complained about the exalted status of Aaron with respect to the priesthood (Num 16:1–31). The story of Korah's contempt and punishment is interpreted as "a reminder to the Israelites so that a strange man does not approach who is not from the offspring of Aaron to offer up incense before YHWH" (Lev 16:40a).

Biblical texts also enumerate strict sanctions for unorthodox priests in Israel:

> There shall not be found in you anyone who passes his son or daughter through fire as an offering, anyone who divines divinings, or reads the right times, or observes signs, or practices witchcraft, or who casts a spell, or consults ghosts or spirits, or seeks oracles from the dead. For an abomination of YHWH is whoever does these things. (Deut 18:10–12)

Texts from Mesopotamia mention all kinds of temple personnel associated with cultic ceremonies or interaction with the god: incantation specialists, diviners, omen experts, astronomers, astrologers, cult prophets, exorcists, conjurers, magicians, singers of liturgy, lamentation singers, musicians, arrangers of the sacrificial table, and boatmen who ferry the cult statues. In Egypt, cultic temples provided communion with the divine, and funerary temples provided communion with the deceased. Mortuary temples, which Egyptians termed "temples of the west" because of their common location on the west bank of the Nile, served to provide for the necessities of the afterlife. Caring for the deity in the cultic temples or for the mummified remains of the deceased in the funerary temples required large numbers of cultic ritualists.

> Among these were the lector priest, responsible for learning and reciting the vast ritual literature; the stolist, who cared for the clothing and other paraphernalia of divine statues; astronomers who kept track of time by observing the heavens and using water clocks and other time-keeping devices; priestly scholars and scribes in the temple's "House of Life" (the scriptorium/library) who accumulated and interpreted the sacred writings; singers and musicians who

played a significant role in temple ceremonies; and, in later times, astrologers who read the fate of the nation and the individual in the stars.[4]

The prohibition against such activities in Israel helped distinguish Israel from the nations around her to ensure "orthodox" worship of YHWH.

Third, on the other hand, the story of the dedication of the young boy Samuel to the temple at Shiloh may indicate that boys could be "donated" to the priesthood by their nonpriestly families. Although Samuel is never called a priest, he performs all the functions of a priest: divination, sacrifice, intercession, and anointing the king. Similarly, the strange story in Judg 17 about a shrine in Micah's house in the hill country of Ephraim records, "There was a young man from Bethlehem of Judah, from the clan of Judah. Now he was a Levite and he was sojourning there (in Ephraim)" (Judg 17:7). In this case, "Levite" seems to be an occupational designation, since the man is descended from the tribe of Judah and not Levi. Micah employs him as his personal priest until the tribe of Dan, migrating from the coastal area near the Philistines to an area north of the Galilee, makes him a better offer. We know that temples in the ANE took in foundlings as a sort of social service agency (see chapter six). Perhaps families also willingly donated their sons to the temple in gratitude to the deity or as a remedy for desperate economic circumstances.

Support of Priests. The biblical material is crystal clear about the economic implications of being a priest—the economic support for a priest should come from the congregation he serves. The summary in Deut 18:1–4 is typical:

> There shall not be for the Levitical priests, all the tribe of Levi, a portion (*ḥēleq*) or inheritance (*naḥălâ*) with Israel; fire-offerings of YHWH and his inherited shares they shall eat. There shall not be for him an inheritance in the midst of his brothers; YHWH is his inheritance just as he said to him. And this will be the just due of the priests: from the people, from the ones offering the sacrifice, whether bull or lamb, he will give to the priest the arm and the jaws and the stomach. Your first grain, your new wine, and your fresh oil, and the first of the shearing of your flock you will give to him.

Although the Levites did not receive an inheritance in the promised land as the other tribes did, they were allotted forty-eight towns and the surrounding pasture lands out of the inheritance properties of other tribes (Josh 21). Confirmation of the special status of priestly land occurs in the account of Joseph's rise to power in Egypt. In desperation over the severity of the famine, the landowners in Egypt begged Joseph to purchase their lands in exchange

---

[4]William A. Ward, "Temples and Sanctuaries, Egypt," *ABD* 6:369–72.

for food. "Only the land of the priests he did not acquire, because it was the prescribed portion for the priests from Pharaoh, and they ate (from) their prescribed due that Pharaoh had given to them; on account of this they did not sell their land" (Gen 47:22).

The temple economy in Jerusalem (or Shiloh or Bethel or wherever) supported temple personnel with shelter, food, and clothing. The priest received a share of the congregation's contributions in return for services rendered. This practice of supporting priests through offerings was widespread throughout the ANE, known as the "prebendary" system, and operative perhaps as far back as 2000 B.C.E. Administrative tablets excavated from the Neo-Babylonian period (sixth century B.C.E.) reveal that prebends ("portions, shares") were an important part of the temple economy in Mesopotamia. A prebend was "the right to an income from the temple in return for the performance of services connected with the cult."[5] Documentation of prebends noted the particular profession, the period of required service, and the temple or god served. The payments regularly included dates or barley and a share of the sacrificial offerings. The quantities of food offered to the Mesopotamian gods could be staggering, and each of the four daily meals required fresh food items. One text, "Daily Sacrifices to the Gods of the City of Uruk," specifies 216 containers of beer, 243 loaves of bread, 50 rams, 3 bulls, plus additional quantities of dates, lambs, ducks, birds, and eggs as the daily fare. There is even a type of postscript to this text detailing which gods will not eat specific types of meat (*ANET,* 343–345). The temple personnel eventually consumed the substantial quantity of leftovers. Tablets from the temple of Ninurta in Nippur list on one side the bread and beer presented as offerings, and on the other side rations allocated to temple personnel. "Significantly, the deliveries of bread for the deities and shrines listed on one side virtually equal the expenditures for personnel on the other."[6] Ration lists from the temple in Sippar also included, in addition to foodstuffs, "an annual allowance of clothing or wool, shoes, blankets, and water-bottles."[7] Apparently, the quantity and quality of the items depended on the recipient's age, status, and type of work performed.

---

[5]A. C. V. M. Bongenaar, *The Neo-Babylonian Ebabbar Temple at Sippar: Its Administration and Its Prosopography* (Uitgaven Van Het Nederlands Historisch-Archaeologisch Instituut Te Istanbul 80; Istanbul: Nederlands Historisch-Archaeologisch Instituut te Istanbul, 1997), 140.

[6]John F. Robertson, "The Social and Economic Organization of Ancient Mesopotamian Temples," *CANE* 1:448.

[7]John D. A. MacGinnis, *Letters and Orders from Sippar and the Administration of the Ebabbara in the Late Babylonian Period* (Grudnia, Poland: Bonami, 1995), 184.

The so-called "Offering Calendar" from the south wall of Rameses III's mortuary temple at Medinet Habu in Egypt (early twelfth century) contains lists detailing the offerings to be brought to the temple on various occasions, including the daily offerings, the monthly feasts, and yearly festivals. The text specifies quantities of various kinds of loaves and cakes as well as jars of beer, amounting to roughly thirty sacks of grain per day. The quantities added to these during the monthly feasts and yearly festivals were small. On the other hand, special festival days called for a large increase in offerings, for example, 46 sacks on Coronation Day and 135 sacks at the Festival of Sokaris.[8] Offerings to the primary god(s) were then redistributed to associated cults, including the royal *ka* chapels and the cult places for deceased private individuals. As in Mesopotamia, offerings reached temple personnel as rations and prebends. It seems likely that most offerings bypassed the gods and went directly to the consumers, since it would be almost impossible to stack on the altar the loaves, cakes, and jars of beer from the specified daily offering amounts.

Abuse of prebends occurred at both ends of the spectrum: priests receiving insufficient prebends and priests taking too much as prebends. At the dedication of the rebuilt walls in Jerusalem, Nehemiah brags that all Israel "gave the daily portions for the singers and the gatekeepers, and they set (it) apart for the Levites, and the Levites set (it) apart for the sons of Aaron" (Neh 12:47). A decade later, Nehemiah discovers that "the portions for the Levites were not given," prompting the Levites to desert the temple area to find sustenance in the countryside (Neh 13:10).

At the other extreme, greedy priests steal more than their share. Eli's sons plucked meat from the cauldron while it was still boiling and, moreover, took meat for roasting by force (1 Sam 2:12–17). Greedy pagan priests in Babylon are described similarly in apocryphal writings: "(The priests) had made a hidden entrance (into the cult statue room), through which they used to go in regularly and consume the provisions" (Bel 13); "The priests sell sacrifices that are offered to the gods and use the money; . . . the priests take some of the clothing of the gods to clothe their wives and children" (Ep Jer 28, 33). Josephus reports that under King Agrippa in the mid-first century C.E. "such was the shamelessness and effrontery which possessed the high priests that they actually were so brazen as to send slaves to the threshing floors to receive the tithes that were due to the priests, with the result that the poorer priests starved to death" (Josephus, *Ant.* 20.181).

---

[8]Jac J. Janssen, "The Role of the Temple in the Egyptian Economy During the New Kingdom," in *State and Temple Economy in the Ancient Near East* (ed. Edward Lipinski; OLA 6; Leuven: Departement Orientalistiek, 1979), 511–13.

Gatekeepers and Keepers of the Threshold: Gate Accountants

The Chronicler reports that a Levite of certain family groups could serve as *šōʿēr,* traditionally translated into English as "gatekeeper." The word is a participle formed from the Hebrew root *š-ʿ-r,* the same root from which the common Hebrew noun *šaʿar,* "gate," is formed. The Hebrew root *š-ʿ-r* is often presumed to be related to the Arabic root, "break through." So the noun *šaʿar,* "gate," denotes the gap in the wall and the wider space inside the wall of a house, temple, or city. The participle is a grammatical form often used for "repeated, enduring, or commonly occurring acts, occupations, and thoughts."[9] So a *šōʿēr* (participle from the root *š-ʿ-r*) is someone who has "repeated, enduring, or commonly occurring acts" at the *šaʿar.* But what acts or occupations did this person carry out at the gate, and how should we translate this word? For now, I will translate *šōʿēr* with the word "gater." Although "gater" is not a generally accepted English word, in this study the form is deliberately chosen to draw attention to the following discussion. One who rules is a ruler and one who bakes is a baker; likewise, one who engages in repeated activity at a gate is a "gater." That is, the usual English suffix to indicate an agent noun is adopted for this occupation as well.

Duties of "Gaters." The Chronicler apparently knew the "gaters" as cultic functionaries with a wide range of duties at the Jerusalem temple throughout its history, as the following citations attest. When David turned the reign of Israel and Judah over to Solomon, he organized the 38,000 Levites, including 4,000 "gaters," who have duties over the temple chambers, over the service of the house of God, over the bread, and for twice daily praise of YHWH (1 Chr 23:28–30). Another account of David organizing the Levites for service indicated that the "gaters" cast lots for their gates. One of the "gaters" was noted as "an adviser with prudence" (1 Chr 26:14). The south gate was assigned to another "gater" and the "house of collections (*bêt hā-ʾăsupîm*)" to his sons (1 Chr 26:15). When the priest Jehoiada was preparing to crown Joash in a secret revolt against Athaliah (ninth century), he assigned as guards for the young king one-third "for 'gaters' of the thresholds and one-third at the house of the king and one-third at the gate of the foundation" (2 Chr 23:4–5). Afterwards, he "stationed 'gaters' at the gates of the house of YHWH, so that no one unclean in any way would enter" (2 Chr 23:19). No

---

[9]E. Kautzsch, *Genius' Hebrew Grammar* (trans. A. E. Cowley; 2d ed.; Oxford: Clarendon, 1910), 357.

mention of "gaters" occurs in the parallel account in 2 Kgs 11; instead, captains of the guards and watchmen stand watch. During Hezekiah's reforms (eighth century), he assigned Levites for service in the temple of YHWH. "And Kore, the son of Imnah the Levite was the 'gater' for the east over the freewill offerings of God, to give the contribution of YHWH and the holiest things" (2 Chr 31:14). Among the first to return to Jerusalem from Babylonian exile (sixth century), the "gaters" were over the work of the service, keepers of the thresholds, over the gates for the house of YHWH, over the temple chambers and over the treasuries (hā-ʾ$\bar{o}$sĕrôt) of the house of God, over the opening every morning, over the vessels of service (checking them in and out), and over the baking ingredients and the rows of bread (1 Chr 9:19–32). In Nehemiah's time (fifth century) the people committed themselves to "bring up to the temple chambers the contribution of the grain, the new wine, and the fresh oil, where are located the vessels of the sanctuary and the priests and the ministers and the 'gaters' and the singers" (Neh 10:40 [39]). A list of the priests and Levites who returned from exile with Zerubbabel includes six men who were "'gaters' keeping watch at the collections of the gates" (Neh 12:25).

We can well understand the role of "gaters" in guarding the entryway into the temple, whether for the safety of those inside (like young Joash) or for preserving the purity of the sacred precincts by keeping out all who were unclean. The Chronicler refers to "gaters" for the ark of the covenant, presumably to prevent damage or theft (e.g., 1 Chr 15:18, 23, 24). Nehemiah stations "gaters" to prevent entry into Jerusalem on the Sabbath (Neh 13:22). But was the occupation of the "gater" solely related to guarding? Three of the above biblical references to "gaters" situate them on thresholds (1 Chr 9:17–18, 22; 2 Chr 23:4). Six other references connect "gaters" with the storage of commodities or vessels (1 Chr 9:26; 23:28; 26:15; 2 Chr 31:14; Neh 10:40 [39]; 12:25). The connection of a "gater" with a threshold is unremarkable, since the threshold was the wooden plank or stone slab spanning the width of the gate. Such a connection means, however, that we may find insight into the role of "gaters" by examining the language associated with thresholds and those who were stationed at them.

"Gaters" and Thresholds. Whereas the Chronicler prefers the participle š$\bar{o}$ʿēr, "gater," the parallel accounts in 2 Kings use the participle š$\bar{o}$mēr, "keeper." Second Kings 12 portrays the priest Jehoiada setting a chest beside the altar in the temple and "the priests who were keepers of the threshold (š$\bar{o}$mĕrê has-sap) deposited there all the silver that was brought into the house of YHWH" (2 Kgs 12:10 [9]). When King Josiah decided to repair the temple (late seventh century), he sent men to the high priest to determine "the silver that was brought to the house of YHWH that the keepers of the

threshold gathered from the people" (2 Kgs 22:4). When King Josiah carried out his religious reforms, he ordered "the keepers of the threshold to remove from the temple of YHWH all the vessels that were made for Baal and for Asherah and for all the host of heaven" (2 Kgs 23:4).

A picture of those stationed at the gates or thresholds (whether termed *šōᶜēr* or *šōmēr*) emerges that involves something other than, or in addition to, guarding, i.e., preventing entry or damage. Even if, at some period in the history of Israel/Judah, persons stationed at gates worked there primarily to prevent entry or damage, by the time of the late monarchy, the keepers of the threshold (the "gaters") were stationed there for another purpose. I suggest that another clue to their purpose is to be found in the Semitic word for "threshold."

In Biblical Hebrew, *sap* means both "threshold" and "basin." The term is used three times in a third-century B.C.E. inscription fragment from Tyre to mean "basin" or "reservoir," also mentioning 1,070 shekels of silver.[10] The related Assyrian word *sippu* means both "doorframe" *and* "container" (*CAD* S:300, 303). An examination of *sap* as "basin" in the Old Testament finds that in all six instances, the Septuagint (the Greek version of the OT from ca. 250 B.C.E.) mistranslates the Hebrew. Once, the Greek simply transliterates the Hebrew *sapōt* as *saphphōth*. Five times *sap* as "basin" is translated with either "door" or "forecourt," the same words used to translate *sap* when the context demands the translation "threshold." For example, the Greek version of the Passover event in Exod 12:22 reads, "Take a bundle of hyssop and dip from the blood that is on the *door* and touch the lintel and both the doorposts from the blood that is on the *door*," when the meaning of the Hebrew in both instances is obviously "in the *basin*."[11] How did the Hebrew word *sap* come to mean both "basin" and "threshold" and cause such confusion for ancient translators? It is possible, of course, that *sap* "basin" and *sap* "threshold" are homonyms that developed independently of each other. It is also possible that the two seemingly independent meanings derived from some common background, for example, collection basins situated at the thresholds of the gates to the temple.[12] We noted above that six references indicate "gaters" connected with the storage of commodities or precious metals. Two references cited above indicate "keepers of the threshold" as collectors of silver from persons entering the temple area. A third reference to

---

[10]G. A. Cooke, *A Text-Book of North-Semitic Inscriptions* (Oxford: Clarendon, 1903), 43–44.

[11]The other examples are: 1 Kgs 7:50 (gold temple vessels); 2 Kgs 12:14 [13] (silver and gold temple vessels); Zech 12:2 (metaphorical "cup of reeling").

[12]For example, see the root *šbᶜ* with the meanings "seven" and "swear an oath," probably diverging from a common background. BDB, 987–90.

the keepers of the threshold indicates their access to (and accountability for?) the cultic vessels for Baal. The Psalmist declares he would rather "serve as a 'thresholder' (a participle form of the root *s-p-p,* from which the noun *sap* also comes) in the house of God than dwell in the tents of wickedness" (Ps 84:11 [10]).

"Gaters" in Mesopotomia. We turn now to the operation of temples in Mesopotamia to examine any possible parallels with the "gater" in the biblical material. In Mesopotamia, although the shrine and altar were the focus of the temple complex from a religious perspective, the temple storehouses functioned as its economic center. The vast majority of excavated Mesopotamian temple archive texts are records of receipt or disbursement into and out of the storehouses. The precision and comprehensive scope of such record-keeping left a paper trail, so to speak, of cuneiform tablets, which can be followed in the reconstruction of the temple economy. Almost all commodities flowed into and out of the temple storehouses at least once in the operation of the temple economy. Significant quantities of agricultural produce needed to be stored in the temple complex before being offered to the deity, sent to workshops for further preparation, or otherwise used.

Texts often refer to storehouses belonging to the temple, as opposed to those belonging to the royal palace, in connection with a divine name, as in "the storehouse of the Šamaš-temple in Larsa" (*CAD* N/1:182). The gate of the storehouse functioned as a point of delivery for barley and dates at the temples in Babylon, Borsippa, Larsa, Nippur, Sippar, and Uruk, accounted for by the "overseer of the storage building" (*CAD* K:64). The temple officials designated specific storage areas for particular goods and products, and they probably assigned areas of the storehouses to particular individuals, as implied in the designation of "the storehouse of the shepherds of Ezida, the wing belonging to PN" (*CAD* Š/3:414). Setting aside storage areas for individuals would certainly facilitate accountability for loss or damages. Many items received from the agricultural and grazing land of the temple were not usable without further processing, necessitating temple workshops and associated skilled personnel.

Temple accounts meticulously documented the issuance of materials from the storehouses to the workshops and their subsequent return. "Letter orders" concerned with the issuing of grains, dates, and oil from the Ebabbar temple in Sippar from the late sixth and early fifth centuries suggest the following steps: (1) A department of the temple sent a request, normally oral, for commodities to the administration; (2) the administration ordered that the commodities be issued from the storehouse; (3) notice of delivery was sent to the accounting department by means of a delivery notice, if requested orally, or by forwarding the letter order from the requesting department;

(4) the information was entered into a master register, the Register of Šamaš, the chief god of the temple.[13]

Temple staff were under strict obligation to safeguard the temple property from misappropriation. This need underlies, for example, a text wherein a storehouse clerk was accused of stealing. When admonished to bring the stolen goods to the administrators of the temple, the overseer of the storehouse swore, "He has not kept anything in his hands. There is nothing for me to bring and show (you)." Not satisfied with his assertion, three doorkeepers of the temple storehouse were questioned, "Is there anything which Anu-shar-uṣur of the supply house has caused to be brought out by you?" In the assembly of the gods, the guards swear, "Everything, as much as the[re is], Anu-shar-uṣur caused to be taken out from the storeroom by . . . and whatever we have seen in his hands . . . [is appropriate]" (*NBAD, #170*).

Translation of "Gater." I suggest, therefore, that the activities associated with the "gater" included, at a minimum, safeguarding the contents of the baskets placed at the thresholds, and perhaps assaying the items deposited, assigning value, and crediting the account of the depositor. These activities are consistent with those documented in the temple archives from Mesopotamia for the storehouse clerks. An introductory accounting textbook describes the three steps of accounting as "1–collection and tabulation, 2–collation and modification, 3–reporting and tabulation."[14] These are precisely the recurring activities of the *šō'ēr,* the "gater." The traditional translation of *šō'ēr* as "gatekeeper" does not communicate the full range of activities and responsibilities of this position. A translation of "gate accountant" or "gate clerk" comes closer to capturing the meaning indicated by the biblical contexts.

Scribes: Storehouse Accountants

We turn now to another common biblical term, the *sōpēr,* traditionally translated as "scribe." The Hebrew word is again a participle, indicating the repeated actions involved in an occupation. A related noun is *sēper,* translated "book" (more precisely, "document" or even "scroll" since codex-form books did not come into existence until long after the Old Testament period). The Hebrew root *s-p-r* has to do with recording information for safekeeping, so the occupation is a "recorder." The information being recorded will influence

---

[13]MacGinnis, *Letters and Orders,* 20–22.

[14]Kenneth W. Perry, *Accounting: An Introduction* (New York: McGraw-Hill, 1971), 8.

what we call the recorder. The translation "scribe" calls to mind a person recording primarily *words*. Unfortunately, as with the traditional translation "gatekeeper" described above, the translation "scribe" does not fully capture the responsibility of this position.

Duties of Sōpēr. When the designation *sōpēr* appears in a list of officials, the exact responsibilities are difficult to define, although the character of the other individuals in the list indicates someone other than a copyist or recorder of words. A list of David's high officials includes the commander of the army, the commander of forced labor, the commander of foreign troops, the historian (*mazkîr*), the *sōpēr,* and the (high) priests (2 Sam 8:16–18 = 2 Sam 20:23–26 = 1 Chr 18:15–17). In 2 Chr 26:11 the divisions of Uzziah's army follow the numbers in the muster made by the *sōpēr* and the official *šōṭēr*. When Nebuchadnezzar sacks Jerusalem in 586 B.C.E., the captain of the Babylonian guard carries off from the temple the chief priest, the second priest, and the three keepers of the threshold, and from the city, the commander of the army, the king's councilmen, the *sōpēr* of the commander who mustered the army, and sixty people of the land (2 Kgs 25:18–19 = Jer 52:24–25).

Four other biblical passages give further details about the responsibility of the *sōpēr*. First, we noted at the beginning of the chapter that the priest Jehoiada set a chest beside the altar, and the priests who were keepers of the threshold deposited all the silver brought into the house of YHWH into the chest. At certain points, the *sōpēr* of the king and the chief priest counted the silver in the chest (2 Kgs 12:11 [10] = 2 Chr 24:11). Second, in 2 Kgs 22:4, King Josiah sent Shaphan the *sōpēr* to the house of YHWH with the instructions, "Go up to Hilkiah the great priest so that he may tally the silver that was brought to the house of YHWH that the keepers of the threshold gathered from the people." Third, Nehemiah claimed as part of his reforms, "I appointed over the treasuries (*ʾôṣārôt*) Shelemiah the priest, Zadok the *sōpēr,* and Pedaiah from the Levites . . . for faithfully they computed and they were responsible to distribute the portions to their brothers" (Neh 13:13). Fourth, Baruch reads the scroll of Jeremiah "in the house of YHWH, in the chamber of Gemariah, son of Shaphan the *sōpēr* in the upper court, at the opening of the new gate of the house of YHWH" (Jer 36:10), indicating a connection between the chamber of the *sōpēr*'s son and the gate of the temple. The duties that these texts associate with the *sōpēr* include counting, tallying, verifying, and then recording, not merely transcribing words. These activities accorded him status in the temple as well as in the king's bureaucracy.

Sōpēr in Mesopotamia. Turning now to the Mesopotamian temple archives, we note that temple officials fastidiously tracked inventories of commodities from storehouse to craftsmen and back again. Recall the discussion in chapter two about the *iškaru* system employed in Mesopotamia to account for raw materials and for finished product. Who were these persons who worked so diligently in the temple storehouses, keeping meticulous records of every item received and disbursed within the temple economy? Sometimes the cuneiform texts refer to these indispensable personnel as "the one over the house of the property," "the one over the house of the barley," and so forth. But the term most used without reference to the particular storehouse was *ṭupšarru*. Although traditionally translated as "scribe," the range of activities and concerns of this person was certainly beyond a recorder of words, a copyist, or even a secretary. These persons functioned in the Mesopotamian temple economy as receiving and disbursing agents of commodities, animals, and precious metals, finished goods inventory clerks, inventory managers, auditors of accounts, record-keepers—in short, accountants.

Sōpēr in Greece. The accounting officials of the Greek temples regularly posted monthly reports, records of business contracts, lists of loan guarantors, and inventories of sacred objects on wooden boards in a public place for the local citizens to scrutinize. Annual audits were conducted, recorded on stelae, and set up in the temple precinct, "where the public might inspect—and doubtless audit—their records."[15]

Translation of Sōpēr. To summarize, then, the Hebrew *sōpēr* was more than a scribe—a copyist or dictation transcriber. He was a counter, a recorder, a ledger-keeper, and an enumerator. Both the *šōʿēr* and the *sōpēr* counted, tallied, and recorded receipts, the *šōʿēr* at the thresholds of the temple gates, and the *sōpēr* for the temple storehouses. Better translations would be "gate accountant" and "storehouse accountant."

Craftsmen

The preparation of sacrificial offerings for cultic worship demanded the work of such artisans as bakers, millers, oil-pressers, vintners, perfumers, weavers, dyers, carvers, and smiths. We have already mentioned the important role of the skilled craftsmen in the construction of the wilderness tabernacle and the First Temple (see chapter two). As an example of unskilled labor, Joshua made the Gibeonites "hewers of wood and drawers of water for the congregation and for the altar of YHWH until this day at the place where he will choose" (Josh 9:27).

---

[15]John Harvey Kent, "The Temple Estates of Delos, Rheneia and Mykonos," *Hesperia* 17 (1948): 243–44; cf. Gary Reger, *Regionalism and Change in the Economy of Independent Delos, 314–167 B.C.* (Berkeley: University of California Press, 1994), 7–9.

Cuneiform texts from the Mesopotamian temple in Sippar illustrate the assignment of raw materials to artisans involved in the preparation and/or manufacture of products in three main categories: food, textiles, and metals. The brewers fermented barley into beer for the fixed and monthly offerings to the deity, apparently of varying quality depending on the available grain. In cases of barley shortage, a type of date wine was produced and offered. Accompanying the alcoholic libations, priests presented the cult statues with breads, porridge, and sweet cakes prepared by the bakers. Millers working for the bakers ground various grains, primarily barley, into flour to be combined with dates or sesame oil for baking. "Soakers" prepared the dates; "oil-pressers" extracted the sweet oil from sesame in successive pressings, to be used not only for baking, but also for illuminating lamps, burning with incense, and lubricating wooden objects. Supporting personnel in the food preparation workshops included measurers, sweepers, fuel suppliers, and porters.

Weavers made up the second major category of craftspersons in the Mesopotamian temple workshops, responsible for the garments to clothe the cult statues. The texts differentiate between weavers of wool and linen, and further between weavers of colored wool and white wool. Associated with the weavers were dyers and cutters of reeds, used to stir the cloth in the dye and as fuel for the dying chemicals. Changing the garments of the gods, referred to in texts as "dirty linen," required the work of washers, bleachers, fullers, and menders. The sackmakers used goat hair to produce the many sacks needed for storing grain and other produce coming into the temple storehouses. Water-drawers, measurers, and porters supported the weaving workshops.

The third main category of craftsmen was comprised of the smiths, workers in gold, silver, or copper, along with skilled workers in leather and wood. In addition, smiths fashioned cultic items, tools, and various implements from iron, bronze, and tin. "The main task of the goldsmiths consisted of the manufacture and repair of golden objects for the adornment of the attire of the cultic statues, often referred to as the 'jewellery of DN' (*šukuttu ša* DN)."[16] Smiths and leatherworkers constructed and repaired the tools for cultivation of the temple's farms (e.g., spades, shovels, sickles, axes, plowshares, bridles, or yokes) as well as the implements needed for the management of the herds and flocks (e.g., knives, shearing clippers, wagon wheels, quivers, or arrows). The smiths fashioned vessels and implements for use elsewhere in the temple complex (e.g., rings for doors, nails, fetters, censers, bowls, or weapons). Carpenters built vehicles (including boats) and furniture, and they carved cultic objects. Other workers soaked, peeled, and bleached reeds to be woven into mats and

---

[16]Bongenaar, *Ebabbar Temple,* 363.

baskets. Leatherworkers rendered glue and varnish from animal hides and converted superior quality skins into parchment.

Here again the Jerusalem temple complex was similar to those in Mesopotamia, utilizing skilled (and unskilled) artisans and craftsmen to prepare and maintain cultic utensils and offerings.

Administrators

Finally, the text from 2 Kgs 12 with which we began the chapter gives some clues as to the administrative personnel at the Jerusalem temple. In verse 11 [10], the two officials who secure and count the silver in the chest are the *sōpēr* of the king and the chief priest. Likewise, in 2 Kgs 22:4, King Josiah sent Shaphan the *sōpēr* to the house of YHWH with the instructions, "Go up to Hilkiah the great priest so that he may tally the silver that was brought to the house of YHWH that the keepers of the threshold gathered from the people." In both passages, the *sōpēr* is an agent of the king and works in partnership with the chief priest to count the collected silver. A hint of a dual administrative structure may also be seen when Hezekiah reestablished the priests and Levites at the beginning of the eighth century, including those refugees from the conquered northern kingdom. King Hezekiah commanded chambers in the temple to be prepared for all the contributions coming in from the people, with Conaniah as leader over the chambers "by appointment of Hezekiah the king and Azariah the leader of the house of God" (2 Chr 31:13). Recall also that in the prophecies of Haggai and Zechariah, the leaders of the temple and community are Zerubbabel, the "governor," and Joshua, the high priest.

Mesopotamian Chief Administrator. Turning to Mesopotamian sources, we find the most extensive documentation of temple administration for the Eanna temple in Uruk and the Ebabbar temple in Sippar during the time of the Persian Empire in the late sixth to late fourth centuries B.C.E. Although these two temple administrations show many similarities, they also differed at the highest levels. The chief administrator in the Eanna temple was the *šatammu*, a title with a long history, going back at least to the days of the Hammurabi dynasty in the seventeenth century B.C.E. In these earlier documents, the *šatammu* did not appear to be solely connected with temples. Not only was he specifically identified with cities or provinces, he also certified the transfer of commodities from one place to another. On the other hand, the role of chief administrator was filled by the *šangû* in the Ebabbar temple in Sippar.

Whether called *šatammu* or *šangû,* the temple administrator, often in the company of the "royal commissioner" (*qīpu*) and/or chief accountant(s) (*tupšarru*), acted as the general manager of the temple. In this capacity he was not only its highest administrative authority, but also its highest legal authority, in fact two inseparable functions. Judicial documents in which high officials appear as characters often dealt with temple business such as the theft of temple property, the personnel of the temple, and problems with the delivery of commodities. Additionally, high temple officials sometimes acted as witnesses to judicial documents in which the temple was not one of the parties. The temple administrator, as the temple's chief executive officer, was responsible for: (1) overall management of the temple assets, including land, animals, and buildings; (2) supervision of temple personnel, including assigning work to staff and directing workmen of all kinds; (3) control over the movement of goods by receiving and issuing commodities from fields, herds, storehouses, and production facilities; and (4) final settling of temple accounts. The documents from the Eanna temple attest that the *šatammu* operated from the temple precinct exclusively, while other temple officials frequently traveled on official business.

Mesopotamian Royal Commissioner. The other high-ranking temple official who managed temple affairs with the *šatammu* or the *šangû* was the *qīpu* "royal commissioner." Appointed and placed in the temple organization by the king, the royal commissioner appeared in land leases, judicial documents, documents dealing with the issue and receipt of commodities, contracts, and promissory notes. Although in many ways his duties overlapped with those of the chief administrator, one of the main tasks unique to the *qīpu* was the supervision of work performed by his workforce away from the temple site. Activities performed by the *qīpu* and his workforce included: making bricks, both mud and baked, determining which workers were used to construct embankments and strengthen the beds of irrigation canals; organizing the harvest and collecting tithes; supervising animal husbandry; paying rations to workers; and dealing with runaway slaves.

Mesopotamian Accountants. Under the Neo-Assyrian and early Neo-Babylonian Empires (eighth to sixth centuries), the temple administration at both Sippar and Uruk included one official called *tupšar Ebabbar/Eanna,* "accountant of Ebabbar/Eanna." With the beginning of Nabonidus's reign in 555 B.C.E., developments in Uruk and Sippar diverged when the *tupšar Eanna* was demoted and between two and four persons held this position jointly. A royal courtier, *bēl piqitti,* was added to the temple staff (see below). After the so-called Nabonidus reforms, the daily management of Ebabbar in Sippar seems to have consisted of the temple administrator, the royal commissioner, and about five accountants. In the sixth year of the reign of Cambyses (ca. 524 B.C.E.), a new "alphabet" accountant who kept records in Aramaic, the *sepīru* or *sēpiru,* joined the temple administration in Sippar, possibly transferring from the state administration.

The fact that the accountants could (apparently) order the issue of commodities without authorization by the temple administrator or the royal commissioner indicates their relatively powerful position in the temple management. The surviving texts consistently portray the *ṭupšarru* issuing and receiving goods, directing workmen and craftsmen, carrying out inspections, settling accounts, and witnessing judicial documents, as well as joining with the *šatammu* or the *qīpu* in managing land or houses. In the Murašu archive from the fifth century, the *sēpiru* accountants made or received payments on behalf of their principals and served as low-level administrative clerks on landed estates.[17] The accountants, traditionally rendered "scribes," were in fact the assistants and the executives of the upper echelon of the temple administration, and as such were responsible for the daily running of the temple, though they were still subordinate to the *šatammu* or the *qīpu*.

Mesopotamian Assistant Administrator. The position of *bēl piqitti Eanna*, "executive assistant of Eanna," introduced under the Babylonian king Nabonidus (555–539 B.C.E.) has a long history, going back into the days of the Assyrian Empire. Like the *šatammu*, he directed workers, received and issued commodities, paid rations and wages, supervised the digging of canals, and witnessed judicial documents. No doubt the administrative managers were ably assisted by clerks, scribes, and secretaries.

Greek Administrators. On the Greek island of Delos in the second century B.C.E., the chief administrators of the Temple of Apollo wore the title *hieropoioi*. Empaneled for a yearly term of service, the maximum number of *hieropoioi* was four, although frequently only two served. Their administrative responsibilities were similar to the *šatammu* or the *šangû* and the *qīpu* in the Mesopotamian temples.

> They oversaw the rental of sacred estates and houses and the collection of rent; hired and paid laborers; granted loans to individuals from the temple funds; disbursed payments to contractors; compiled inventories of the vast body of dedications Apollo collected; bought items necessary for ritual and the running of the temple; and last, but not least, recorded their activities on inscriptions published annually.[18]

Once again, we see the personnel situation at the Jerusalem temple mimicking the personnel configurations at the temples of the surrounding nations.

---

[17] Matthew W. Stolper, *Entrepreneurs and Empire: The Murašu Archive, the Murašu Firm and Persian Rule in Babylon* (Istanbul: Nederlands Historisch-Archaeologisch Instituut te Istanbul, 1985), 22.

[18] Reger, *Regionalism and Change,* 7–8.

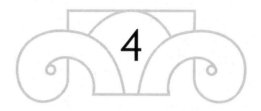

Temple Income

The previous two chapters examined the economic impact of temple construction and the staffing practices of the Jerusalem temple as compared to ANE and Mediterranean peers. In this chapter we turn to the question of temple income. We have already seen in chapter three that the temple personnel were entitled to economic support in exchange for their services. Obviously, the temple needed some form of "income" to fulfill its role in society as the place of communication with the divine. From what sources did the temple in ancient Israel receive income? How did temple officials collect it? What happened to it? And how does information about temple income in ancient Israel compare with temple income in other parts of the ANE?

Land Ownership

The temple was a central organizing institution in ancient societies. Mediator between the deity and the people, the temple exercised power vis-à-vis the crown and the community. And, in ancient times no less than today, power attracted wealth (and vice versa). In ancient societies the primary form of wealth was land and its productive use. The produce of agriculture, flocks, and herds could be consumed by the owner's household or traded for silver or other necessities. Owners could hire laborers for wages or lease the land in a sharecropping arrangement.

Jerusalem

As we will see, all major temples in Mesopotamia owned land and controlled its production. In some cases, temples controlled vast landed estates.

Did the Jerusalem temple own land and control production for the benefit of divine service? Despite vigorous debate among scholars, the issue of land-ownership by the Jerusalem temple remains unresolved. The biblical texts are not definitive as to the issue of landownership by the temple, since tantalizing hints on both sides of the issue exist in the biblical canon.

The strongest argument marshaled on behalf of temple landownership involves the various legal stipulations regarding land inheritance and redemption in biblical texts. Levitical regulations govern the dedication of individual houses and fields to YHWH, i.e., to the control of the priests.

> When a person consecrates his house as holy to YHWH, the priest shall assess it; whether good or bad, just as the priest assesses it, thus it shall stand. . . . If a person consecrates part of a field of his (inherited) possession as holy to YHWH, your assessment before me shall be its seed; a homer of grain in exchange for fifty shekels of silver. . . . When the field goes forth in the Jubilee, it will be holy to YHWH as a devoted field; it will belong to the priest as his (inherited) possession. (Lev 27:14, 16, 21)

If the field "will belong to the priest as his (inherited) possession," then is the field, for all practical purposes, the property of the temple? According to Ezra 10:8, whoever fails to obey the summons to assemble in Jerusalem, "by order of the leaders and the elders, all his movable property will be devoted" [to the temple? to the priests?]. Although the Levites do not participate in ancestral inheritance of property, they do receive cities and surrounding fields to be used for familial support.

> YHWH spoke to Moses in the desert plain of Moab at the Jordan, at Jericho, saying, "Command the children of Israel so that they will give to the Levites from the inheritance of their possession cities to live in; also, open lands surrounding the cities you shall give to the Levites. The towns will belong to them to live in and the open lands will be for their beasts and their movable property and all their animals. (Num 35:1–3)

Since these lands belong to temple personnel, are they, in effect, properties of the temple?

A second argument in favor of landownership by the temple are narrative and legal texts that refer to animals sacrificed by the priests on behalf of others, without specifying the source of the animals. For example, suppose the congregation incurs guilt by erring unintentionally. Then, "when the sin that they sinned becomes known, the congregation shall offer up a young bull, a male of the herd, as a sin-offering and they shall bring it before the Tent of Meeting" (Lev 4:14). In the exaggerated narrative of the grand Passover celebration under King Josiah (640–609 B.C.E.), the Chronicler reports, "the leaders of the house of God gave to the priests for Passover offerings

2600 (sheep) and 300 cattle . . . the chiefs of the Levites contributed to the Levites for Passover offerings 5000 (sheep) and 500 cattle" (2 Chr 35:8–9). Understandably, there might be a time lag between the donation of animals and their use in specific cultic rituals. Did the temple maintain corrals, pens, or stables near the temple courtyard? Or did the temple in fact own herds of animals for use in cultic rituals, restocked by individual donations? Some have argued that the prophet Amos was a herdsman for the temple. Amos 1:1 describes him as "among the herdsmen" (*nōqĕdîm*) of Tekoa. Parallels are known in Akkadian (*nāqidu*) and Ugaritic (*nqdm*), where the "herdsmen" appear in a list of vocations just before "priests" and "holy ones." Even if Amos were not a member of the temple personnel per se, he could have been under contract with the temple to manage a portion of the temple flocks.

A third argument revolves around the large amounts of land allocated to the temple and the priests in Ezekiel's vision (see especially Ezek 45). Obviously idealistic in its scope, the vision may still reflect the authentic custom of temple landownership.

Counterarguments, however, seem equally persuasive. First, property devoted to YHWH fell under the authority and control of the priests. But, even when ancestral lands had been consecrated to YHWH, the owner maintained the right of redemption. "If the one who consecrated it wishes to redeem the field, then one-fifth of the silver of your assessment will be added to it, and it will belong to him" (Lev 27:19). Nehemiah lamented that the Levites have "forsaken the house of God" in Jerusalem to return to their fields in the countryside, and discovered that "the portions of the Levites were not given" (Neh 13:10) as required by law for their support (Neh 12:44). It is reasonable to posit that these Levitical fields were leased out to agricultural workers while the owner was on assignment in Jerusalem for extended periods of time, as it would not always be economically prudent to leave land fallow. Second, the text's lack of specificity regarding the source of sacrificial animals does not necessarily mean that the temple "owned" the animals, or even stabled them. Third, the utopian vision of Ezekiel does not necessarily correlate with actual circumstances in Judah in any given historical period. Further, Ezekiel's compelling imaginative construct may have been deliberately designed to counter the existing situation of nonownership of land by the temple.

In discussing the probability of temple landownership, we must also consider the general assertion by YHWH that "the land is mine" (e.g., Lev 25:23). If there is any historical reality underlying this claim, the land belonging to YHWH must have certainly been land owned by the temple and administered by the priestly personnel. In the Leviticus context, ownership of the land by YHWH is the warrant for not selling the land in perpetuity.

Since the land belongs ultimately to YHWH, land sales really function only as long-term leases. There is no specific admonition against private land ownership here. Rather, the assertion "the land is mine" is akin to YHWH's claim, "Every wild animal of the forest is mine, the beasts of a thousand hills; I know every bird of the mountains, and the moving things of my fields are mine" (Ps 50:10–11). As Creator of heaven and earth, YHWH owns all things, yet appoints humankind as stewards of the land and animals.

The cumulative biblical evidence does not allow unequivocal statements regarding landownership by the Jerusalem temple. Inasmuch as the crown held property and the crown and temple were the two major societal institutions in Israel/Judah, it may be reasonable to infer that the temple held land. Writing in the first century C.E., Philo relates, "The revenues of the temple are derived not only from landed estates but also from other and far greater sources which time will never destroy" (Philo, *Spec. Laws,* 1.76). On the other hand, if the temple staff farmed tracts of land and engaged in animal husbandry, one would expect certain residual information to remain in the biblical texts, including support of the necessary skilled personnel and collection and disposition of the yields. Thus, it is uncertain whether the temple owned land.

Whether or not the temple in Jerusalem owned land with herds and flocks, we may reasonably assume that from time to time the temple needed to purchase animals from the community. Specific cultic rituals demanded particular animals, for example, "a red heifer without defect, in which there is no blemish and on which no yoke has lain" (Num 19:2b). National festivals required large numbers of animals in Jerusalem. The national Passover festivals under Hezekiah (2 Chr 30) and Josiah (2 Chr 35) enumerate bulls and sheep in the thousands.

Mesopotamia

Even if the biblical evidence for land ownership by the Jerusalem temple is ambiguous, the record is crystal clear for temples in Mesopotamia. Perhaps the greatest source of temple income in Mesopotamia was landownership. One scholar offers this definition of the Babylonian temple: "It is essentially the house in which a god lives, manages his wordly [*sic*] business, is served by his household and his people, and, through his own success, ensures the happiness and prosperity of his city and her inhabitants."[1] The Mesopotamian

---

[1]Edmond Sollberger, "The Temple in Babylonia," in *Le Temple et le Culte* (Uitgaven Van Het Nederlands Historisch-Archaeologisch Instituut Te Istanbul 37; Leiden: Nederlands Historisch-Archaeologisch Instituut te Istambul, 1975), 34.

temple complex, with its fields and flocks, storehouses and stables, production facilities and personnel, constituted a self-sustaining household functioning as an economic unit in itself. Within this autonomous economic unit, temple assets (lands, herds, facilities, stores, personnel) were put to productive use in order to generate the food, clothing, tools, furnishings, and ritual items that the deity and the deity's household could use.

Thousands of excavated tablets from temple archives confirm that land and animals were important components of the temple's economy in the first millennium B.C.E. Historian Robert Adams reports that the Eanna temple in Uruk was "surely one of the largest landed economic establishments of the time."[2] The temple precinct covered more than 60,000 square meters (approx. 15 acres), including upwards of 150 storage facilities. Two millennia earlier, the Baba Temple in Uruk possessed over 11,000 acres and 1,000 workmen.[3] At the end of the seventh century and in the sixth century, the most important temples in Mesopotamia—Esagila in Babylon, Eanna in Uruk, Ebabbar in Sippar, Ezida in Borsippa—owned vast amounts of land and thousands of animals. For instance, the temple Eanna possessed 5,000–7,000 head of cattle and 100,000–150,000 head of sheep, and according to one document, it received within a year more than 11,000 pounds of wool from sheep belonging to the temple. One piece of property yielded almost 50,000 bushels of barley for the same temple in a year.[4]

The temple's agricultural land provided the produce necessary for the feeding of the god and the god's household, the temple personnel. The general designation in temple documents for land, as well as other assets of the temple, was "property of (Divine Name/Divine Title)." Particular types of land were specifically designated in the cuneiform texts as "uncultivated land of the temple of" (Divine Name), "field," "grain field," and "orchard set with date palms." Sometimes the location of the land was specified with reference to other (known) property as in "field on the bank of the royal canal." Temple archives preserve thousands of receipts for produce from temple fields, gardens, and groves: barley, emmer, spelt, wheat, dates, sesame, garlic,

---

[2]Robert M. Adams, *Heartland of Cities: Surveys of Ancient Settlements and Land Use on the Central Floodplain of the Euphrates* (Chicago: University of Chicago Press, 1981), 190.

[3]Adam Falkenstein, *The Sumerian Temple City* (Los Angeles: Undena, 1974), 7–8.

[4]Muhammed A. Dandamaev, "State and Temple in Babylonia in the First Millenium B.C.," in *State and Temple Economy in the Ancient Near East* (ed. Edward Lipinski; OLA 6; Leuven: Departement Orientalistiek, 1979), 589; Waldo H. Dubberstein, "Comparative Prices in Later Babylonia (625–400 B.C.)," *AJSL* 56 (1939): 26.

mustard seeds, vegetables, reeds, wood, and honey. Texts mention various personnel responsible for the cultivation of the temple's vast agricultural acreage: farmers of various crops, orchardkeepers, diggers of canals, reed cutters, straw carriers, gardeners, plowmen, plow leaders, ox drivers, and teamsters. In addition, archers did duty on temple land as protectors of the arable land and its cultivators. The agricultural produce was regularly delivered to the temple storehouses, where accountants inventoried and receipted it. From there, the priests took produce directly to the shrine for presentation to the cult statue.

Land suitable for grazing was variously termed "land drained by ditches," "land first emerging from inundation," "marshy soil affected by salinity," "reed marsh," "drained land," "cultivated grain fields," and "drained territory" in the texts, terms that seem to indicate land unsuitable for agriculture. Animals bred and tended on temple land included sheep, goats, cattle, donkeys, oxen, birds, ducks, hens, geese, and fresh- and saltwater fish. Although some large animals were raised as draft animals, most were destined for the deity's dining table. Texts mention a wide range of personnel engaged in animal husbandry: herders of cattle, sheep, goats, asses, she-asses, and pigs; herder supervisors; shepherds and sheepshearers; branders; fishermen of fresh water, brackish water, and sea; tenders of horses and felines; fatteners of cattle, sheep, and birds; and birdkeepers. These personnel were entrusted with the care of, and accounting for, the animals.

Texts indicate a strict accounting for the flocks and herds of the temple, no doubt reflecting the value—monetary and religious—of the animals to be sacrificed to the deity. The herdsmen were required to account for all the animals in their care, being held responsible for losses from their neglect or carelessness, but not for losses by accident or destruction by wild beasts. Nor was maintenance of the initial flock of animals sufficient. Increases in numbers as well as quantities of wool were expected in the annual inspection. For the Eanna temple in Uruk, the required increases were apparently "2/3 per head of sheep and 1 per head of goat, as well as 1½ minas of wool per sheep and 5/6 mina per goat. It may be that they were allowed to keep any increase and woolage above this target, in addition to having disposal of the milk and milk products all through the year."[5] The cattle (and other animals?) belonging to the Eanna temple in Uruk were branded with a star, the symbol of the resident deity Ištar. In one text, two temple herdsmen swear by the gods to come to Uruk for "a reckoning of the large and small cattle, property of Ishtar of Erech and Nanâ," otherwise "they will commit a sin against god and king" (*NBAD*, #137). In another, "the shepherds gave bribes to the governor and

---

[5]MacGinnis, *Letters and Orders,* 10.

the temple administrator (and as a result no accounting was made)" (*CAD* Š/3:247). As on farms, archers guarded the herds and flocks.

The "herdsman/shepherd of the regular offerings" was responsible for the supply of sacrificial animals from the temple flocks and herds. He apparently coordinated his activities with the stables so that animals could be transported from the grazing lands to the temple area. A text from the Eanna archive lists the sheep given to the shepherd of the fixed offering apportioned by day for the month of Ab in the first year of Cambyses (529 B.C.E.)—five or six sheep per day for the fixed offering and four to six sheep per day for the monthly offering (*NBAD*, #148). The herdsman of the regular offering had to meet the same strict standards of accountability as the grazing herdsmen. A text from Uruk describes an audit of the activity conducted by Shuzubu, the herdsman of the regular offering in the final three years of the reign of Nabonidus (536–539 B.C.E.). "During that time this man received no less than seven thousand and thirty-six animals and had disposed of six thousand eight hundred and sixteen, leaving a balance of two hundred and twenty. According to the figures on the tablet, the audit shows that [Shuzubu's] accounts were correct."[6] In addition to the use of animals for the deity's dining pleasure, priests slaughtered sheep in order to "read" the entrails, as evidenced by omen texts and by the mention of diviners and omen experts in ration texts. Records indicate receipt into the storehouses of large amounts of animal by-products: hides, wool, goat's hair, eggs, and milk.

Large-scale agriculture and broad-based animal husbandry in Mesopotamia, principally on the part of crown and temple, prospered not only from dedicated irrigation efforts but also from the relative peace of the Neo-Babylonian and Achaemenid (Persian) Empires in the sixth to fourth centuries. Skirmishes or even serious uprisings occurred at the accession of a new ruler, but these rebellions, primarily in the outlying provinces, did not significantly affect the stability of the agricultural center of the empire in southern Mesopotamia. Such stability allowed for the accumulation of significant surplus crops, which the temple rationed out from its depositories to personnel throughout the year. As the temple's acreage grew and the consequent yield flowed into the storehouses, strategies for managing production quantities were utilized by the temple. The most straightforward alternatives were (1) to retain full ownership of the land under production, disposing of the excess yield not utilized in the internal temple economy, or (2) to utilize alternative landownership and cultivation strategies so that production quantities coming into the temple economy would roughly approximate its needs. The latter leads to a discussion of leases and sales of agricultural land.

---

[6]Archibald Tremayne, *Records from Erech: Time of Cyrus and Cambyses (538–521 B.C.)* (New York: AMS, 1925), 13.

Land Sales and Leases. The Mesopotamian temple archives are noticeably silent on the topic of land sales. Presumably, the fine climate, rich soil, and extensive irrigation network that made Mesopotamia such an important breadbasket of the ancient world would have made landownership a desirable proposition, especially in times of peace. As long as seed, tools, and workers could be supplied, the outcome was more or less predictable. Also, the crown had donated at least some of the acreage owned by the temples, and it may not have been politically astute to dispose of that land. Texts indicate that the temple in Uruk owned roughly 30,000 acres in the regions of Sippar and that the temple in Sippar owned estates in Uruk, the ancient equivalent of land swapping between the temples. This would make economic sense if the crops grown on the distant land somehow supplemented the crops of nearby land.

In contrast to the dearth of economic texts regarding land sales, hundreds if not thousands of texts document land leasing as an activity of the temple. Of course, land leasing was not exclusively restricted to the temple nor to the middle centuries of the first millennium. The crown as well as private individuals also leased land to tenant farmers. The Code of Hammurabi (c.1700 B.C.E.) contains a dozen laws related to the leasing of grain fields or date groves. Leasing arrangements benefited both the community and the temple by allowing it to cultivate arable land when it did not directly control adequate numbers of farmers. The value of tenant farming was captured by lamenting, "My field is like a woman without a husband because it is without a tenant farmer" (*CAD* E:305). The standard leasing contract specified the lessee, the lessor, the amount of rent to be paid, the particular production measure to be employed, the delivery date, the delivery place, the witnesses, the scribe, and the date of the contract. Apparently, some land leased by the temple was subsequently subleased to other parties. If the temple arranged to lease substantial acreage to a few people, allowing them to sublease smaller portions of the land to others, the temple could reduce the number of direct tenants, thereby reducing the effort required to administer the tenancies. In one leasing contract for Eanna land, a woman was the sublessee responsible for the rent and was assured that the measure to be used was the same standard used by the temple's own gardeners (*NBAD,* #66).

Land leasing arrangements probably contributed to the standardization of weights and measures. Lessors and creditors, including the temple and the state, used their own measures by which they received and lent commodities. Evidence from the Neo-Babylonian and early Persian periods suggests varying standards of measurement. The "king's measure" came to replace the various temples' measures as the standard, although by the late fifth century, the royal standard measure had weakened to the point where multiple measures were once again employed.

Land leasing contracts generally called for a percentage share of the crop designated as *imittu*, "estimated yield," "impost," or "rent." The lessor apparently had the right to fix the percentage of the crop to be remitted by the tenant farmer. Naturally, representatives of the landowner often carried out this responsibility. Land leasing contracts regularly contained the phrase "charged against," the same phrase used in standard debt contracts of the time (see chapter five), emphasizing the legal liability of the lessee to remit a share of the crop to the lessor as payment for the use of the land. Since the acreage of the land under lease was not generally specified, the property simply being identified as "the rental area of [Personal Name]," we are unable to calculate the percentage share of the crop usually due as rent. Evidence from the Old Babylonian period (mid-second millennium B.C.E.) indicates that the tenant farmer typically took two-thirds, while the owner of the field took one-third of the yield. The Code of Hammurabi sometimes awards two-thirds to the owner and sometimes calls for equal distribution of the field's yield between owner and tenant farmer. A Neo-Babylonian text (sixth century B.C.E.) apportioning the *imittu* of several fields generally allocates 25% to the gardeners, 15–25% to various individuals (workers?), and the remaining 50–60% to the temple's representative, of whom the land was *ina pāni*, "at the disposal" (*NBAD*, #59). Contracts also provided for natural disasters: "If a man leases his field to a cultivator and receives the rent for his field, and afterwards the storm-god Adad devastates the field or a flood sweeps away the crops, the loss is the cultivator's alone."[7]

In the Neo-Babylonian period, the share of the crop paid by the lessee to the lessor was termed *sūtu* when the lessee was a semifree dependent of the temple. The rations of these semidependent personnel could be deducted from the amount of *sūtu* owed to the temple as rent. Generally contracts fixed *sūtu* payments in advance, in contrast to *imittu*, which was based on assessment of the crop yield. On several occasions, the temple administration in Sippar sent a letter ordering the "overseer of the *sūtu* payments" to issue commodities collected as *sūtu* rent directly to temple personnel working away from the temple complex, bypassing the temple storehouses.[8] The overseer kept the letter as proof of disbursement when he settled his accounts on the Register of Šamaš at the Ebabbar temple.

Like most administrators in charge of a large organization, the temple staff tried to negotiate the best deal with tenant farmers from the commu-

---

[7]Martha T. Roth, *Law Collections from Mesopotamia and Asia Minor* (SBLWAW 6; 2d ed.; Atlanta: Scholars Press, 1997), 89 §45. Cf. §46 where the yield should be divided if the catastrophic damage occurs *before* the rent is paid, i.e., the loss should be shared between tenant and owner.

[8]MacGinnis, *Letters and Orders*, 20.

nity. In two examples from prospective lessees, one potential lessee offered to increase the inflow of grain to the temple and assume responsibility for maintenance of the irrigation canal feeding the property (*NBAD,* #90). The second potential lessee offered to decrease the outflow of materials from the temple and make an additional cultic offering (*NBAD,* #182).

The evidence of leasing or selling houses is not extensive enough to answer questions of specific terms of the lease or sale. In the temple archive from Sippar there is "the one in charge of the houses," who collected the rent for temple-owned houses. Annual rental amounts ranged from one-third shekel for "collapsed" houses to more than twenty shekels for more sophisticated dwellings.[9]

Management of Animals. The management of land related closely to the cult's need for ceremonially clean or ritually specific animals. For example, one special ritual used a pregnant cow, bought at a price three and four times its typical market value.[10] The temple's economy expanded into the local (or regional) community to locate and purchase the particular animal needed for the cultic rituals.

Numerous texts testify to the receipt of dead animals or carcasses into the temple storerooms, presumably unrelated to ritual slaughtering at the altar. Freshly dead animals could be distributed as rations to temple personnel if the animal had not died of disease. Or the temple could sell the carcass, another expansion of the internal temple economy into the local community. For diseased animals, the hides may have been usable for leather or some of its byproducts. A letter to Assyrian King Esarhaddon notes how hides of diseased sheep were saved even though the meat was rejected (*RCAE,* #75). Part of animal husbandry management included introducing new animals into the herd and culling other animals. Temple archives record the buying and selling of animals, again illustrating the temple's economic influence into the community or region. We noted above how temple animals were placed "at the disposal of" (*ina pāni*) temple herdsmen and shepherds. The temple could also lease animals to persons outside the temple complex. The owner was entitled to a fixed percentage of the milk, wool, and young offspring, and the shepherd kept the remainder. Interestingly, these arrangements were often termed *iškaru,* the same term noted in chapter two (in connection to the wilderness tabernacle) for raw materials given to craftsmen, who were then contractually responsible for finished products.

---

[9]A. C. V. M. Bongenaar, "Money in the Neo-Babylonian Institutions," in *Trade and Finance in Ancient Mesopotamia* (ed. J. G. Dercksen; Leiden: Nederlands Instituut voor het Nabije Oosten, 1999), 164–65.

[10]Dubberstein, "Comparative Prices," 31.

Egypt and Greece

The issue of landownership by Egyptian temples is more difficult than in Mesopotamia, since the Egyptian temple was more closely related to the state government, perhaps even as "one branch of the government administration."[11] The granaries at Thebes, whether crown or temple, functioned as an integrated unit under one central accounting system. Although we should guard against exaggerating the state-temple connection in Egypt since the temple managed to attain some economic independence through trade, state control of and access to royal funerary temple revenue was effective throughout Egypt's history.

Whatever the ultimate ownership claims, Egyptian temples controlled vast tracts of land, in the proximity of the temple and in distant territories. "Some scholars argue that by 1165 temples owned one-third of all arable land; others believe that, two centuries later, they owned most of it."[12] Since the state had significant control over all revenue, to say temples "owned" land is not necessarily to say temples absolutely controlled revenues from land. According to the Wilbour Papyrus (mid-to-late first millennium B.C.E.), a temple's land was divided into three categories. On large farms directly cultivated and harvested by the temple staff, approximately 30% of the harvest flowed into the temple storehouses while 70% went to rations and wages. Relatively small farms were leased on a long-term basis to cultivators whose rent was a share of the harvest, generally 6%. Very small plots generated no surplus at all for the temple storehouses, but were able to sustain the cultivators.[13] In the Ptolemaic period (third century B.C.E.), temple lands were regularly allotted to high-level state employees whose wealth consisted of land and houses and the rights to income from the temple for services performed.

Unlike the Mesopotamian and Egyptian temples, there is scant evidence of land ownership by Greek temples. Vast acreages did not play a part in the temple economy as a way to care for the gods and the gods' households, although there were receipts of rents from sacred estates and houses.

---

[11]Barry J. Kemp, "Temple and Town in Ancient Egypt," in *Man, Settlement and Urbanism* (ed. Peter J. Ucko, Ruth Tringham, and G. W. Dimbleby; Cambridge, Mass.: Schenkman, 1972), 659. Janssen agrees, stating "the temples were a specialized state organization [like the army] with wide economic consequences." Janssen, *Role of the Temple,* 509.

[12]David O'Connor, "The Social and Economic Organization of Ancient Egyptian Temples," *CANE* 1:320.

[13]Ibid., 323; Kemp, *Temple and Town,* 658.

Summary

Many factors affected temple ownership of land, including the full range of socioeconomic and political influences. It is striking, however, that in the irrigation economies of Mesopotamia and Egypt that engaged in large-scale grain agriculture, temples owned large amounts of land, as did the crown. By contrast, in the rainfall economies of Greece and Judah that engaged in small-scale agriculture, temples do not appear to have been substantial landowners. I suggest, therefore, that land ownership by temples was at least partially related to the issue of water supply (irrigation vs. rainfall). Where an administrative bureaucracy was needed to manage widespread irrigation and large-scale agriculture, the temple appeared to fulfill an institutional role as a landowner. When the geography and climate favored small-scale agriculture manageable by individuals, the temple did not own large estates.

Tithes

Jerusalem. Significant contributions flowed into the Jerusalem temple as a result of the obligation of the people to present tithes of their crops and their increase in flocks and herds. Related to the Assyrian term *ešrû* and the Hebrew number ten, *ʿeśer,* the tithe in Israel/Judah was termed *maʿăśēr,* one of many designations for contributions to the temple.

> You will bring there (the place YHWH will establish his name) your whole burnt offerings (*ʿōlôtêkem*), your sacrifices (*zibḥêkem*), your tithes (*maʿśĕrôtêkem*), the contribution (*tĕrûmat*) of your hand, your vows (*nidrêkem*), your freewill offerings (*nidbôtêkem*), and the firstborn (*bĕhōrōt*) of your cattle and your flock. (Deut 12:6)

The priestly book of Leviticus details the circumstances under which the various offerings are to be made to YHWH. Regulations apply to the whole burnt offering (*ʿōlâ*), grain offering (*minḥâ*), offerings of well-being (*šĕlāmîm*), sin offering (*ḥaṭṭāʾt*), guilt offering (*ʾāšām*), votive offering (*neder*), and freewill offering (*nĕdābâ*). Rituals are prescribed for ordination of priests, purification of a woman after childbirth, cleansing of leprosy, purification after bodily discharges, slaughter of animals, the Day of Atonement, and the appointed festivals. As the divinely ordained means of reconciliation (divine/human and human/human), the sacrificial system resulted in significant transfer of economic wealth from the community to the temple and priests. Succinctly summarized by YHWH, "They shall not appear before me empty-handed" (Exod 23:15b). Levitical stipulations specify the quantity of the tithe as one-tenth and the items subject to tithe as agriculture and animals.

> Every tithe of the land, whether seed of the land or fruit of the tree, belongs to YHWH; it is holy to YHWH. If a person redeems his tithe, he will add a fifth to it. Every tithe of herd and flock, every one that passes under the staff, the tenth one will be holy to YHWH. (Lev 27:30–32)

While the Levitical regulations understand local shrines as recipients of the agricultural and animal tithes, the Deuteronomic regulations have in mind the centralization of worship in Jerusalem, necessitating allowances for the transport of the tithe.

> You shall surely give a tithe of all the produce of your seed that comes forth from the field year by year. And before YHWH your God in the place where he will choose to establish his name, you will eat a tithe of your grain, your new wine, your oil, and the firstborn of your herd and your flock, in order that you may learn to fear YHWH your God forever. But if the way is so long for you that you are not able to carry it, because the place is so distant where YHWH will choose to establish his name when YHWH your God blesses you, then you will exchange it into silver and you will bind up the silver in your hand and you will come to the place which YHWH your God will choose for it, and you will exchange the silver for [whatever you desire]. (Deut 14:22–26)

Obviously, silver is easier to transport than sheep or baskets of grain. The Deuteronomic provisions for eating the tithe apply to sustenance during the journey, not to the total consumption of the tithe upon arrival in Jerusalem, else there would be no (economic) purpose to requiring the tithe. The Deuteronomic provisions for partial consumption of the tithe, as well as mandatory attendance at the Jerusalem festivals, would "give the peasants additional positive motivation to go up to the capital to do the king's new thing" (2 Kgs 23:22–23).[14]

Biblical writers use the abundance of tithes brought to the temple in Jerusalem to convey the abundant blessing of YHWH on the faithful king and community, as well as the eager obedience of the people.

> He (Hezekiah) told the people who were residing in Jerusalem to give the portion of the priests and Levites, in order that they might be resolute in the law of YHWH. As the word spread, the children of Israel had in abundance grain, new wine, oil, and honey, and all the produce of the field, so they brought the tithe of all the abundance. As for the children of Israel and Judah residing in the cit-

---

[14]W. Eugene Claburn, "The Fiscal Basis of Josiah's Reforms," *JBL* 92 (1973): 16–17.

ies of Judah, they also brought the tithe of the herd and flock and the tithe of holy things set apart for YHWH their God, and they piled them up in heaps. . . . Then Hezekiah said to prepare chambers in the house of YHWH, so they prepared [them]. And they brought the contribution, the tithe, and the holy things faithfully. (2 Chr 31:4–6, 11)

The prophet Malachi denounces the people for cheating God when they offer imperfect tithes.

> Should a mortal rob God? Yet you are robbing me. So you said, "In what are we robbing you?" The tithe and the contribution! With a curse you are cursed for you are robbing me, all the nation. Bring every tithe to the storehouse (*bêt hāʾôṣār*) so that there will be food in my house. (Mal 3:8–10)

In the apocryphal tale of Tobit, he illustrates his righteousness by testifying about his generosity with the tithe.

> But I alone went frequently to Jerusalem for the festivals, as it has been written for all Israel in an everlasting decree. Once I had the first fruits of the crops and the firstlings of the flock, the tenth of the cattle, and the first shearings of the sheep, I would hurry off to Jerusalem. I would give them to the priests, the sons of Aaron, at the altar; likewise the tenth of the grain, wine, olive oil, pomegranates, figs, and the rest of the fruits to the sons of Levi who were serving in Jerusalem. Also for six years I would save up a second tenth in silver and go and spend it in Jerusalem. A third tenth I would give to the orphans and widows and to the proselytes who had attached themselves to Israel. I would bring it and give it to them in the third year, and we would eat it according to the decree that was decreed about it in the law of Moses and according to the commandments that were commanded by Deborah, the mother of my father Tobiel, for my father had died and left me an orphan. (Tob 1:6–8)

Clearly the tithe represented a major source of income for the Jerusalem temple, whether understood as an obligatory tax or as a voluntary contribution. Tithes of animals and agricultural produce, especially grain, wine, and oil, would have supplied the shrine and altar with the requisite sacrifices and the temple personnel with food and clothing. The people deposited their tithes in Jerusalem, though some texts describe the role of the Levites as collectors of the tithes.

> The first of our coarse meal, our contributions (*tĕrûmōtênû*), the fruit of every tree, the new wine, and the fresh oil we will bring to the priests, to the store chambers of the house of our God, and the tithe (*maʿśar*) of our land to the Levites, for it is the Levites who collect the tithe in all the cities of our labors. (Neh 10:38[37])

Perhaps the people gave the tithes to the Levites who transported them to Jerusalem. By the agency of the Levites, then, all the people "brought" tithes to Jerusalem.

Further, biblical texts indicate that the Levites, who were supported by the tithes of the people, also paid it themselves.

> When you receive from the children of Israel the tithe that I am giving to you from them as your inheritance, then you shall offer from it the contribution of YHWH, a tithe from the tithe. (Num 18:26)

> And the Levites are collectors of tithes in all the cities of our labor . . . and the Levites shall bring up the tithe of the tithe to the house of God, to the chambers, to the storehouse. (Neh 10:39[38])

Mesopotamia. When we turn to the subject of the tithe in Mesopotamia, we find that the practices are remarkably similar to those in Israel/Judah. The Mesopotamian term most commonly translated as "tithe" was *ešrû*, representing approximately one-tenth of a person's income. In the Old Babylonian period (mid-second millennium B.C.E.), the term *miksu* appears as a general term for revenue, primarily from agricultural activities, imposed in proportions of one-tenth and due to both state and temple. But obligatory inflows to the temple were also described as various kinds of "taxes" and "tribute," even though these same terms were also used with reference to obligations to the state. Note the terminology used by leading scholars in the field who characterized the tithe as a kind of tax: "The major source of temple revenue consisted of various kinds of taxes, the most important being the tithe";[15] "The income of the temple came from taxes (especially tithes)."[16] Inasmuch as the tithe was compulsory, it functioned as a tax. At least ten percent of a farmer's produce was not available for familial consumption.

A text from the Eanna temple archive in Uruk accounts for various types of income from the third through the seventh year of Nabonidus (530s B.C.E.). Sprinkled throughout the account record, among the details of rent received from lessees and cultivators, are phrases like the following: "500 GUR of barley, 137 GUR of dates of the tithe" (*NBAD*, #227). Most often the name of the relevant deity was documented in the formula "(dates and/or barley) tithe that is the property of" Divine Name. Although the vast majority of tithe records appear to be based on a percentage of agricultural yield, one could also remit tithes on other bases: "One mina of silver, the tithe, which [PN] has given for his getting well to Bēl and Bēltija for the removal of rubble from

---

[15]Dandamaev, "State and Temple," 593.
[16]MacGinnis, *Letters and Orders,* 7.

Esagila" (*CAD* E:369). In the Larsa period (eighteenth century B.C.E.), a trader provided with private funds paid ten percent of the increase to the Ningal temple.[17] The tithe obligation was most frequently met with barley and dates, but also with other grains, silver, wool, and animals. Apparently nothing escaped the rule of the tithe; a text from the time of Darius (521–486) mentions a tithe of a cedar branch, and Jesus criticizes the Pharisees for tithing mint, dill, and cumin while ignoring justice and mercy.[18]

In Mesopotamia "the official in charge of the tithe" collected it, remitting the proceeds to the temple storehouses where accountants settled individual tithe accounts. In at least one text, the official also participated in the inspection of the tithe commodities.[19] Sometimes the officials in charge of the tithe, at the behest of the temple administration, distributed tithe collections on site, bypassing the temple storehouses. The right to collect temple tithes could be sold to persons outside the temple complex; presumably, the collector retained any commodities collected above the agreed amount, a situation ripe for corruption.

Tithe texts from Babylon, Borsippa, Kish, Marada, Nippur, Sippar, Ur, and Uruk mention eleven different deities.[20] Although tithes may have been remitted to minor temples, it is more likely that the main temple of each region functioned as the central temple, eventually receiving the tithes from the surrounding area. The places of delivery were further specified as the "storehouse" or the "gate," locations staffed with temple accountants.

An interesting aspect of temple tithes is the question of who was obligated to pay them. Every resident paid tithes from their agriculture and herds, each to the temple closest to where he or she held land or grazed a herd. Assyrian King Esarhaddon (680–669 B.C.E.) inquired as to the payment of the "customary dues" to the god Ashur by government officials and received a listing of names in reply; "none of these has given the customary dues of barley and spelt" (*RCAE*, #43). Evidence suggests that even temple personnel paid tithes to the temple from their income, including the *šangû* (chief administrator) of the Ebabbar temple and the royal courtiers appointed to the temple administration. One text records the tithe paid by the

---

[17]Maria DeJong Ellis, "Taxation in Ancient Mesopotamia: The History of the Term Miksu," *JCS* 26 (1974): 219 n. 40.

[18]Grazia Giovinazzo, "The Tithe *ešrû* in Neo-Babylonian and Achaemenid Period," in *Le Tribut dans l'Empire Perse: Actes de la Table Ronde de Paris 12–13 Décembre 1986* (ed. Pierre Briant and Clarisse Herrenschmidt; Travaux de l'Institut d'Études Iraniennes de l'Université de la Sorbonne Nouvelle 13; Paris and Louvain: Peeters, 1989), 100; Matt 23:23.

[19]MacGinnis, *Letters and Orders,* 128.

[20]Giovinazzo, "The Tithe *ešrû*," 96–98.

"chief of the king's waters," a royal official in the temple hierarchy possibly in charge of irrigation.[21]

Until the rise of Cyrus and the Achaemenid dynasty in 539 B.C.E., the royal family had paid tithes to the temples like all other citizens: Belshazzar paid a sheep tithe; Nabonidus delivered the tithe rights to six gold mines to the Ebabbar temple.[22] At the accession of Cyrus, the official policy regarding royal tithes reversed. Although subjects in the Achaemenid realm were obligated to support temples through tithes, the Achaemenids themselves did not pay temple tithes.

Egypt. The textual evidence for the collection of tithes by the temple in Egypt is not nearly as extensive as in Mesopotamia. Perhaps the main support for the temples came from the royal administration, and thus indirectly from the populace. A Ptolemaic decree (third century B.C.E.) presented Khnum, the ram-god of the First Cataract region, with "a tithe of the yield of fishing, hunting, snaring, cattle raising, mining, and various handicrafts and a tithe of precious imports into Egypt."[23]

Taxes

As we noted in the introductory chapter, terminology relating to taxation is confusing. Whereas we normally associate "taxes" with an obligatory payment to the government and "tithes" with the temple, the situation was not so segregated in the ANE. Particularly since the biblical texts are theological documents and not economic receipts, information relating to taxation and the Jerusalem temple is particularly elusive. By contrast, excavated temple archives from Mesopotamia are primarily administrative and economic documents. In earlier sections we have begun by looking at the biblical texts, and then moved to the other ANE texts to provide background information. In the case of taxation, it will be more productive to reverse the order, since the ramifications of taxation and the temple are much clearer in Mesopotamia. Once we have examined taxation in Mesopotamia, we will turn to taxation in Israel/Judah.

Mesopotamia

Terminology. The following kinds of taxes illustrate the diversity of compulsory exactions in Mesopotamia. The *ḫamussu*-tax, literally "the fifth," was

---

[21]Bongenaar, *Ebabbar Temple*, 137.

[22]Giovinazzo, "The Tithe *ešrû*," 104; Raymond P. Dougherty, *Records from Erech: Time of Nabonidus (555–538 B.C.)* (YOS 6; New York: AMS Press, 1920), 12.

[23]Porten, *Archives from Elephantine*, 25.

mentioned in a Neo-Assyrian text, an indictment against state administration officials: "Up to the present moment, none of the high officials of your land has brought the tribute of the city of Barhalza. . . . May the king question the scribes of the governor of Barhalza . . . saying, 'Wherefore have you not given the tribute for Ashur' for non-payment of tax into the temple" (*RCAE*, #532). A portion of an annual tax collected from merchants, military commanders, and others, the *igisû*-tax, was forwarded to gods and temples (*CAD* I-J:41–43). In a Neo-Babylonian text, a supervisor gave the following instructions: "Point out to the workmen the part of the (field) impost which goes as *n.*-tax [*nisihtu*-tax] so that they may move the barley" (*CAD* N/2:271). Assyrian King Sargon (721–705 B.C.E.) states, "I imposed on them a *s.*-tax [*sibtu*-tax on animals] on cattle and sheep and goats (to be paid) annually to Bēl (and the son of Bēl)" (*CAD* Ṣ:166). Another text implies that the animals collected for the *sibtu*-tax were supplied for the regular offerings of the temple (*CAD* Ṣ:167). The *qīpu*, "royal commissioner," of the Ebabbar temple in Sippar was obliged to pay the annual *nāmurtu*, "gift," to the temple consisting of five sheep, one cow, and two lambs.[24]

The temple also received "tax income" in the form of conscripted labor called *ilku,* a term usually denoting the military service due to the state in return for a grant of agricultural land. Perhaps the temple was also due labor services in some measure by the community, or perhaps the king redirected the *ilku*-service due to the crown by assigning it to the temple. One text reports *ilku*-barley as destined for the temple: "to measure out the *i.*-income collected from the farmers, consisting of 150 gur of barley, to the temple of Šamaš" (*CAD* I-J:77).

The general term for temple revenue of all kinds appears to have been *irbu,* covering offerings, tithes, taxes, and fees paid in silver, commodity staples (barley, dates, sesame), sheep, or other animals. One may call these forms of temple revenue "taxes" in that they were obligatory payments from persons in the temple's district and represented a form of institutional exaction. Presumably, the community believed that temple tithes and taxes were necessary to house, clothe, and feed the gods. In return, the gods ensured fertility and prosperity. But temple tithes and taxes did not exhaust the duty of farmers and herders. They were also obligated to pay taxes to the crown for the administration of the state. Before turning to the role of the temple in the collection of state taxes, it is necessary to review briefly the subject of taxation in Mesopotamia.

The study of taxation in first-millennium Mesopotamia involves not only the confusing terminology related to royal income already mentioned,

---

[24]Bongenaar, *Ebabbar Temple,* 40.

but enormous complexities in the levels of taxation. Scholars often draw a distinction between "taxes" and "gifts" in Mesopotamia, so that "taxes" represent the systematic exaction of surplus from subjugated populations, whereas "gifts" belong to the sphere of benevolent rule and the consent of the governed. Herodotus' statement is offered as the parade example: "In the reign of Cyrus and Cambyses after him there was no fixed tribute, but payment was made in gifts" (Herodotus, *Hist.* 3.89). But the statement probably says more about the perceived role of the early Achaemenid dynasty as benevolent despots than about the economic extraction systems in the Persian Empire. The terminological debate is sometimes based on the qualitative level of goods (commodities for taxation vs. prestige goods for gifts) and the rank of the parties (inequality for taxation vs. parity for gifts); that is, the peasants paid "taxes" and the nobility gave "gifts." Whatever the terminological distinctions, all contributed to the maintenance of the royal bureaucracy.

Still another part of the difficulty in describing taxation in Mesopotamia relates to the terminology of "tax" vs. "tribute." The amounts that subject regions within the empire paid to the central government were known as "tax," whereas amounts paid by countries subdued but still governed by a local ruler and an Assyrian appointee were known as "tribute." Political decisions regarding inclusion of a territory in the state system determined if a payment was tax (inside the redistribution system) or tribute (outside the redistribution system). Such tribute was probably brought annually directly to the king, not through the provincial system, and consisted exclusively of nonbulk items, with the exception of horses. The distinction between "tribute" and "booty" is sometimes traced to the reign of Tiglath-pileser III (744–727), who abandoned the custom of plundering and devastating conquered regions in favor of imposing continuing tribute collected by an Assyrian bureaucracy. Previously, the distinction between tribute and booty was practically meaningless since the prospect of Assyrian invasion (and the impending plundering) prompted the threatened area to offer equivalent tribute as appeasement. Tribute is connected with formal requisition—"the robbery is indirect."[25]

The Persian imperial taxation system included all sorts of compulsory payments. For purposes of this study, the term "taxes" refers to the resources exacted by the ruling political power, who then exercised control over the re-

---

[25]Henri J. M. Claessen, "Tribute and Taxation or How to Finance Early States and Empires," in *Le Tribut dans l'Empire Perse: Actes de la Table Ronde de Paris 12–13 Décembre 1986* (ed. Pierre Briant and Clarisse Herrenschmidt; Travaux de l'Institut d'Études Iraniennes de l'Université de la Sorbonne Nouvelle 13; Paris and Louvain: Peeters, 1989), 51.

distribution of said resources. In modern economies the federal government uses both monetary policy and fiscal policy to influence levels of economic activity. Taxation is an instrument of fiscal policy, the level and composition of receipts and expenditures. Taxation comprises an important part of government receipts and can be adjusted by manipulating the goods or services subject to tax, the rate of tax, and the exemptions to tax. At a socioeconomic macrolevel, taxation serves the goal of redistribution of resources from some portions of society to others.

In Mesopotamia, taxation redistributed resources from taxpayers through the king to the military and aristocracy primarily, and secondarily to the rest of society. Taxation, tribute, booty, and gifts flowed into the palace household without much trickle-down effect on the private sector. Royal building projects were completed by conscripted or deported labor gangs who drew rations from the palace estates.

Basis of Taxation. The fundamental basis for state taxation was the exaction of agricultural produce and labor. The state received a share of agricultural produce from land owned outright by free citizens, land given to military and other officials, and royal land worked by dependent tenants. Although tax rates are not precisely known, some rates attested in the Neo-Assyrian Empire are 10% for grain and 25% for straw, an indication that straw for building material and animal fodder was in relatively short supply.[26] The following text suggests a tenth proportion due to the crown in the Neo-Babylonian period: "15 *kur* of barley, tithe for the 11th year (which) PN has delivered to the storehouse (for) royal income."[27]

As with tithe payments to the temples, terminology related to state income—agricultural produce or personnel service—from state land is confusing. As mentioned above, *ilku*-service obligations were attendant upon allotments of land by the crown to private citizens. The plots of land carried the obligation of military service as archers ("bow-land"), cavalry ("horse-land"), or charioteers ("chariot-land"). For convenience, any military fief is commonly referred to as "bow-land" regardless of specific services rendered. In return for royal grants of land, the beneficiaries of similar occupation organized themselves into a group called *ḫaṭru,* whose members outfitted themselves with weapons, horses, and/or chariots as needed for the particular military service. They were additionally responsible for deliveries of various

---

[26]J. N. Postgate, "The Economic Structure of the Assyrian Empire," in *Power and Propoganda: A Symposium on Ancient Empires* (ed. Mogens Trolle Larsen; Copenhagen Studies in Assyriology: Mesopotamia 79; Copenhagen: Akademisk Forlag, 1979), 205.

[27]Giovinazzo, "The Tithe *ešrû,*" 105.

kinds, including flour, silver, and the *bāru*-tax. Over time the *ilku*-military service obligation was gradually fulfilled through substitution of personnel, then by payments in kind, and then by monetary payments.

Besides the association of men into a military *ḫatru* (with a land grant as reward), the state exacted labor resources by conscripting men for the army and for building projects. The Assyrian king Esarhaddon (680–669 B.C.E.) boasted, "I added craftsmen, scribes, shield-bearers, scouts, farmers, shepherds and gardeners to the mighty forces of Assur and greatly increased the royal contingent of the kings my fathers before me."[28] Some time later when the Achaemenid rulers had subdued the Neo-Babylonian regime in 539 B.C.E., they added a new administrative layer requiring support by the populace. The Achaemenid administration demanded payments and services to be used outside Babylonia in their capital cities. Tablets from Persepolis catalogue precious gifts from all over the empire as well as thousands of workmen from many ethnic groups working on building the new capital in exchange for rations.

Supporting the royal bureaucracy required enriched yields that could be levied, increased efficiency of exaction and distribution, and new forms of taxation. Although land was the fundamental basis for taxation, the state augmented the land-based tax in order to secure additional sources of income. Devising new types of taxes on commercial activity was an especially efficient means of generating income, since merchants and consumers already encouraged the movement of goods. An added benefit to the empire of increased commercialization was the breakdown of traditional patterns of familial economic self-sufficiency and an increased dependency on the central government for economic well-being. In addition to shares of agricultural produce, various other state exactions for shipment of goods, animals, and personal valuation were due. Royal tax income drew on a wide variety of sources: percentages of production; shares of increases in herds and flocks; tax on production of craftsmen; head tax; harbor charge; crossing fees; canal fees; bridge tolls; import duty; overland customs tax; fee for shipments of monetary items; purchase tax for local markets; and a user tax for public facilities by merchants. Note the various items recorded in a letter to an Assyrian king inventorying the taxes received from a particular province:

> Two talents of silver, twenty mana of silver, a garment of elephant hide, fifty chitons, ten under-garments, three lamakarti vessels of fish, twenty strings (?) of fish, one thousand fish, the whole being taxes; one circlet (?) of gold, twenty plates of silver, four under-garments of cotton, fifteen tent coverings (?) of the

---

[28]Postgate, "Economic Structure," 211.

land of Hasai, ten chitons, ten large under-garments—the total receipts. This (is) the total for the palace. (*RCAE,* #568)

The items were directed to the palace, the lady of the palace, the crown prince, the steward of the palace, the scribe of the land, the commander-in-chief, and other military officers.

Subjects of Taxation. Who owed taxes in Mesopotamia? Generally speaking, everyone was subject to some form of enforced exaction by the state administration unless specifically exempted by periodic royal proclamations of freedom, which monarchs proclaimed at their accession to the throne or in periods of political or economic crisis. These proclamations generally included restoration of towns and temples, pardon of rebels and prisoners, repatriation of exiles, redistribution of land, cancellation of debt slavery, and relief from royal exactions of commodities and/or labor, either temporarily or permanently. In short, these "freedom decrees" offered political freedom as well as debt relief. Individuals or cities received these freedoms as a reward for special service or loyalty to the king. Occasional proclamations of freedom by the king were politically expedient tactics to rectify economic conditions harmful to the state and generate goodwill toward a benevolent ruler, thus weakening potential political rivals.

In the Achaemenid Empire, land owned by the Persian nobility was tax-exempt by statute. In fact, those who actually worked the noble's land often carried immunity from state taxes as well, thus increasing the amount of income flowing into the noble's treasury and insuring his continued allegiance to the crown. In a letter to Assyrian King Esarhaddon a royal astrologer informs the king that the tax exemption should be extended from a month to a year based on the omens observed (*RCAE,* #74). Kings could grant whole cities exemption from taxes and conscripted labor: "I established freedom from encumbrances for this city, no deductions may be made from its barley, and no tax is to be paid from its straw" (*CAD* Z:32).

The comprehensive taxation system primarily supported the royal establishment and the army. Although often termed "redistributive," taxes were actually redistributed in a small percentage of the total economy, paying for the lifestyle of the elite and the waging of war. Assessed by the provincial governments, military *ilku*-service and tax payments of grain and other commodities provided for the maintenance of garrisons throughout the empire, which in turn provided security to farmers and herders. Evidence suggests regions supplied royal needs by rotation. Herodotus thus explains that the maintenance of the king and his army was undertaken by Babylonia for four months per year and by the rest of Asia for the remaining eight months per year, concluding, "Thus the wealth of Assyria is one third of the whole wealth of Asia" (Herodotus, *Hist.* 1.192).

Assessment and Collection. With a wide section of the population liable to taxation, an elaborate assessment and collection process arose. Obviously, the king would have delegated the collection of taxes to royal officials. In a letter to King Esarhaddon, the royal astrologer instructs the king to "write to the abarakku official, the sinew of (your) hands. The skins are plentiful. *Let* him collect the tax *from* the shepherds" (*RCAE*, #75). In another letter to the same king, royal servants ask for instructions regarding wine received for which there is no storage space (*RCAE*, #86). Darius I reorganized the empire he inherited in 521 B.C.E. into twenty satrapies and assessed taxes for each satrapy based on the acreage of cultivable land and the type of crop produced. The full collection of taxes was the responsibility of the provincial satrap, who no doubt enlisted local officials to gather and transport the various commodities to regional collection centers. Although some goods went directly from taxpayer to crown, the temples also probably collected portions of royal taxes. Consider the following text:

> PN, PN2, PN3, and PN4 have taken an oath by DN and the king (saying) "We shall estimate the yield in dates due from the 'bow'-land of PN5 for the year 4 of RN, we shall be responsible (lit. see) until the (entire) yield that pertains (to it) enters into Eanna." (*CAD* I-J:123)

We noted earlier that the crown granted bow-land to private citizens in exchange for military service and commodity deliveries, i.e., taxes. This text specifies that the requisite yield in dates be remitted to the Eanna temple in Uruk.

Contributions to the crown of food or precious metal were frequently collected in a *quppu*, "basket" or "cash box." In a text from 561 B.C.E. a high-ranking official reports that his messenger deposited 12 1/2 shekels of silver into the *quppu* basket.[29] Although this text leaves the precise location of the basket in the city unclear, we have ample evidence that items destined for the crown were collected by means of a *quppu* in the temple precincts supervised by officials termed "the ones in charge of the (wicker) cash box of the king." Dandamaev terms this official, "the state financial agent in the temple."[30]

> Thirty shekels of silver, offerings, from the wicker cash-box of the king, (collected) at the gate from the ninth of MN until the 24th of MN. (*CAD* I-J:175)

> x silver came into the collection boxes at the gate. (*CAD* B:20)

---

[29]Raymond P. Dougherty, *Neo-Babylonian and Persian Periods* (vol. 2 of *Archives from Erech;* New Haven: Yale University Press, 1933), #86. In this case the *quppu* basket specifically carries the determinative for "wood."

[30]Dandamaev, "State and Temple," 590.

Collection boxes at the gates would ensure comprehensive coverage of all those entering the temple precincts. And we have already seen that the "gater" (*šōʿēr*) was a gate accountant.

The following text makes clear that the cash box of the king was separate from the cash box of the temple:

> The royal cash box in Eanna together with the cash box of the *šatammu* office, all the shares of the king and of the *šatammu* official, as much as there is . . . (*CAD* Q:309)

The royal collection basket at the gate was designated for income from individuals, while another *quppu* at the altar collected the royal share of the sacrificial offerings.

> Throw the breast cut of the sheep from the main morning (meal of the god) into the king's cash box (*CAD* Q:309).

Lower in rank than the officials in charge of the *quppu* in Sippar were the "guardians" (*maṣṣartu*) of the cash box and the supervisors of the cash boxes of the smaller sanctuaries. Texts testify to "the guardian of the cash box of Bēlet (=Ištar) of Akkad, the guardian of the cash box of the temple of Gula and the treasurer of Bunene."[31] Just as the *šōʿēr* was a "gate-keeper" and a "gate-accountant," the "guardians" were not simply guards physically protecting the cash box. They were also treasurers. It is not hard to imagine that contributors perceived the keepers of the basket at the temple gate as guards. If the "contributions" were obligatory, and evidence points in that direction, then surely the personnel supervising the royal collection baskets made sure that each person entering the temple deposited his food or precious metal for the crown.

Since most contributions at the local level were in-kind payments whose value varied, officials were necessarily assayers of value. Keepers of the basket were called upon to value the produce delivered by farmers as tax payments. Additionally, donors dropped payments in silver into the basket at the gate in the form of rings, wires, miscellaneous silver cuttings, and other objects of varying quality. In the temple foundry, smiths smelted the silver payments into bars of uniformly high quality and standard size. The following texts document the process:

> 9 3/4 shekel of gold, being the revenue of the month Aiaru were given to E. and (his) goldsmiths for smelting.[32]

---

[31]Bongenaar, *Ebabbar Temple,* 102.

[32]A. Leo Oppenheim, "A Fiscal Practice of the Ancient Near East," *JNES* 6 (1947): 117.

Smelt the silver of the revenue [collected] at its gate [i.e., of the temple].[33]

[. . .] mina of silver from the revenue (collected) at the gate of the storehouse have been smelted [and] 1 mina 39 1/2 shekel of silver were lost in the refining.[34]

The incoming silver of the gate and that of the temples of Anunnītu and Gula was handed over by Kurbanni/Saggillu, who is known as the guardian of the cash box of the temple of Gula, to be smelted and casted.[35]

Herodotus describes a similar procedure by King Darius I for tribute and taxes received in gold:

The tribute is stored by the king in this fashion: he melts it down and pours it into earthen vessels; when the vessel is full he breaks the earthenware away, and when he needs money he cuts off as much as will serve his purpose. (Herodotus, *Hist.* 3.96)

At this point, we note that one of the top officials in the temple administration was the *qīpu*, "royal commissioner," appointed by the crown to comanage the temple complex with the *šangû* or *šatammu*, "chief administrator" (see chapter three). The crown, therefore, had an on-site representative to monitor tax payments.

We noted in chapter three how the owners of rights to temple income known as prebends could sell them to others. In the following two texts, future income related to the *sūtu* tax (here noted as *s.*-tax) has been sold by the crown to individuals:

two and one-half minas worth of salt-water fish, dates, garlic, and wool, the *s.*-tax of PN (and others), PN2 has purchased (from the palace) for five-sixths mina of silver—he will receive the wool (from the taxpayer) at the time of the wool plucking, and he will then pay the palace five-sixths mina of silver under seal. (*CAD* S:424)

x silver, the value of salt-water fish, x silver, the value of forty gur of dates, (being) the *s.*-tax of PN for the 25th year of Hammurapi, which PN (hereby undertakes to) give to PN2 (the man to whom the palace has sold the proceeds of the tax). (*CAD* S:424)

The temple served as the central registry for real estate transactions, witnessing contracts and archiving deeds. In this capacity, the temple had a built-in tracking system for monitoring payments related to production from

---

[33]Ibid.

[34]Ibid.

[35]Bongenaar, *Ebabbar Temple,* 108.

agricultural or grazing lands. Since the temple administration already maintained accounts by individual for the payments of tithes, the infrastructure was in place to account for the payment of taxes by individuals to the crown via the temple. The farmer or herder made his delivery to one collection site, and the crown took advantage of the temple administration already in place. Although the temple was obliged to deliver taxes to the crown, substitute commodities or equivalent silver could be delivered depending on the needs of the internal temple economy. In the text cited above documenting the receipt of thirty shekels of silver into the basket of the king at the temple gate, "eleven shekels of silver were given (to) PN (to buy) gold, twelve shekels of silver were given for casting objects for the temple" (*CAD* I-J:175).

An obvious advantage to collecting royal taxes at the temple was the implied sanctioning by the resident deity. A text from the Eanna archive in Uruk recorded Nabonidus' question to the chief administrator (*šatammu*) of the Esagila temple in Babylon: "How much of the property of the Lady-of-Uruk has come up to Babylon?" Weisberg suggests the king was asking about delayed royal taxes. If so, the collection point was the Esagila temple.[36] As agents of the Persian Empire, temples were incorporated into the government regulated system of land tenure and the network of taxgathering organizations. Temple administrators, therefore, were de facto tax collectors for the state.

Egypt

Tax collection in Egypt seems to have been the responsibility of government agencies concerned with collecting, storing, and disbursing revenues, a role for which the temples were ideally suited. A fleet of barges made repeated landings along the Nile to collect grain from small landholders for transportation to the temple granaries in Thebes. One scholar even suggests the burial of boats near funerary temples was related to the collection of taxes by divine powers.[37] By the Ptolemaic period (third century B.C.E.), the state banks were the collection agencies for state money taxes, while the state granary system received and accounted for taxes in kind and rents in kind due to the provincial government from Egyptian citizens. The "Customs Account" (475 B.C.E.) recorded customs payments to royal storehouses from incoming ships, as well as dues on the export of the mineral natron. "For each of the documented forty-two ships, customs officials collected the duty *(mndt²)* or

---

[36]David B. Weisberg, "A Neo-Babylonian Temple Report," *JAOS* 87 (1967): 9.

[37]Dieter Arnold, "Royal Cult Complexes of the Old and Middle Kingdoms," in *Temples of Ancient Egypt* (ed. Byron E. Shafer; Ithaca, New York: Cornell University Press, 1997), 36.

the tithe *(mᶜšrᵓ)* for the royal treasury."[38] The extant correspondence from Arsames, the Persian satrap of Egypt in the fifth century B.C.E., includes a letter adjudicating a dispute over land inheritance. Arsames granted the petitioner's request with the provision, "Let him hold-(it)-as-heir and P A Y to my estate the land tax just as formerly his father Pamun had been P A Y I N G."[39]

As the primary means for organizing, storing, and disbursing revenue for state needs within regional contexts, the temples were key elements in maintaining state revenue and providing economic stability for Egypt as a whole. Janssen suggests that the "vexing" question of whether Egyptian temples paid taxes is solved by understanding that temples were a branch of government administration, and therefore, would not have paid taxes. "Nobody has ever suggested that the Granary or the army paid taxes; why then should temples do so? There is indeed not a single shred of evidence for a temple tax."[40] While the Egyptian temples may not have been taxed per se, they were obligated to provide corvée labor to the state, else there would be no need for an exemption granted by Amenhotep III to the cult personnel of Amun at his first *sed*-festival around 1370 B.C.E.[41] The exemption from the obligations of state service freed the temple personnel from state labor so they could dedicate themselves exclusively to serving the state god. The temple was also obligated to supply food and commodities to the necropolis workmen of the state. Average monthly rations were 4 sacks of emmer wheat for bread, and 1.5 sacks of barley for beer, sufficient supplies for a family of six to eight adults. Produce taken in by royal funerary temples was sent to royal capitals to be distributed for support of palace and city, then to the sun temple for each funerary cult, then to the funerary temple, and finally to the mortuary priests of the cemetery around the pyramid.

Israel

Basis of Taxation. With this background of temples and taxes in the ANE, we turn to the Jerusalem temple. In addition to tithes of agricultural produce and animals, Israelites paid a shekel tax to support the Jerusalem temple economy.

> This is what every one who passes by to be registered will give: half a shekel in the shekel-measure of the sanctuary (the shekel is twenty gerahs), half a shekel as a contribution (*těrûmâ*) to YHWH. (Exod 30:13)

---

[38]Porten and Yardeni, *Textbook of Aramaic Documents,* 3:xx.

[39]Ibid., 1:118.

[40]Janssen, "Role of the Temple," 509.

[41]José M. Galán, "The Ancient Egyptian *Sed* Festival and the Exemption from Corvée," *JNES* 59 (2000): 256.

> We establish on ourselves a commandment to charge ourselves one-third of a shekel per year for the service of the house of our God—for the rows of bread, the regular grain offering, the regular whole burnt offering, the sabbaths, the new moons, the appointed festivals, the sacred donations, and the sin offerings to make atonement for Israel—for all the work of the house of our God. (Neh 10:33–34 [32–33])

It may be that the tax evolved from a one-time assessment for the construction of the wilderness tabernacle to an annual obligation for cultic services.

The beginning of chapter three quoted a passage from 2 Kings at length to illustrate the roles of the temple personnel. The parallel passage in 2 Chronicles specifically mentions the Mosaic tax and describes the collection and disbursement procedure under king Joash (836–797 B.C.E.).

> The king commanded and they made one chest (*ʾărôn*) and they set it at the gate of the house of YHWH to the outside. And a call went out in Judah and in Jerusalem to bring to YHWH the tax (*maśʾat*) that Moses, the servant of God, imposed on Israel in the wilderness. All the princes and all the people rejoiced and brought and deposited [it] in the chest until its completion. Then, on the occasion that one brought the chest to the officers of the king under supervision of the Levites and they saw how abundant the silver was, the accountant (*sōpēr*) of the king and the official of the chief priest came and they emptied the chest and lifted it and returned it to its place. Thus they did day by day and they gathered silver in abundance. And the king and Jehoiada gave it to do the work of the service of the house of YHWH. (2 Chr 24:8–12)

We have already described texts from Mesopotamian temples that document the placement of a basket, *quppu,* at the temple gate and at the altar for the express purposes of collecting silver taxes and obligatory sacrificial offerings. So we should not be surprised to find a chest (*ʾărôn*) at the temple gate in Jerusalem for the purpose of collecting silver. We noted already the similarity in the supervisory personnel, the king's accountant and the priestly official, with those in Mesopotamian temples.

Diaspora Jews scattered throughout the Mediterranean basin collected the shekel tax locally and shipped it to the Jerusalem temple. As Philo describes the process,

> In fact, practically in every city there are banking places for the holy money where people regularly come and give their offerings. And at stated times there are appointed to carry the sacred tribute envoys selected on their merits. (*Spec. Laws* 1.78)

Binder further explains, "In Greco-Roman literature, the word *tameia* ('banking places'), when used in connection with *hieros chremata* ('sacred monies'), uniformly denotes a temple treasury. . . . Because most of the money contributed to the synagogues was transported to the main sanctuary, one might even say they were 'branches' of the central repository."[42] The Roman governor in northern Syria appropriated funds destined for the Jerusalem temple in excess of 100 pounds of gold,[43] on the pretense that Judah was a foreign country. The governor had to defend himself before the Roman Senate but escaped severe sanctions after an effective defense by Cicero. Later Roman legislation specifically protected all funds bound for the Jerusalem temple under the laws governing sacrilege. When the steady flow of currency into Jerusalem ceased with the destruction of the Second Temple in 70 C.E., Emperor Vespasian broadened the definition of those obligated to pay the shekel tax, significantly increasing the amounts flowing into Judah from the Diaspora.

Other compulsory obligations, although not called a "tax," included, among other things, providing wood for the altar (Neh 10:35 [34]), paying a fine of twenty percent to the priests when the wronged party is not available (Num 5:8), and forfeiting the yield of the vineyard to the sanctuary if it is planted with two kinds of seed (Deut 22:9).

But temple tithes and taxes did not exhaust the financial obligations of farmers and herders. They were also compelled to pay various taxes to the reigning political authority for the administration of the state, including the support of the royal household, just as was the case in Mesopotamia. Samuel enumerates a lengthy list of ways that a king will exact revenue and/or service from his subjects.

> This will be the custom of the king who reigns over you: Your sons he will take and set for himself in his chariots and as his horsemen, so they will run before his chariots, and to set for himself commanders of thousands and fifties, to cultivate his cultivable land and to harvest his harvest, and to make his weapons of war and his chariot equipment. Your daughters he will take for perfumers and cooks and bakers. Your best fields and vineyards and orchards he will take, so he may give them to his servants. Of your seed and your vineyards he will take a tithe, so he may give it to his officers and servants. Your best male and female servants and young men and your donkeys he will take, so they may do his work. Of your flock he will take a tithe and you will be servants for him. (1 Sam 8:11–17)

Scholars have suggested that the reorganization of the administrative districts under Solomon expressly provided for the regular and efficient collec-

---

[42]Donald D. Binder, *Into the Temple Courts: The Place of the Synagogues in the Second Temple Period* (SBLDS 169; Atlanta: SBL, 1999), 428–30.

[43]Salo W. Baron and Arcadius Kahanm, *Economic History of the Jews* (New York: Schocken Books, 1975), 14.

tion of taxes.[44] In the postexilic commonwealth, the peasants complained that the exactions for the king were ruinous:

> We borrowed silver for the tribute (*middat*) of the king [on] our fields and our vineyards. (Neh 5:4)

> Look, we are slaves today, and as for the land that you gave to our fathers to eat its fruit and its goodness, look, we are slaves on it. For its abundant produce belongs to kings that you set over us because of our sins; over our bodies they are ruling, and with our beasts for their pleasure, and we are in great distress. (Neh 9:36–37)

As we saw in chapter two (Second Temple), the letter sent to the Persian king Artaxerxes mentions three types of exactions paid by the province Beyond the River into the imperial coffers: *mindâ*, *bĕlô*, and *hălāk* (Ezra 4:13, 20; 7:24). The *middâ* or *mindâ* was a tribute tax paid in silver or in kind to the king personally. The *bĕlô* was probably a poll tax based on a person's capacity to work, and the *hălāk* was a "land tax" based on property ownership. These exactions of the king appear to be regularized in quantity and timing. But the Israelite king could also exact occasional taxes, as evidenced by the following text.

> . . . and he [Pharaoh Neco] set a punishing fine on the land, one hundred talents of silver and a talent of gold. . . . Now as for the silver and the gold Jehoiakim gave to Pharaoh, he taxed the land to give the silver according to the word of Pharaoh, according to each assessment he exacted the silver and the gold from the people of the land to give to Pharaoh Neco. (2 Kgs 23:33, 35)

In Herod's time, "the direct income tax on agricultural produce reached one third or one quarter from cereals and one half from fruit, and this was only one of the taxes collected. There were also indirect taxes, fixed taxes, and temporary taxes."[45]

Subjects of Taxation. As in other areas of the ANE, everyone in Israel/Judah bore some form of enforced exaction by the reigning political authority, including the temple, unless specifically exempted. The 1–2 Maccabees relate that "government officials received five thousand shekels of silver every year from the services of the temple" (1 Macc 10:42) and that when Lysias, the guardian of the king and the man in charge of the government, came

---

[44] 1 Kgs 4:7–19; see, e.g., Gösta W Ahlström, "Administration of the State in Canaan and Ancient Israel," *CANE* 1:59; Sean E. McEvenue, "The Political Structure of Judah from Cyrus to Nehemiah," *CBQ* 43 (1981): 359.

[45] Magen Broshi, "The Role of the Temple in the Herodian Economy," *JJS* 38 (1987): 31.

against Jerusalem, "he intended to make the city a home for Greeks and to subject the temple to a silver levy just as he did on the sacred places of the other nations" (2 Macc 11:2–3). But if the crown wished to curry favor with the personnel or patrons of the temple, the temple and its cultic ritualists were logical candidates for tax exemptions. Late biblical and deutero-canonical texts indicate that the Second Temple was tax-exempt at least on particular occasions, if not as a more general policy.

> To you we make known that as for all the priests, Levites, singers, persons at the doors, temple slaves, and servers of the house of this God, it is unlawful to impose on them tribute (*mindâ*), poll tax (*bĕlô*), and service tax (*hălāk*). (Ezra 7:24)

> Now I release you and free all the Jews from the taxes and the salt tax and the crown levies, and instead of the one-third of seed and the one-half of the fruit of trees that I should receive, I free them from this day. . . . And let Jerusalem and its regions be holy and free with respect to the tithes and the tax. . . . All are free of the taxes even on their cattle. (1 Macc 10:29, 31, 33)

Josephus reports that Antiochus III decreed that all temple personnel "shall be relieved from the poll-tax and the crown-tax and the salt-tax which they pay" (Josephus, *Ant.* 12.142). Antiochus goes on to grant a tax remission to all Judeans for three years and to reduce future taxes by one-third (Josephus, *Ant.* 12.143–44).

Assessment and Collection. This wide-ranging set of taxes required an elaborate assessment and collection process. We have already noted the role of the Levites in the collection of tithes from areas removed from Jerusalem and of the "gaters" in collecting, assaying, and accounting for contributions. Moreover, we noted the use of a container in the temple precincts in which silver was deposited, to be counted by a pair of officials, one royal and one priestly. These procedures closely resemble those in Mesopotamian temples.

Moreover, temple texts from Mesopotamia document the smelting of incoming silver by smiths into ingots of a standard size and quality. In a seminal article in 1936, Torrey proposed a similar process by means of a foundry in the Jerusalem temple. Silver offerings of various shapes and sizes were melted down and recast under the supervision of a temple official.[46] In a later article, Torrey cites Eissfeldt's report on excavations at Ras Shamra offering supporting evidence. "Eissfeldt further remarks that at Ras Shamra earthenware containers were found filled with a great variety of objects of bronze, silver, or gold: earrings, finger rings, bars and pieces of all shapes—evidently

---

[46]C. C. Torrey, "The Foundry of the Second Temple at Jerusalem," *JBL* 55 (1936): 255–56.

intended to be melted down. Some portion of this was found in the 'library' belonging to the temple complex; and he raises the question whether the temple of Ras Shamra may not have had their foundries."[47]

As we have seen, under monarchic rule, Israel/Judah brought exactions of various commodities to the temple as directed by priestly instruction and by royal command. By centralizing cultic practices at the Jerusalem temple and destroying all other cultic sites, all commodities—tithes and taxes—would move toward the capital city.

When Israel/Judah no longer enjoyed independence, the rebuilt Second Temple probably served as a central collection site for government taxes. Any funds from the royal treasury that went toward building the temple would have been amply recouped by taxes collected in Israel/Judah and remitted to Persian authorities. The Second Temple administrators, the sociopolitical leaders of the restoration community, were the de facto tax collectors in the Persian province of Yehud.

Gifts

From the Crown. Scholars agree that the king, from the earliest days of the ANE, contributed funds and materials for the (re-)building of the temple for the deity. The biblical texts give ample witness to the generosity of kings with regard to the Jerusalem temple. The Bible depicts David and Solomon as the magnanimous benefactors of the First Temple, providing building materials, produce and animals for sacrificial offerings, silver and gold, and dedicated gifts of war booty. King Asa (913–873 B.C.E.) donated silver, gold, and cultic vessels (1 Kgs 15:15 = 2 Chr 15:18). King Hezekiah (726–697 B.C.E.) repaired the doors of the temple and contributed supplies for sacrificial offerings at the rededication ceremony (e.g., 2 Chr 29:3; 30:24; 31:3). In the postexilic commonwealth, the cost to rebuild the temple was to be furnished by the royal treasury, along with additional gifts of gold and silver (Ezra 6:8; 7:15; Neh 7:70).

In Mesopotamia, several texts demonstrate that the crown made donations of agricultural land to temples. In some cases, these lands were granted as bow-lands. In other cases, the land seems to have been contributed to the temple without any specific obligation. In a letter to King Sargon of Assyria (721–705 B.C.E.), the writer complains of noncompliance with the king's orders to appropriate a private field for the temple in the reconstructed city of

---

[47]Idem, "The Evolution of a Financier in the Ancient Near East," *JNES* 2 (1943): 301.

Dur-Sharrukin (*RCAE*, #480). In another text, a private citizen must contribute his son to the Eanna temple in payment of a debt. In addition, he donates a field to the temple, but retains the right to some future income from it (*NBAD*, #18).

One of the king's duties as ruler of the nation was to supply regular and occasional offerings to the temple: "He established his (Šamaš's) regular offerings and installed PN, the temple administrator of Sippar and diviner (to oversee them)" (*CAD* S:201). A text from Uruk detailed the sheep, oxen, geese, doves, and eggs provided by King Nabonidus (555–539 B.C.E.) for the offerings on specific days (*NBAD*, #123). In another text from Uruk, the king gave 20 jars of wine, 5 jars of honey, 10 leather bags, and 2000 loads of date palms in addition to the normal Dilmun dates offered on the first day of the month.[48] Belshazzar donated alum to the Eanna temple when he was crown prince.[49] The New Year's Festival in Babylon furnished a particularly appropriate opportunity for the king to display his wealth and military achievements in the form of tribute and exotic booty, some portion of which were subsequently given to the temples.

The largesse of the king at the Babylonian New Year's festival often included prisoners of war. The deportation of captured people and resettlement of them as laborers in temple precincts was a common policy of Assyrian kings. Sennacherib (704–681 B.C.E.) presented captives from the Puqudu tribe, identified as "the spoil of my troops" to the Ištar temple in Uruk at the time of a New Year festival.[50] Another document from the time of Sennacherib records the gift of several persons, including families, to the temple of Zababa: "total, 41 souls, men of Arbela (citizens of the town of Arbela!)."[51] The Assyrian king Ashurbanipal (669–627 B.C.E.) boasted that he presented the choicest of people and booty from Elam.[52] Captives and free citizens alike were probably put to work under supervision in the temple's fields and workshops.

The temple may have been entitled to conscript (corvée) labor from the citizens of the district surrounding it, as implied in the following instructions

---

[48]David B. Weisberg, *Guild Structure and Political Allegiance in Early Achaemenid Mesopotamia* (New Haven: Yale University Press, 1967), 9.

[49]Paul-Alain Beaulieu, *Legal and Administrative Texts from the Reign of Nabonidus* (YOS 19; New Haven: Yale University Press, 2000), #287.

[50]Bustenay Oded, *Mass Deportations and Deportees in the Neo-Assyrian Empire* (Wiesbaden: Otto, Harrassowitz, 1979), 115.

[51]V. A. Jakobson, "The Social Structure of the Neo-Assyrian Empire," in *Ancient Mesopotamia: Socio-Economic History* (ed. I. M. Diakonoff; Moscow: Nauka, 1969), 295.

[52]Oded, *Mass Deportations*, 114.

to the chief administrator (*šangû*): "Tell PN the *š[angû]* to give you x field from the corvée field(s) of the temple of Sin" (*CAD* Š/1:378). In the discussion on taxation, we noted that persons had an *ilku*-obligation to the state in return for grants of land. In some cases, persons could be assigned to temples to fulfill part of their obligation: "He belongs to the temple of Ninurta with regard to *i.*-duty and corvée work"; "I am appointed to the *i.*-duties for Ezida on my father's (i.e., your) behalf" (*CAD* I-J:76). Reassigning *ilku*-payments from the crown to the temple shifted the administrative burden from the palace to the temple storehouse accountants.

Another category of personnel given to the temple was the *širku*, "oblate, consecrated servant," a person donated and dedicated to the god(s) of a local temple. "The translation 'oblate' conveys the circumstances that *širku*'s were socially, juridically, and economically bound to the temples, but were not religious personnel active in the performance of the cult" (*CAD* Š/3:110). Apparently, to be marked with a star signaled that the *širku* was devoted to the deity for life, not unlike the branding of animals belonging to the temple. In return for their work, the temple oblates received lodging, food, and clothing. Temple oblates worked in the fields, among the temple flocks and herds, or as general laborers under supervision. In the Sippar texts, oblates were frequently found away from the temple precincts doing agricultural work for the *qīpu* of Ebabbar. Neither slave nor free, their freedom of movement restricted, oblates could not be sold by the temple administration as slaves, but could be hired out to others outside the temple complex. Oblates were occasionally reported in the ration lists as "fugitive," indicating a certain dissatisfaction with their lack of freedom.

Related to the long-standing obligation of the king to (re-)build temple sanctuaries and provide offerings and sacrifices was the presentation of items for the cultic shrines or for the performance of rituals, including jewelry and procession boats. The Babylonian crown prince Belshazzar gave a golden "tongue" to the sanctuary of the goddess Anunnītu in Sippar in the tenth year of Nabonidus (ca. 545 B.C.E.).[53] Apparently, the temple even received exotic gifts from foreign kings: "Three white horses *they have brought* with housings of silver, and *upon* the copper bands *of* the housings there is written: 'From Tammaritu, which the king of Elam has sent *for* Ishtar of Uruk'" (*RCAE*, #268).

As in Mesopotamia, the Egyptian temple received extravagant gifts of land, commodities, people, and cultic items from the Pharaoh. The temple administered crown land (*khato*-land), which carried the obligation of royal service, an arrangement similar to that of the *ilku*-land of Mesopotamia.

---

[53]Bongenaar, *Ebabbar Temple,* 241.

Along with grants of mineral resources, the Pharaoh sometimes granted the services of workmen to work the mines and transport the minerals to the temple. At the Egyptian *sed*-festival, the king gave male and female singers and dancers in the royal administration to the temples. In Tutankhamun's restoration stela (mid-fourteenth century), the king boasts that he has "filled the storehouses (of the temples) with male and female dependents and with the products of his majesty's booty."[54] Prisoners of war and other slaves were regularly donated to the temple districts. These "gifts" from the crown may not have conveyed permanent ownership rights; rather, the crown allocated the land, minerals, and workers to the temple as "government institutions" with ultimate authority retained by the Pharaoh.

From Individuals. The biblical texts describe all manner of offerings to the temple by the ordinary people of the land. The Exodus accounts of the building of the tabernacle detail the extravagant gifts from everyone:

> gold, silver, and bronze, blue and purple and scarlet stuff and fine twined linen, goats' hair, tanned rams' skins, goatskins, acacia wood, oil for the lamps, spices for the anointing oil and for the fragrant incense, onyx stones, and stones for setting, for the ephod and for the breastpiece. (Exod 25:3–7 = 35:5–9)

The people brought so many gifts that Moses had to restrain them (Exod 35:6–7). According to the Chronicler, the people at the building of the First Temple

> gave for the service of the house of God five thousand talents and ten thousand darics of gold, ten thousand talents of silver, eighteen thousand talents of bronze, and a hundred thousand talents of iron. And whoever had precious stones gave them to the treasury of the house of YHWH. (1 Chr 29:7–8)

In thanksgiving for deliverance from King Sennacherib of Assyria in 701 B.C.E., "many brought an offering to YHWH to Jerusalem" (2 Chr 32:23).

In later centuries, wealthy individuals were generous patrons of the temple in Jerusalem. Ben Kattin donated twelve spigots and a pulley for the laver; Ben Gamala donated gold lots to replace the boxwood ones previously used; Alexander of Alexandria, brother of Philo, contributed the gold and silver plating for the gates of the sanctuary; Nicanor of Alexandria installed the famous copper gates of Corinthian craftsmanship that allegedly required the strength of twenty men to maneuver.[55]

---

[54]Galán, "Ancient Egyptian *Sed* Festival," 256–57.
[55]Baron and Kahan, *Economic History of the Jews,* 13; Yehoshua M. Grintz, Bezalel Porten, and Shmuel Safrai, "Temple," *EncJud* 15:980.

Similar practices obtained elsewhere in antiquity. In Mesopotamia, private citizens made spontaneous, voluntary contributions to temples in "payment" of divine favor hoped for or already received, including a sun disk, silver, and linen garments for healing by the deity. In a text from the Borsippa temple, a man donates "1 mina of silver . . . the fixed sacrifice for Zababa and Ninlil" for the period from Nisan to Adar in the 5th year of Artaxerxes (*NBAD,* #204). Evidence does suggest support of Egyptian temples by individuals as well as the state. Excavations at a shrine in Lower Egypt uncovered ancient silver vessels, three of which are inscribed in Aramaic, "That which Ṣēhā᾿ bar ᶜAbd-ᶜAmrū brought-in-offering to [the goddess] han-᾿Ilat."[56] In Ptolemaic times the temples were centers of the healing arts, no doubt in return for a gift from the petitioner. Apparently, the temples in Greece relied almost exclusively on donations from wealthy patrons and pious peasants. After a military victory, successful warriors donated tithes in the form of tripods or statues. The goddess Athena received one-sixtieth of the incoming money tribute from the allies of Athens as a firstfruits offering for safeguarding the public revenues.[57] Certainly, votive gifts expressed thanksgiving for favorable oracles and for successful healing rituals.

Consistent with the broader practice of the ANE, the temple in Jerusalem was the destination of people "dedicated" to the deity. Earlier biblical traditions know the *nāzîr,* "Nazirite," one set apart from the community for service to YHWH, marked by unshaven hair and abstinence from alcoholic drink (e.g., Num 6:2; Judg 13:5; 16:7). Later traditions list among the temple personnel the *nĕtînîm,* "temple servants," apparently given to the temple for cultic service (e.g., 1 Chr 9:2; Ezra 2:43; Neh 3:31). These personnel are the Judean equivalent of the *širku* of the Mesopotamian temples. Perhaps prisoners of war were donated to the temple in Jerusalem as in Mesopotamia, although we cannot be certain: "You (Lord) went up to the height, you led captives, you received gifts from mortals" (Ps 68:19 [18]).

Another potential source of labor for the cult came from those who fled to the Levitical cities of refuge (Num 35). The law is succinctly given in Exod 21:12–14:

---

[56]Isaac Rabinowitz, "Aramaic Inscriptions of the Fifth Century B.C.E. from a North-Arab Shrine in Egypt," *JNES* 15 (1956): 2.

[57]Jack M. Balcer, "Ionia and Sparda Under the Achaemenid Empire the Sixth and Fifth Centuries BC: Tribute, Taxation and Assessment," in *Le Tribut dans l'Empire Perse: Actes de la Table Ronde de Paris 12–13 Décembre 1986* (ed. Pierre Briant and Clarisse Herrenschmidt; Travaux de l'Institut d'Études Iraniennes de l'Université de la Sorbonne Nouvelle 13; Paris and Louvain: Peeters, 1989), 11.

Whoever strikes a person so that he dies, surely he will be put to death. But when he does not lie in wait, but God puts the opportunity in his hand, then I will appoint a place where he may flee. But when a person acts rebelliously against his companion to kill him by shrewdness, from my altar you will take him to die.

The sanctuary, of course, has a long history of being an inviolable place of refuge. The question arises, however, as to the occupation of the manslayer now that he has relocated to the city of refuge and claimed sanctuary at the altar. As discussed above, it is possible to understand the Levitical properties as "belonging" to the temple, worked by temple personnel, with the agricultural and animal yield supporting the personnel and the shrine. Perhaps those who fled to the Levitical cities of refuge were similarly understood as "belonging" to the cult, put to work on "temple" land, thus serving temple personnel and the shrine.

Trade

Barter trade has long functioned in ancient economies as a reciprocative means of exchange. Trade is an economic technique of managing shortages and surpluses.

Mesopotamia. Mesopotamian temple personnel received prebends or rations, primarily of barley, dates, and wool, which they could then trade outside of the temple infrastructure for other necessities. Economically speaking, this process was sustainable only if the individuals had access to trading outlets and controlled sufficient quantities to command a fair trade. Merchants and trading agents who were working pockets of the international routes through Mesopotamia and the eastern Mediterranean basin facilitated the exchange of native produce among regional economies. The institution of the temple in Mesopotamia could take advantage of economies of scale not only to be able to partake of, but to stimulate, barter trade. Excess commodities in the temple storehouse were traded for other needed commodities, principally silver. Such trade was no doubt presented as sanctioned by the local deity: "Lord Enlil, the merchant of the wide earth, Lord, whose wife is the trader of the Earth" (*ANET* 576:10–11).

One of the simplest examples of barter trade is a transfer of fine oil from the Esagila temple in Babylon to the Eanna temple in Uruk. The text is an affidavit from a temple worker that "up to the time when at Éanna it arrived, no-one had touched it" (*NBAD*, #124). One of the more interesting texts concerns the disposal of old liquor from the temple storehouse (*NBAD*,

#188). Evidence demonstrates that the Eanna temple in Uruk had trade centers in Babylon, Borsippa, and Larsa. The archives from Uruk recorded receipt of income from ships and disbursement of silver to use for boat rental, presumably for trade along the lengthy waterways of Mesopotamia.[58] Over one thousand years earlier, archives from the Ur III period show that the temple employed sailors and merchants to trade its goods in foreign seaports, perhaps even monopolizing trade in Ur. Neumann describes "balanced accounts" from this period in which the commodities entrusted to the merchants ("debits") are compared to the commodities acquired in exchange by the merchants ("credits") to produce a positive or negative "balance."[59] The barter trading of commodities, by land or by sea, demonstrates the interaction that the temple had with other economies as it sought to balance its supplies with its demands.

Jerusalem. The biblical texts give ample evidence that Israel's neighbors to the north, Tyre and Sidon, were the "trader of the nations," plying ships throughout the Mediterranean basin and the Persian Gulf (e.g., Isa 23:1–8; Ezek 27:1–25). Situated at the crossroads of Africa and Asia, Israel/Judah was ideally located to take advantage of trade routes.

One well-known reference to trade occurs in the story of Joseph and his scheming brothers. We pick up the story after the brothers had thrown Joseph into a well and stolen his fashionable coat.

> They sat down to eat; then they lifted their eyes and looked and—can you imagine!—a caravan of Ishmaelites was coming from Gilead. Their camels were carrying gum, balm, and myrrh, walking to go down to Egypt. Judah said to his brothers, "What profit is there if we kill our brother and conceal his blood? Come on, let's sell him to the Ishmaelites so that our hands will not be against him, for he is our brother and our flesh." And his brothers listened. When the Midianite traders passed by, they drew him up and brought Joseph up out of the well, and they sold Joseph to the Ishmaelites for twenty (measures of) silver. So they brought Joseph to Egypt. (Gen 37:25–28)

The biblical texts also describe the trading activities of Solomon and attribute the acquisition of temple building materials to him (1 Kgs 9:26–28; 10:22, 28). But is there any evidence that the Jerusalem temple as an institution was involved in trade?

---

[58]Raymond P. Dougherty, *Time of Nebuchadrezzar and Nabonidus* (vol. 1 of *Archives from Erech;* New Haven: Yale University Press, 1923), #384.

[59]Hans Neumann, "Ur-Dumuzida and Ur-DUN: Reflections on the Relationship Between State-Initiated Foreign Trade and Private Economic Activity in Mesopotamia Towards the End of the Third Millennium BC," in *Trade and Finance in Ancient Mesopotamia* (ed. J. G. Dercksen; Leiden: Nederlands Instituut voor het Nabije Oosten, 1999), 45.

There are two tantalizing hints that traders were associated with the temple. First, the enumeration of the repair of the walls around Jerusalem under the direction of Nehemiah states, "After him Malchijah, one of the goldsmiths, made repairs as far as the house of the temple servants and the traders, in front of the gate of the muster and as far as the roof chamber at the corner" (Neh 3:31). The syntax could be interpreted to mean there was one lodging place accommodating temple servants and traders in service of the temple. Trading activities would be necessary for the temple to acquire, for example, the exotic spices needed to mix the incense and the anointing oil for cultic use (Exod 30:22–25, 34–38).

Second, the final assertion of Zechariah's apocalyptic visions is: "And there shall not be a trader (*kĕnaʿănî*) again in the house of YHWH of Hosts in that day" (Zech 14:21). Hebrew *kĕnaʿănî* is related to the Akkadian *kinaḫḫu*, "red-purple wool," which lent its name to the greater region of the Phoenician coast, known for the abundance of shellfish with red-purple dye. Hebrew *kĕnaʿănî* is the trader of red-purple dyed cloth. The virtuous woman in Prov 31:24 supplies the *kĕnaʿănî* with her woven cloth. The affiliation of the trader with the temple in the Zechariah text is unclear: is the trader defiling the sacred precincts with commercial enterprise, so that Zechariah hopes for a return to a purely cultic atmosphere? Or, is the trader acting on behalf of the temple, so that Zechariah envisions a day when all cultic supplies are readily available, obviating the need for barter and exchange with the nations?

The biblical evidence does not allow for definitive statements regarding temple traders. The Mishnah describes the trading of temple surpluses in the rabbinic period. The importance of the temple as a societal institution, its location along the ANE trade routes, and the need to manage surpluses and shortages combine to suggest that trading would be a reasonable economic activity of the Jerusalem temple.

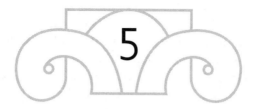

5

Temple Expenses

Having examined the major sources of temple income—tithes, taxes, and gifts—we turn now to the question of temple expenses. How did temple personnel put the income derived from tithes, taxes, and trade to use? What were the categories of temple expenses and how did these expenditures further the mission of the temple as the place of communication with the divine?

Personnel

As already noted, a major expense of the temple was the provision of shelter, food, and clothing to priests and other personnel. A large proportion of the tithes brought into the temple economy must have gone toward their support. In addition to the priests and Levites, biblical texts attest to the utilization of specialized labor for skilled and unskilled tasks. As an example of unskilled labor, Joshua made the Gibeonites "hewers of wood and drawers of water for the congregation and for the altar of YHWH until this day at the place where he will choose" (Josh 9:27). More skilled laborers could fill the roles ascribed to Bezalel, of whom YHWH says, "I have filled him with the spirit of God, with wisdom, intelligence, knowledge, and with every work, to plan the plans and to work in gold, silver, and bronze, to engrave stone for settings and to engrave wood, to do every work" (Exod 31:3–4 = 35:31–33). Specialized labor for the temple from outside Judah required payment of wages. Thus, for supplying timber and crafting furniture, King Solomon "gave Hiram [of Tyre] twenty thousand kors of wheat as food for his household and twenty [thousand] kors of beaten oil; thus Solomon gave to Hiram year by year" (1 Kgs 5:25 [11]).

In the great landed estates of the Mesopotamian temples, temple personnel were a resource in the temple economy, to be managed just as agriculture or animals or surplus stores were managed. More agricultural personnel were needed in the harvest seasons; supplemental workers were wanted in the birthing or shearing seasons; specialized labor was required for the fashioning of particular jewelry or tools. The temple managed its personnel needs by hiring workers from the community. Temple archives from Mesopotamia document the payment of wages to fullers, brick-molders, weavers, porters of asphalt and reeds, canal diggers, brick-makers, ship-pullers, coppersmiths, straw carriers, and gardeners, among others. Temples benefited when masters apprenticed their slaves to craftsmen, in order to increase the slave's skills and the master's profits. Temples also secured temporary personnel by requiring labor as one of the terms of a loan, often in place of interest charges. The majority of disbursement texts for wages list the person's name, the commodity to be paid as wages, the period of time covered by the disbursement, and sometimes the person's profession. In the discussion of temple personnel in chapter three we noted the distribution of prebends to certain (high-ranking) temple personnel, primarily barley, wool, and shares of the sacrificial offerings. Likewise, rations were issued to (lower-ranking) temple personnel, primarily barley, dates, and wool. Only careful comparison of the personnel lists with the disbursement tablets can confirm whether the commodities were being issued as "prebends" or "rations" to temple personnel or as "wages" to non-temple personnel. Even if the distinction cannot now be easily made between prebends/rations to temple personnel and wages to hired laborers, it should be obvious that all were expenses of the temple economy. Further, the commodities issued to hirelings exited the internal temple economy to be consumed in the local or regional economies.

The sale or leasing of prebends was another interesting feature of the temple economy as it relates to temple personnel. Since the prebendary office was hereditary, the owner of the prebend could sell, lease, bequeath, pledge, or assign his rights to the income in whole or in part. There was a contract transferring the prebendary right, with the person taking over the duties of the prebend called the *epišānūtu,* "performer." A simple contract is illustrated by the following texts:

> The daily duties of the oxherd prebend of Ezida belonging to PN which are at the disposition of PN2 for performance from the year x to the year y. (*CAD* E:240)

In the following text, the performer takes over prebendary rights from the temple *mubannûtu,* "cook":

(Sale) of his entire share in the mubannûtu's prebend, his entire share in the "buckets" of the goddesses, his share in the tail meat of the ox and the (pertinent) hides, his entire share in the . . . -s of the goddesses, (and) his entire share which he owns with his brothers and partners which pertains to the mubannûtu's prebend. (*CAD* Z:148)

Of course, as prebends were divided up among persons and into fractions of time, the contracts became more complicated. Two prebendary lease contracts from 485 B.C.E. specify that the performers would pay sesame and oil to the prebendary oil pressers as compensation for the associated rights (and duties) for fifteen days, and that performers would pay emmer, sesame, and honey for the rights (and duties) of the sweet cake baker's prebend for thirteen specific cultic ceremonies.[1] In these contracts the performers compensated the prebendaries with the same commodities they received from the temple's storehouse to complete their duties. For example, the sweet cake baker would have received emmer (a type of grain), sesame, and honey from the temple storehouses in order to bake sweet cakes for presentation to the deity and ultimate consumption by the priests. The performers, therefore, were expected to use the quantities of commodities issued from the temple storehouses to perform the required duties and compensate the prebendaries. Presumably, the remaining commodities provided the performer's personal income. Efficiency in use of commodities is thus encouraged. By the Hellenistic period (late fourth century), women often appear as principals, as distinct from the Late Babylonian period (mid-sixth century) when they appeared as coprincipals with their husbands or sons.[2] The sale of prebendary rights to nontemple personnel clearly expands the temple economy into the local or regional economies.

Taxes

We demonstrated in chapter four that the temple was a likely collection point for state taxes. The taxes collected at the temples, therefore, had to be delivered to the king: "They have taken the workmen belonging to the temples to (transport) the tax barley of the palace" (*CAD* B:232). More likely, silver equivalent to the value of the agricultural taxes was delivered to

---

[1] Bongenaar, *Ebabbar Temple,* 265.
[2] Gilbert J. P. McEwan, *Priest and Temple in Hellenistic Babylonia* (Wiesbaden: Steiner, 1981), 117.

the palace, perhaps along with the regular deliveries of the *quppu* basket containing the royal share of the sacrificial offerings.

As we discussed in chapter four, the cessation of the royal tithe to the temple at the rise of the Achaemenid dynasty did not prompt the elimination of taxes due from the temple to the crown. Certainly some temple cities claimed their exemptions from previous regimes or were granted exemptions by the Achaemenids. But there does not appear to have been a full exemption from state taxes for temples across the board. Under the Achaemenids, most temples were obligated to pay in-kind taxes of animals, grain, dates, beer, and wool. On the other hand, there is no evidence that temples paid taxes to the crown in the Hellenistic period (beginning in the late fourth century). The lack of evidence may not reflect the actual practice; rather, evidence may be lacking because records were written on parchment or papyrus rather than on cuneiform tablets as in earlier periods. We know that persons working in the temple economy paid at least some taxes. The following texts describe a variety of taxes paid by temple personnel.

> Concerning the increase of the cattle and sheep of Bel, Nabu, and Nergal, which the governors seized . . . (*RCAE*, #464, referring to the *ṣibtu* tax on animals)

> What I have received from the gold of Adad which (is) in the *k.*-office. (*CAD* K:237, where *k.*-office stands for the *kāru* office or harbor station that collects transport taxes)

> The agent (for the collection) of the *b.*-tax from the temple oblates. (*CAD* B:120, where *b.*-tax stands for the *bāru* tax, the same tax on barley due from bow-lands)

> Two shekels of silver, under seal, the *i.*-tax of PN, the chief singer. (*CAD* I-J:42, where *i.*-tax stands for the annual *igisû* tax)

It seems reasonable that the crown would have imposed as many different kinds of taxes on as many different people as possible to be able to support a lavish lifestyle for the king and his entourage. Accumulation of wealth by the royal family underscored their status and prestige in the ANE. We noted above, however, that cities—and perhaps especially temple cities—could be declared exempt from taxes for a period of time. The following two texts are examples of specific exemptions:

> Indicate how much silver is temple assets(?) so that it will not be subject to a payment of *š.*-fee on route [referring to the *šaddu'atu* fee paid to the harbormaster on shipments of merchandise and monetary items]. (*CAD* Š/1:46)

> I canceled the *ilku*-duties for all the categories of temple personnel and thus freed them. (*CAD* I-J:77)

In Greece multiple revenues flowed into the state administrative coffers from tithes, taxes on precious metals, and taxes on various commercial transactions. In some cases, Greek temple personnel were exempt from state taxes, as were the temple personnel in Mesopotamia. In a missive to Gadatas, the provincial satrap of Ionia, King Darius I (521–486 B.C.E.) praised him for cultivating nonindigenous fruit trees, but threatened him with punishment for levying a tax from the sacred gardeners of Apollo.[3]

Royal Provisioning

Israel/Judah. In addition to paying tithes and taxes to the temple and state, the people were responsible for supplying provisions for those in the political bureaucracy. Solomon's redistricting plan resulted in twelve areas, intentionally differentiated from the twelve traditional tribes.

> Solomon had twelve appointees over all Israel and they supplied the king and his household, one month per year was assigned to each to supply. . . . (The people of Israel and Judah) were bringing a gift (*minḥâ*) and serving Solomon all the days of their lives. . . . (The appointees) also brought the barley and the straw for the horses and the steeds to the appointed place, each in his order. (1 Kgs 4:7, 21, 28)

Since all manner of produce came into the temple from tithes, offerings, vows, and taxes, the temple was in the best logistical position to apportion food and fodder for the royal household. More importantly, the ideology of offering produce to the deity would mitigate the perceived burden on the populace—it is more palatable for the peasant to make an offering to the deity than to pay taxes to the king.

Mesopotamia. As we have seen, the Mesopotamian temple storehouses received the production of vast agricultural acreages as well as foodstuffs that individuals gave as tithes and taxes. Herds and flocks grazed on temple lands, and even more animals were contributed by the crown for daily offerings. After being offered to the gods in daily meals, part of the food went to support the temple personnel working in the fields and workshops. A portion of the food was obligated to the crown for provisioning the royal table via the king's basket by the altar into which sacrificial remains were deposited, and there was also the cash box of the king by the gate. A royal servant declares, "The dues of Nabu I have brought to the crown prince my lord" (*RCAE,* #187). The obligatory

---

[3]Marcus N. Tod, *A Selection of Greek Historical Inscriptions to the End of the Fifth Century B.C.* (Oxford: Clarendon, 1933), 12–13.

feeding of the king, the provincial satraps, and the imperial army was part and parcel of the taxation redistribution system of the Achaemenid period. The "king's table" was one method of redistributing items from the king down to the nobility and the soldiers, as several texts illustrate.

> By the first day of MN PN will deliver in the palace of Amanu two hundred vats of good beer made from dates which were given to him from (the stores of) Eanna for the š. of the king. (*CAD* Š/3:377, where š. stands for *šuṣbuttu*, "provisioning")

> From the bread, beer (etc. allotted to Šamaš, Aja, and Bunene), half of the king's share is the allowance of the š. (*CAD* Š/1:379, where š. stands for *šangû*, "temple administrator")

> Gather into Eanna the barley (which is) the daily sustenance of the king.[4]

A longer text concerns "eighty large sheep, the property of Innina of Erech and Nanâ," that is, of the Eanna temple in Uruk. These sheep were "brought from the stable of Innina of Erech . . . on the seventeenth day of Marchesvan, the second year of Cambyses" as provisions for the king. The text warns the sheep's trustee that if he does not deliver it for the provisioning of the king, "he will commit a sin against Gobryas, the governor of Babylon and the Land beyond the River." One scholar supposes that since the Land beyond the River is mentioned, an area that included Judah, the text may refer to preparations made in Syria-Palestine as Cambyses began mustering his forces for a campaign against Egypt in 525 B.C.E.[5]

Similarly, evidence from Uruk suggests that at regular intervals, the *quppu* basket was taken to Babylon to provide food and silver for the king's support. In the text cited below, an urgent reproach was given for neglecting the *tabnîtu* basket, the "well-arranged basket" of the king. Apparently, these were reed baskets of special construction, possibly stronger and more ornate.

> The king approaches. Why have ye neglected the tabnîtu basket of the king for the third month? Bring the tabnîtu basket to the king. . . . Why have ye slaughtered a lamb of the plain (desert) for the tabnîtu basket of the king and according to your wish slain a lamb worth 1 1/2 shekels of silver for 1/4 of a (shekel) of silver for the holiday? Do not delay with reference to the sacrifices of the gods and the tabnîtu basket of the king. Put all things in order and keep the watch of the gods and the king. Slaughter a large lamb for the tabnîtu basket of the king.[6]

---

[4]Raymond P. Dougherty, "Cuneiform Parallels to Solomon's Provisioning System," *AASOR* 5 (1923–4): 27.

[5]Idem, *The Shirkutu of Babylonian Deities* (New York: AMS Press, 1923), 43–44.

[6]Dougherty, "Cuneiform Parallels," 30–31.

The temple was also responsible for providing rations for those who transported the basket of the king.

Furthermore, the temple frequently provided rations for those who traveled for the empire. A text from the forty-second year of the reign of Nebuchadnezzar (604–562), from the temple archive in Uruk is a receipt for dates used as provisions for Babylonian military officials in the city of Tyre. Another Uruk temple text under the same king documents the provisioning of flour for the two men in charge of the sustenance of the king and his soldiers who were with him in Tyre. Still a third text describes military equipment for four soldiers disbursed by the temple.[7] Temple archives from Telloh document provisions for government messengers during the Ur III period (early second millennium).[8] The accumulated evidence suggests that the temples supplied the crown with considerable amounts of produce and animals: "sheep and goats, cattle, barley, sesame, dates, wine, beer, spices, oil, butter, milk, wool, and also to furnish fodder for the royal cattle, and provisions for state officials and for the labourers of the royal estates."[9]

It is a small step from supplying food and equipment for the royal military to supplying persons for the royal military. Not surprisingly, temple oblates offered a pool of men to swell the ranks: "The three hundred oblates left with PN for military service" (*CAD* Š/3:108). Another text documents the use of temple oblates by the crown: "PN, an oblate of Ištar of Uruk, who is in shackles (and assigned to chopping straw in the royal stables)" (*CAD* Š/3:107); "PN the gatekeeper of the royal š. (and other officials) spoke as follows: 'PN2, the oblate of the Lady of Uruk who had been held in the royal š., opened his iron shackles and fled'" (*CAD* Š/3:413, where š. stands for *šutummu*, a storehouse). Temple slaves tended royal cattle, manufactured bricks for the palace, cut reeds, and performed whatever tasks were needed. Further, the conscripted oblates were supposed to bring along their own provisions, as indicated when an official complains that the temple oblates he received did not have any provisions (*CAD* S:173).

Evidence suggests that conscription by the crown was not limited to temple oblates. Citizens of the empire, including temple personnel, were obliged to supply labor "in the households of Persian kings and nobles as bakers, cooks, cup-bearers, door-keepers, physicians, eunuchs, etc."[10] For example, "PN, the cupbearer of the Lady-of-Babylon, PN2 his sister (or wife),

---

[7]Idem, *Neo-Babylonian and Persian Periods*, #135.

[8]George A. Barton, *Haverford Library Collection of Cuneiform Tablets or Documents from the Temple Archives of Telloh* (Philadelphia: Winston, 1904–1914), 11.

[9]Muhammed A. Dandamaev, "Achaemenid Babylonia," in *Ancient Mesopotamia: Socio-Economic History* (ed. I. M. Diakonoff; Moscow: Nauka, 1969), 309.

[10]Ibid.

PN3 the stone mason, total of three (deportees from Babylon) subject to work for (or in) royal š[utummu]." (*CAD* Š/3:413). In one text, the king (unexpectedly) paid silver to the temple treasury for providing deliverymen.[11]

In Egypt the temple also supplied food and commodities to the necropolis workmen of the state, as we have seen. Average monthly rations were four sacks of emmer wheat for bread, and one and one-half sacks of barley for beer, sufficient supplies for a family of six to eight adults.[12]

Produce taken in by royal funerary temples was sent to royal capitals to be distributed for support of palace and city, then to the sun temple for each funerary cult, then to the funerary temple, and finally to the mortuary priests of the cemetery around the royal tomb.

Appropriations

The income and expenses of the temple economy we have described so far are, for the most part, orderly and systematic. Subjects paid tithes and taxes into the temple storehouses according to recognized standards; the crown made gifts to facilitate repair of temple facilities and provide for the regularized cultic rituals; the temple distributed commodities and precious metals to the royal household at regular intervals. But the reality of the temple economy was not so idyllic. The king's role as (re-)builder, supplier of offerings, exemptor, and protector apparently permitted a degree of management involvement in the affairs of the temple, no doubt seen as interference at times by temple authorities. Occasionally, the interest of the crown in temple assets led to diversion or outright appropriation of temple treasures.

Jerusalem. There is ample evidence in the biblical texts of the local monarch appropriating the treasures of the Jerusalem temple in order to appease the aggression of a foreign power.

> Now Asa, (king of Judah), took all the silver and gold that was remaining in the treasuries of the house of YHWH and the treasuries of the house of the king and he gave them into the accountability (*bĕyad*) of his servants, and King Asa sent them to Ben-hadad, the son of Tabrimmon, the son of Hezion, the king of Aram, who was dwelling in Damascus, saying, "Let there be a covenant between me and you, between my father and your father, for I am sending you an appeasement gift (*šōḥad*) of silver and gold. Go, break your covenant with Baasha, king of Israel, that he may withdraw from me." (1 Kgs 15:18–19 = 2 Chr 16:2–3)

---

[11]Dougherty, *Nebuchadnezzar and Nabonidus*, #184.
[12]Janssen, "Role of the Temple," 509.

In response to tribute levied by King Sennacherib of Assyria in the late eighth century, Hezekiah plundered "all the silver that was found in the house of YHWH and in the treasuries of the house of the king. At that time, Hezekiah stripped off the doors of the temple of YHWH and the doorposts that Hezekiah, king of Judah, overlaid, and he gave them to the king of Assyria" (2 Kgs 18:14–16). Interestingly, the parallel accounts in Isa 36 and 2 Chr 32 contain no account of any levy or plunder.

Further, there is evidence of foreign powers and native rulers plundering the temple treasures directly, including Pharaoh Shishak of Egypt (935–914 B.C.E.) (1 Kgs 14:26 = 2 Chr 12:9) and King Jehoash of Israel (799–784 B.C.E.) (2 Kgs 14:14 = 2 Chr 25:24). The biblical narrative foreshadows Nebuchadnezzar's plunder of the temple by narrating King Hezekiah's welcome of emissaries of Merodach-baladan, crown prince of Babylon. Hezekiah "showed them the treasure house, the silver, the gold, the spices, the fine oil, and all his armory, all that was found in his treasuries. There was nothing that Hezekiah did not show them in his house and in all his kingdom" (2 Kgs 20:13 = Isa 39:2). According to the account in 2 Kings, in the eighth year of his reign (597 B.C.E.), Nebuchadnezzar, the king of Babylon "carried out all the treasures/ies of the house of YHWH and the treasures/ies of the house of the king, and he cut up in pieces all the vessels of gold that Solomon, king of Israel, had made for the temple of YHWH, just as YHWH had spoken" (2 Kgs 24:13). The parallel account in 2 Chr 36:7 indicates that Nebuchadnezzar carried off "some of the vessels of the house of YHWH" and deposited them in "his temple in Babylon." In the nineteenth year of his reign (586 B.C.E.), King Nebuchadnezzar "burned the house of YHWH and the house of the king and all the houses of Jerusalem; every great house he burned with fire" (2 Kgs 25:9). He carried off all the accoutrements of temple service—pillars, stands, sea, pots, shovels, snuffers, incense dishes, firepans, and bowls (2 Kgs 25:13–17 = Jer 52:17–23). More than four hundred years later, Antiochus Epiphanes plundered the Jersualem temple: "He entered into the holy space in arrogance and he took the golden altar, the lampstand for the light and all its utensils, the offering table, the cups, the bowls, the golden censers, the curtain, the crowns, and the gold plating on the front of the shrine; he stripped off everything" (1 Macc 1:21–24a).

Less offensive than outright plunder was the appropriation of temple funds for city maintenance. "The viaduct for the [red] cow and the viaduct for the scapegoat and the strip of scarlet which was between its horns and [the maintenance of] the pool of water and the wall of the city and the towers thereof and all the needs of the city came out of the remainder in the chamber" (*m. Šeqal.* 4:2). According to Josephus, when the temple renovations were completed and the construction workers needed additional work, King

Agrippa II "did not veto the paving of the city with white stone," while paying their wages from temple funds (Josephus, *Ant.* 20.222).

Mesopotamia. One concrete expression of the oversight (or interference) exercised by the king in Mesopotamia was the appointment of members of the temple hierarchy in positions as priests, labor supervisors, inspectors, and fiscal agents. The high priest of the Ebabbar temple in Sippar also served as the chair of the royal judicial court. Given that the temples were important socioeconomic institutions in the community, the king would naturally have wanted a measure of control in the temple administration. As crown prince and governor of Babylonia, Belshazzar was involved with the administration of the Eanna temple in Uruk: he showed interest in the use of religious paraphernalia, and entrusted some sheep belonging to the temple to his shepherds.[13] The last Babylonian king, Nabonidus, leased temple lands to individuals outside the temple staff, who then generated profits from the land and paid the requisite taxes to the king and tithes to the temple.[14] "The Neo-Babylonian kings owned prebends in local temple organizations. Nabonidus, for example, reinstalled old prebends, created new ones, and aborted yet others in Eanna at Uruk."[15]

One text describes the gift of three white horses from the king of Elam for the goddess Ištar of Uruk. But the author admits: "Because of the king my lord I feared and I did not give them to the temple. Now the shepherds (who) brought the three horses I have sent to the king; and when I saw the copper bands which were written upon, I forwarded them to the king my lord. May the king my lord do according as he wishes" (*RCAE,* #268). In another text, the diversion of temple assets to the king was accomplished by a royal representative in the temple administration: "When the man who is in charge of the basket brought four male oxen, among them three clean (pure) ones, from Ina-ṣilli-Nanâ, the slave of Nabû-aḥ-iddin, he did not tell us. He apportioned them for the offering of the king."[16] In the two texts below, the writer complains to the king that the governor has seized temple assets.

> The governor of the city of Dur-Sharrukin earlier opened my seal. . . . Your house of the god and of the king my lord he opened, the money he took out, as the prefect and the governor of Nineveh and Arbela take out money from the temples. Let him bring it, it is the treasure of the god and of the king my lord. (*RCAE,* #339)

---

[13]Dougherty, *Records from Erech,* 12.

[14]Amélie Kuhrt, "Nabonidus and the Babylonian Priesthood," in *Pagan Priests* (ed. Mary Beard and John North; Ithaca: Cornell University Press, 1990), 147; MacGinnis, *Letters and Orders,* 11.

[15]Bongenaar, *Ebabbar Temple,* 141.

[16]Dougherty, "Cuneiform Parallels," 27 n. 13.

> Concerning the increase of the cattle and sheep of Bel, Nabu, and Nergal, which the governors seized; . . . (*RCAE,* #464)

Neither were temple assets and treasuries secure from foreign appropriation. Invading armies frequently plundered the temple's wealth, some of which eventually made its way into temple treasuries in the homeland of the foreign army.

No less than today, items in the temple storehouses and workshops were subject to theft by employees. In chapter three, we cited the sworn testimony of the storehouse overseer that a certain clerk had not misappropriated anything belonging to the temple and noted the use of the debt agreement clause *ina pāni* to assign precious materials to craftsmen in the temple workshops. Despite these precautions and the presence of guards, inventory shrinkage due to theft was a cost of doing business.

> The golden tablet which disappeared from the temple of Ashur has been seen in the possession of Kurdi-Nergal, the sculptor. At this moment the gold is in his hands. . . . The gold is gone, should not the king take account of it? Let them (also) question at the same time those who partake of the gifts pertaining to the temple of Ashur. (*RCAE,* #429)

> . . . Nabuepush the kalu priest of Ea has made a robbery in the temple of Ekur. The mass (?) of gold from upon the splendid (?) vessel which is before Ishtar he stripped off and carried away. Nabuiddina the temple guard found it in his. . . . Nabuepush who committed the robbery is a kalu priest. There is no one except him in the shrine. (*RCAE,* #1389)

Greece. In the Greek city-states there appear to be no specific examples of tapping temple resources for secular needs, but there was the suggestion to appropriate the riches of the temple of Branchidae during the Ionian revolt.[17] The account of temple treasuries being usurped by the city of Athens in the fifth century B.C.E. is probably a religious fiction, since the transferred funds were the war reserve of the people stored in the temple.

Community Welfare

Jerusalem. Widespread evidence in the biblical sources demonstrates a concern for the marginalized of society, theologically and ethically grounded in YHWH's rescue of the people from Egypt (e.g., Exod 22:21; Deut

---

[17]Chester G. Starr, *The Economic and Social Growth of Early Greece, 800–500 B.C.* (New York: Oxford University Press, 1977), 39.

10:17–19). The oft-repeated Deuteronomic formula "the widow, the orphan, and the resident alien" (e.g., Deut 24:19–21) sounds a refrain in the legal material calling the community to care for those without societal protection. The concern for the needy is nowhere more eloquently expressed than in the Psalter, the cultic hymnbook of ancient Israel/Judah. In poems ranging from lament to praise, YHWH is depicted as the helper of the needy and the refuge of those in any kind of trouble. For example, "Out of the devastation of the poor, out of the groaning of the needy, now I will rise up, says YHWH; I will place them in the safety for which they pant" (Ps 12:6 [5]). Various categories of the less fortunate are depicted in Psalm 146, one of the "Hallelujah" songs ending the Psalter collection.

> Happy is the one whose help is the God of Jacob,
> whose hope is in YHWH his God,
> maker of heaven and earth, the sea and all that is in them,
> the keeper of faithfulness forever,
> doing justice for the oppressed, giving food to the famished.
> YHWH is unbinding prisoners; YHWH is opening blind eyes;
> YHWH is raising up bowed-down ones; YHWH is loving righteous ones;
> YHWH is protecting resident aliens; orphan and widow he will restore,
> but the way of the wicked he will pervert. (Ps 146:5–9)

Because YHWH is "gracious and merciful, slow to anger, and abounding in steadfast love," the needy of whatever circumstance plead for YHWH to send help from the sanctuary. For example, "May he send your help from the sanctuary (*qōdeš*), and from Zion may he sustain you" (Ps 20:3 [2]). Indeed, part of the divine duty was to care for the weak, as is seen in God's admonishment of other gods in the divine council:

> How long will you judge unjustly and show partiality to the wicked? Give justice to the weak and the orphan; execute righteousness for the afflicted and the destitute; rescue the weak and the needy, deliver them from the hand of the wicked. (Ps 82:3–4)

In fact, the deity who is not able to protect and feed the needy is not divine at all.

> They never deliver a person from death nor rescue the weak from the strong. They never restore sight to a blind person, they never rescue a person who is in distress. They never take pity on a widow nor do good to an orphan. . . . Therefore, how does one suppose or call them gods? (Ep Jer 35–39 [36–40])

The Jerusalem temple, the place where YHWH chose to establish his name, was situated in society as an institution commissioned to enact the character of YHWH as protector of the poor and needy. The other ANE societal institution charged with caring for the needy was the monarchy:

> He (the king) delivers the needy crying out for help, and the poor, and the one who has no helper. He has pity on the weak and the needy, and the lives of the needy he rescues. From oppression and violence he redeems their life, and their blood is precious in his eyes. (Ps 72:12–14)

The temple, constructed under the auspices of the king and supported by the king's generosity, could act as institutional agent on his behalf in society. YHWH interceded on behalf of the needy through the agency of the temple to bring about justice and righteousness. That is, the Psalter's metaphors derive from a socioeconomic reality located in the economic role of the temple. The Psalter—and the temple underlying the imagery—was concerned with the needy in two basic ways: protection (especially of the fatherless) and feeding.

The orphan, the son or daughter without protection and economic support of a father, is of particular concern in the Psalter. YHWH is labeled as "helper of the orphan . . . to do justice for the orphan" (Ps 10:14, 18). This gracious action of YHWH is performed in the context of YHWH as king (10:16). Two psalms hint at the role of the temple in providing permanent shelter for the orphan.

> Father of orphans and pleader for widows, God is in his holy habitation.
> God is setting the solitary in a household. (Ps 68:6–7aa [5–6aa])

> If my father and my mother abandon me,
> then YHWH will gather me up. (Ps 27:10)

As noted earlier, the "house of the god"—the temple—was supported by the "household of the god"—the temple personnel. The psalmists assert that the household of God will accommodate those without a household, namely, the fatherless orphan. Perhaps, like the *širku* of Mesopotamia and the *nāzîr* or the *nĕtînîm* of Judah, orphans worked in the temple precincts in return for shelter, food, and clothing.

The second category of help attested in the Psalter is the feeding of the hungry or poor. For example, "The poor will eat and be satisfied" (Ps 22:27a [26a]). Again, the Psalter offers tantalizing hints of the temple's role in providing food to the less fortunate in the community.

> Look, the eye of YHWH is toward those who fear him,
> to those who hope for his steadfast acts of love,
> to deliver their lives from death,
> and to keep them alive in the famine. (Ps 33:18–19)

Taste and see that YHWH is good.
Happy is the mighty one who seeks refuge in him. (Ps 34:9 [8])

How precious is your steadfast act of love, O God,
that mortal children take refuge in the shadow of your wings.
They are satiated from the grain of your house
and from the river of your delights you give them drink. (Ps 36:8–9 [7–8])

For YHWH has chosen Zion; he desired it for his dwelling place;
"This is my resting place forever; here I will dwell for I desired it.
I will abundantly bless its provisions; its poor I will satisfy with food;
its priests I will clothe with salvation; and its faithful will give a ringing cry."
(Ps 132:13–15)

(YHWH) establishes peace in your (Zion's) territory;
with an abundance of wheat he satisfies you. (Ps 147:14)

With storage facilities for surplus commodities, the Jerusalem temple would
have been the logical candidate to supply wheat to the community in time of
shortages. The temple of YHWH on Zion would have embodied the gra-
ciousness of YHWH by serving as a food pantry for the poor.

Also reminiscent of the broader ANE culture was the periodic benevolence of the king, usually in connection with a religious ceremony. After
King David brought the ark into Jerusalem with great rejoicing (to the dis-
may of his wife Michal),

> David finished offering the burnt offerings and the peace offerings and he
> blessed the people in the name of YHWH of Hosts. And he distributed por-
> tions to all the people, to all the multitude of Israel, to men and women, to each
> one cake of bread and one raisin-cake, so all the people went to their houses.
> (2 Sam 6:18–19 = 1 Chr 16:2–3)

The most explicit care of the community by the temple is in relation to
the Deuteronomic understanding of the tithe. Beyond the legal provisions in
place to provide for the needy in the regular course of life, a portion of income ordinarily directed to the temple was to be diverted to the marginalized
of society.

> At the end of three years you shall bring forth every tithe (*maʿśar*) of your pro-
> duce in that year, and you will store it up in your gates. So the Levite, for he has
> no portion nor inheritance with you, the resident alien, the orphan, and the
> widow who are in your gates shall come, so they may eat and be satisfied, in
> order that YHWH your God may bless you in every work of your hand that you
> do. (Deut 14:28)

Mesopotamia. As in Jerusalem, the Mesopotamian temple cared for the needy or marginalized of society, including the poor, the orphan, and the widow. A text from 587 B.C.E. documents the withdrawal of barley "for sick people," probably from the Eanna temple in Uruk.[18]

A specialized altruistic function of the Mesopotamian temple was to ransom prisoners of war when the prisoner did not have sufficient means of his own. Consider one of the laws of Hammurabi (ca. 1700 B.C.E.):

> If there is either a soldier or a fisherman who is taken captive while on a royal campaign, a merchant redeems him and helps him to get back to his city—if there are sufficient means in his own estate for the redeeming, he himself shall redeem himself; if there are not sufficient means in his estate to redeem him, he shall be redeemed by his city's temple; if there are not sufficient means in his city's temple to redeem him, the palace shall redeem him; but his field, orchard, or house will not be given for his redemption.[19]

A letter written by Hammurabi echoes the role of the temple and the merchant (*tamkārum*) in ransoming captives: "As to Sin-ana-ḤE.GAR-lippalis, the son of Manimum, whom the enemy has captured, give ye 10 shekels of silver from the Sin temple to his tamkārum and redeem him."[20] Since the merchant (*tamkārum*) traveled frequently, he would be an appropriate liaison between captive and temple. Merchants were still attached to the temples in the first millennium, trading temple surpluses for profit or for commodities not available in Mesopotamia. We may reasonably assume that the temple continued its charitable role as redeemer of captives beyond the Old Babylonian period, although the evidence is spotty.

Egypt. In Egypt, a considerable number of people outside the temple precincts received a share of the temple offerings, "not unlike the parish-relief boards of Christian churches."[21] Charity toward the poor was encouraged in the following New Kingdom Wisdom text of Amen-em-opet (tenth century):

> If you find a large debt against a poor man,
> Make it into three parts;
> Forgive two, let one stand;
> You will find in it a path of life. (*ANET,* 423)

---

[18]David B. Weisberg, *Texts from the Time of Nebuchadnezzar* (YOS 17; New Haven: Yale University Press, 1980), #142.

[19]Roth, *Law Collections,* 87 §32.

[20]Rivkah Harris, "Old Babylonian Temple Loans," *JCS* 14 (1960): 129.

[21]Janssen, "Role of the Temple," 515.

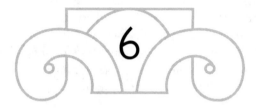

Temple as "Bank"

As we noted in the introductory chapter, the scholarly discussion of the temple has been primarily concerned with the development of Israelite religion and its relationship to neighboring cultures. Although recent scholarship has acknowledged some impact of the temple on economic life, the acknowledgement is most often characterized by a general statement on the economic role of temples in the ANE. The following statements are paradigmatic:

> The Jerusalem temple constituted an economic entity in its own right.[1]

> The economic weight of the temple was a tangible reality in the city-state with its influence felt in every domain of political, social and economic life of the community.[2]

> The temples of ancient Mesopotamia were powerful factors in the society and economy of ancient Mesopotamian urban communities. The resources controlled and created, and the lives and livelihoods sustained, were crucial to the prosperity and stability—the survival—of the communities.[3]

If scholarship moves beyond general claims for the temple's importance as an economic institution in ANE society, the common notion is that temples functioned as "banks" in antiquity. The following statements are typical:

> The Temple, with its treasures and its treasuries, was a national bank of sorts.[4]

---

[1]Shimon Applebaum, "Economic Life in Palestine," in *The Jewish People in the First Century: Historical Geography, Political History, Social, Cultural and Religious Life and Institutions* (ed. Shmuel Safrai and M. Stern; Philadelphia: Fortress, 1976), 683.

[2]A. Leo Oppenheim, "The Mesopotamian Temple," *BA* 7 (1944): 60.

[3]Robertson, "Social and Economic Organization," 1:443.

[4]Carol L. Meyers, "Temple, Jerusalem," *ABD* 6:350–69.

Temples functioned as the banks of antiquity, and to extend the metaphor, the temple storehouses were the bank vaults.[5]

Many of the larger temples throughout the Achaemenid empire were wealthy institutions with their own land holdings and work force, their own capital in specie and produce from which they advanced loans, serving more or less the same function as banks and credit unions today.[6]

But the description of the ancient temple as a "bank" is imprecise and inaccurate. More precisely, temples functioned as "treasuries" or "depositories," a place for the storage and retrieval of (precious) commodities and metals *by the depositor.* Temple archives demonstrate that the temple held deposits by individuals but did not allow others to access them or in any other way use the negotiable instruments that complete the definition of "banking." Temples lent their own property, not that of others on deposit with the temple (see Loans below). If the temple used the deposits at all, it was acting as a broker at the direction of the depositor, who retained the risk of the use. The defining issue is the accountability for risk. A broker-intermediary does not assume any risk; a banker-intermediary assumes risk as a creditor. So temples were not "banks" in antiquity. Rather, the more precise designation for the role of the temple in antiquity would be "financial intermediary." As collector, user, and disburser of goods and financial services, the temple transferred value from contributor to consumer. In this chapter, we explore the actions of the temple in its role as financial intermediary for the community.

Sacred Space

Jerusalem. Temples could function in an economic role in ancient societies because it was first of all sacred space connected with the deity. Even if we conclude that the Jerusalem temple did not hold title to land, the temple "owned" its sacred precincts. As sacred space, it was a particularly appropriate place for swearing oaths, performing specific cultic rituals, discerning the divine will, and rendering judicial decisions. The biblical texts amply document the temple as a place to swear oaths. At the dedication of the First Temple, King Solomon implored YHWH to hear and judge rightly when a sinner "swears an

---

[5]John W. Wright, "Guarding the Gates: 1 Chronicles 26.1–19 and the Roles of Gatekeepers in Chronicles," *JSOT* 48 (1990): 76.

[6]Joseph Blenkinsopp, "Temple and Society in Achaemenid Judah," in *Second Temple Studies: 1. Persian Period* (ed. Philip R. Davies; JSOTSup 117; Sheffield: Sheffield Academic Press, 1991), 23.

oath before your altar in this house" (1 Kgs 8:31 = 2 Chr 6:22). If a servant wished to remain with his master beyond the term of service, "his master shall bring him near to God, bring him near to the door or to the doorpost, and his master shall pierce his ear with an awl, and he shall serve him forever" (Exod 21:6). Although the exact location of the doorpost is not specified, a doorpost, "near to God" would be the local sanctuary.

Naturally, the sacred space was an appropriate place to seek the divine will. When the Benjaminites advanced against other armed Israelite tribes, "the Israelites inquired of YHWH, for the ark of the covenant was there (Bethel) in those days" (Judg 20:27). The divine answer is simply recorded as "So YHWH answered/said." But sometimes the divine answer was mediated through mechanical devices known as Urim and Thummin, perhaps something like dice. For example, to settle a dispute King Saul inquired of God, "O Lord God of Israel, why have you not answered your servant today? If in me or in Jonathan my son there is wrongdoing, O Lord God of Israel, give Urim; but should you say wrongdoing is in your people Israel, give Thummin" (1 Sam 14:41, Greek version).[7] The devices indicated the guilt of Saul and Jonathan and cleared the people. Confirming that King Saul had fallen out of divine favor, the biblical narrator notes, "When Saul inquired of YHWH, YHWH did not answer him, neither by dreams, nor by Urim, nor by prophets" (1 Sam 28:6). This is all the more poignant when we realize that Saul's name (*Šāʾûl*) is a pun on the verb "inquire" (*šāʾal*), a technical cultic term for seeking the divine will. As a result of the nonresponsiveness of YHWH, King Saul sought out a "medium in Endor" (1 Sam 28:7).

As we would expect, temple functionaries charged a fee for witnessing oaths and performing ritual acts. When Saul could not locate his father's donkeys, his attendant suggested consulting a "man of God in this town." A conversation ensued over how to pay for the services of such a person.

> Saul said to his attendant, "Suppose we go. What would we bring to the man, since the bread in our sacks is gone? There is no present to bring to the man of God. What do we have?" But the attendant answered Saul and said, "Look! A quarter shekel of silver is found in my hand. I will give it to the man of God so he will declare to us our way. (1 Sam 9:7–8)

A common prophetic critique is the greed of the priests: "Its (Israel's) priests teach for a bribe" (Mic 3:11); "everyone is greedy for unjust gain;

---

[7] The Greek version is used here for translation because the Hebrew version is incomplete. Due to the repetition of the address "O Lord God of Israel" and the similar phrases "give Urim" and "give Thummin," scholars believe the scribe's eye skipped from the first address all the way to the final petition, leaving a truncated version of the original manuscript. See the standard commentaries on 1 Samuel for further comment.

from prophet to priest, everyone deals falsely" (Jer 6:13 = 8:10). By charging for the use of its sacred space and personnel, the Jerusalem temple turned space and people into productive assets, not unlike the common practice today of charging for the use of a sanctuary or synagogue (and a pastor or rabbi) for a wedding.

Mesopotamia. The role of the oath in legal decisions when witnesses were not available is well documented in the ANE. Increasingly, oaths sworn at temples played a decisive role in binding contracts and commercial enterprises. Some of the texts found in the Mesopotamian temple archives appear to concern business dealings between private individuals. A sixth-century Neo-Babylonian text from Borsippa specifies that the settlement of a suit between individuals was recorded on the "tablet of Nabû," the local deity, with the result that, "Their legal proceedings with each other are ended" (*NBAD*, #115). Other texts document decisions concerning slaves, transfer of a dowry, theft of property, summons to court, settlement of an estate, terms of loans, and business partnership agreements.

Evidence also suggests that the Mesopotamian temple was involved in real estate recordkeeping, perhaps because the temple staff was skilled in the recording arts. The temple of Bēl in Babylon maintained the "Register of Bēl," which functioned as a central register for all real estate transactions.[8] Warranty deeds were among the texts discovered in the temple archives. In one deed specifying the land to be transferred and the price of the land in silver, an additional amount of barley was given for which no purpose was specifically stated (*NBAD,* #6). The purchaser paid silver and a small amount of barley, yet could meet the seller's price by paying silver. Then, for what purpose was the barley given? I propose that the small amount of barley (or silver or other commodity) was taken by the temple as a commission for recording and archiving the deed. It seems reasonable to posit that the temple would have charged some fee for witnessing oaths and legal documents. The temple's primary responsibility was the care of the gods through regular ritual and occasional festivals, "but it could also undertake privately commissioned ceremonies, such as burials and perhaps extispicies (divination by reading entrails)."[9] In this way, the Mesopotamian temple turned its sacred space into a productive asset.

In the second and first centuries B.C.E., the island of Delos in the Mediterranean, now part of Greece, was transformed into "the center of a trans-Mediterranean trading network, and more specifically into the nerve center

---

[8]Fritz M. Heichelheim, *An Ancient Economic History* (2 vols; Leiden: Sijthoff's, 1958), 2:71.

[9]J. N. Postgate, "The Role of the Temple in the Mesopotamian Secular Community," in *Man, Settlement and Urbanism* (ed. Peter J. Ucko, Ruth Tringham and G. W. Dimbleby; Cambridge, Mass.: Schenkman, 1972), 813–14.

of the Roman republican slave trade, functioning as a duty-free port and a 'boomtown' of economic development."[10] The topography of the island indicates that each marketplace (*agora*) resembled a distinct and separate sanctuary that would have contained altars and statues of gods. Oaths sworn in the names of these gods facilitated the business transactions conducted in the *agora*. Apparently, one of the purposes of the religious fraternal organizations formed on Delos in the second century B.C.E. was to swear oaths for one another in commercial transactions, a striking example of the interplay between temple and private commerce.

Deposits

Just as oaths in the sanctuary enjoyed divine backing, do too did depositors expect divine protection of their goods in the temple, which provided a secure depository. The most common vocabulary for the storage areas of valuable commodities in the Jerusalem temple during the monarchic period is *'ôṣār*, often specified as *'oṣar bêt YHWH*, "the storehouse of the house of YHWH," or *'ôṣār bêt ham-melek*, "the storehouse of the house of the king." The word is used both for the storage location of precious commodities (i.e., treasury), and for the stored commodities themselves (i.e., treasure). The Septuagint translates the Hebrew *'ôṣār* with the Greek word *thēsauros*, derived from the Greek verb that means "to store up, gather, save." The later biblical texts seem to prefer the word *liškâ*, "chamber," for the storage areas surrounding the Second Temple and for the living and/or working locations of temple personnel. In Ezra and Nehemiah, the Septuagint translates *liškâ* with *gazophylakion*, probably a composite word from the Persian word for "treasury" (*ganj*) and the common Greek word for "prison" (*phylake*).[11] In Chronicles, the Septuagint chooses *pastophorion*, a word normally associated with the chamber of the marriage bed, perhaps appropriated because of the exquisite garments associated with the marriage bed, and then more generally, for precious items of any kind.

According to the texts, the storage locations held silver and gold, cultic vessels, wine, oil, wood, "devoted" and "sacred" things, and, more generally, tithes, contributions, and stores. Nehemiah summarily calls offerings of grain, wine, and oil *tĕrûmâ*, no matter the motivation (tithe, tax, votive, freewill, etc.). Postbiblical literature specifies the particular use of various cham-

---

[10]Nicholas K. Rauh, *The Sacred Bonds of Commerce: Religion, Economy, and Trade Society at Hellenistic Roman Delos, 166–87 B.C.* (Amsterdam: Gieben, 1993), xv.

[11]*BDAG*, 186.

bers, e.g., for vows of valuations, freewill offerings, anonymous gifts, vessels, etc.[12] The three levels of storerooms around the three sides of the temple, each story with approximately thirty chambers, housed the cultic supplies needed to carry out the prescribed rituals as well as the commodities contributed by the people.

The most common items that Israelites donated to the temple for cultic use were, according to the texts, silver and gold, along with "sacred" and "devoted" things. The notable exception to the use of the contents of the treasury for cultic purposes is the distribution of "the spears and the shields that belonged to King David that were in the house of YHWH" (2 Kgs 11:10 = 2 Chr 23:9). Even in this case, the priest used the stored items to protect the legitimate king of Judah who hid in the temple for six years. Similar incidents include the sword of Goliath left at the shrine in Nob (1 Sam 21:10 [9]) and weapons left by Alexander the Great in a Persian temple (1 Macc 6:2). The temple functioned alongside a royal treasury, not as the royal treasury. Evidence for the Jerusalem temple as a depository for private individuals does not appear until the later centuries of the first millennium in the deuterocanonical texts. Before we turn to these texts of the Hellenistic period, we will review the depository practices of temples in ancient Mesopotamia and ancient Greece.

Mesopotamia. Numbers of texts indicate the role of the Mesopotamian temple as depository for the community. Of course, not everyone realized the benefit of the temple's security, as this text makes clear: "And let no one bar you from any of your silver which is safeguarded in the hole in your field."[13] For those who chose the temple over their back yards, goods "held in safekeeping" could include silver, tin, barley, doors, and even slaves and fields. No wonder temple treasuries were often looted by conquerors or by the local king for warfare or other ventures. Despite this risk, persons in the community would have deposited their precious commodities in the temple storerooms in confidence that (1) the deity would protect the treasured items, and (2) the excellent temple administrative staff would keep meticulous records. The temple was always open, so to speak, so access to one's personal treasure was assured. Excavations in Ur have revealed storerooms and offices at the back of the ziggurat terrace accessed directly through the Nabonidus gate, and the Nebuchadnezzar gateway may have been connected also with a late version of the Ningal temple.[14]

---

[12]Grintz et al., "Temple," 15:981–82.

[13]Steven W. Cole, *Nippur IV: The Early Neo-Babylonian Governor's Archive from Nippur* (Chicago: University of Chicago Press, 1996), #106.

[14]L. Woolley and M. E. L. Mallowan, *Ur Excavations IX: The Neo-Babylonian and Persian Periods* (London: Skilton, 1962), 5.

Initially, the temple labeled, sealed, and stored items with the intention of returning them to their owners exactly as deposited. As time passed, however, the depositor could convert his wealth into an income-earning asset by allowing access to the item by the temple. In antiquity, deposits converted into loans produced income for the depositor and permitted the temple access to the deposited commodity for a limited period, perhaps as a way of temporarily managing shortages in the temple economy. Modern banks would take the next step: allowing access to deposits by third parties via loans.

Greece. The most extensive information related to role of the temple as a secure depository is from ancient Greece. Concerning the temple of Artemis at Ephesus, Dio Chrysostom wrote:

> You know about the Ephesians, of course, and that large sums of money are in their hands, some of it belonging to private citizens and deposited in the temple of Artemis, not alone money of the Ephesians but also of aliens and of persons from all parts of the world, and in some cases of commonwealths and kings, money which all deposit there in order that it may be safe, since no one has ever yet dared to violate that place, although countless wars have occurred in the past and the city has often been captured. Well then, do they go on and take any of these monies when any need arises, or do they "borrow" them at any rate— an act which, perhaps, will not seem at all shocking? No; on the contrary, they would sooner, I imagine, strip off the adornment of the goddess than touch this money. ("To the People of Rhodes," *Discourse* 31.54–55, LCL)

In Olympia, Delphi, Delos, Miletus, Ephesus, and other temple districts of Greece, large treasuries accumulated from at least the eighth century B.C.E. from votive gifts and pious donations. The temple on Delos stored both its own savings and those of the city-state, as did the temples in classical Athens.

By the fifth century B.C.E., Greek temples had developed a thoughtfully organized deposit system. Secular private institutions had arisen in response to the increasing need for credit in the mercantile economy of the Mediterranean basin. These private entities were called *trapeza,* after the tables used to display the coins; the English word "bank" derives from the "bench" used by the moneylenders. Both sacred temple and secular private banks accepted deposits in two forms: the closed deposit and the *depositum irregulare.* The closed deposit was safeguarded in sealed containers of clay, leather, metal, or wood. A label recorded the name of the owner and the contents, which were only available to the depositor or his authorized agents. The depositor showed one half of a token, the other half of which the temple matched. Agents had to demonstrate their delegated authority to access the closed deposit by presenting a *symbolon,* usually the depositor's signet ring, which was matched to the seal on the deposit container.

The regulations regarding *depositum irregulare* were more open, although a written contract was still required. Withdrawals could be made more easily and further funds could be deposited by the owner or by anyone the owner authorized. There is evidence that the owner of an account could have access to funds in a location other than that of the initial depository, the first evidence of the modern letter of credit. A man from Athens requested that his funds deposited with a private *trapeza* in Athens be made available to him when he arrived in Miletus.[15] It may be that funds from the account of one customer could be transferred to the account of another customer without any cash changing hands, the so-called *giro* transfer. In a lively commercial trading economy, this ability to make payments to another without using actual currency would have expedited trade immensely and stimulated economic growth.

Jerusalem. With this background information from Greece and Mesopotamia in mind, we return to the deuterocanonical biblical texts of the late first millennium. These writings indicate a depository system used by the temple that is remarkably similar to Greece.

> He (Simon) explained (to the governor) about the untold wealth filling the treasury (*gazophylakion*) in Jerusalem, with the result that the total of the balances was incalculable. . . . But the high priest indicated that deposits belonged to widows and orphans, and even some belonging to Hyrcanus, the son of Tobias, a man appointed to prominent authority—thus the impious Simon misrepresented—the total of the silver was four hundred talents, and two hundred of gold. (2 Macc 3:6, 10–11)

> (Simon reported to the governor:) "Many myriads of items of wealth have been deposited in the Jerusalem treasuries not available for the common use of the priests." . . . And the people uttered indignant complaints against the matter and considered it outrageous if those whose custom it was to deposit and who trusted in the temple treasury (*thēsauros*) would be deprived (of their deposits). (4 Macc 4:3, 7)

Josephus, the first-century C.E. historian, describes the wealth in the temple treasuries, apparently entrusted to the safety of the temple rather than left to the Romans.

> They further burnt the treasury-chambers, in which lay vast sums of money, vast piles of raiment, and other valuables; for this, in short, was the general repository of Jewish wealth, to which the rich had consigned the contents of their dismantled houses. (Josephus, *J. W.* 6.282)

---

[15]William Linn Westermann, "Warehouses and Trapezite Banking in Antiquity," *Journal of Economic and Business History* 3/1 (November 1930): 41.

The book of Tobit describes the practice of leaving a deposit with a private individual. Tobit said to his son Tobias,

> "Now I will indicate to you the ten talents of silver that I deposited with Gabael, the son of Gabria, in Rages of Media." . . . Then Tobias said to him, "How will I be able to obtain the silver if I do not know him?" Then he gave to him the receipt . . . And he (Tobias) gave him (Gabael) the receipt, so he brought forth the little bags with the seals intact and he gave (them) to him. (Tob 4:20; 5:2–3; 9:5)

Sealed bags and depository receipts are reminiscent of the depository procedures described for temples in Greece in the latter half of the first millennium.

Loans

Israel/Judah was heir to and participant in the broader ANE culture with respect to supporting the twofold institutional system of temple and state through extractions of agricultural production, herds, and other property. Tithes and taxes paid to temple and state substantially narrowed the economic margins of the peasant agriculturists. Wealth became increasingly concentrated in the upper echelons of society, who used it to generate more wealth, to the further deterioration of the economic situation of the common peasant, the ancient version of "the rich get richer while the poor get poorer." With the erosion of family- or tribal-based communities in favor of urbanized populations, the peasant farmer in dire economic straits looked outside the family for economic assistance. In order to acquire seed grain, peasant farmers would execute a debt instrument to be repaid from the proceeds of the next harvest. Lending, therefore, bridged the gap between available capital and the agricultural cycle. In this situation short-term credit was in the best interest not only of the farmer, but also of the creditor who depended on the farmer's surplus as tithes and/or taxes. A farmer with no seed grain, and thus no harvest, was a farmer who could not pay tithes or taxes to the temple and state. Both institutional loans and private loans may have been operative in Judah in the first millennium. Although the biblical texts do not document loan contracts listing the temple as the creditor, the surplus commodities in the temple storerooms as well as the gold and silver in the temple treasuries would have made the temple a logical choice as the community's lender. As we will see, the Mesopotamian temple was heavily involved in lending.

Jerusalem

The biblical texts do distinguish between "lending" and "being a creditor." A prophecy of the universal impact of YHWH's action in the earth lists six pairs of opposites:

> And it will be, as the people, so the priest; as the servant, so his master; as the maid, so her mistress; as the buyer, so the seller; as the lender (*malweh*), so the borrower (*lōweh*); as the creditor (*nōšeh*), so the one who has a creditor (*nōšeʾ*) on him. (Isa 24:2)

Exod 22:24 [25] regulates lending activity in the community:

> If you lend (*talweh*) my people silver, the poor with you, you shall not be to him as a creditor (*nōšeh*), you shall not set interest (*nešek*) on him.

Just as in modern society, "interest" was the amount to be paid by the debtor in addition to the principal amount of the loan in order to compensate the lender for the use of the principal. According to economic theory, the general level of interest rates is set by the interaction between the demand for credit and the supply of credit. The array of rates in the economy is determined by the perceived risk of the investment by the credit suppliers. Manipulation of interest rates is a strategy in monetary policy to make credit more or less attractive to lenders or borrowers. Fully collateralized obligations with a short maturity date carry a lower risk than unsecured debt with a distant maturity date and, hence, a lower interest rate.

Apparently, a temporary exchange between two parties *without* any stated compensation was encompassed by the Hebrew verb *lāwāh*. In its basic verbal stem Qal, the verb means "borrow"; in its causative stem Hiphil, it means "lend" (lit. "cause to borrow"). An exchange of goods to be repaid with *explicit* compensation for the transaction was in the purview of the Hebrew verb *nāšāʾ* and its homophone *nāšāh*. The biblical texts exhort the faithful to lend (*lāwāh*, in the Hiphil), i.e., without interest, out of abundance of goods and generosity of spirit. For example, "Good is the one who shows favor and lends, who supports his words with justice. For he will not be shaken forever, as a perpetual remembrance the righteous will be" (Ps 112:5–6). The punishment of YHWH on the unfaithful is evident when resident aliens lend out of their abundance to the needy Israelites inhabiting of the land: "The resident alien who is in your midst will ascend over you higher and higher, but you will descend lower and lower. He will lend to you, but you will not lend to him. He will be the head and you will be the tail" (Deut 28:43–44). Wickedness consisted in failing to repay the principal amount of the loan: "The wicked one borrows but does not repay, but the righteous one shows favor and gives" (Ps 37:21).

The extant evidence from Mesopotamia illustrates the diverse ways creditors received compensation for the risks taken in lending their assets: interest, collateral, guarantors, repayment penalties, and default provisions (see below). The biblical texts describe the creditor's compensation for the risk of loss exclusively in terms of interest and collateral.

Lending at Interest. We noted above the apparent compensation associated with the verb *nāšā²* or *nāšāh,* indicated by its related noun *maššā²,* "interest." The verb *nāšak* and its related noun *nešek* also indicate interest as compensation for the loan. In typical Hebrew fashion, the simple basic stem Qal means "pay interest," while the causative stem Hiphil means "charge interest" (lit. "cause to pay interest"). The root meaning of the verb is "bite," calling to mind the expression "taking a bite out of my income." The Septuagint translates with *ektokizō,* "take out interest," and the related *tokos,* "interest." The Greek root of these words, *tiktō,* means "cause to come into being; produce," and connotes the ability of the asset to "produce" income in the form of interest. An asset generating interest payments is a *productive* asset. Ezekiel pairs *nešek,* "interest," and *tarbît,* "increase," as compensation available to the creditor, although the righteous took neither. In condemnation of the abominable city, the word of YHWH declares, "They take a bribe in order to shed blood; interest (*nešek*) and increase (*tarbît*) you take; you violently take control of your neighbors by extortion; you have forgotten me—an oracle of the lord YHWH" (Ezek 22:12). The difference in the two expressions of compensation is explained by one scholar as

> . . . one being inoffensive, *tarbît* "increase", which is generally taken to mean "(moderate) interest". The other, *nešek,* since it implies *savagery* (parallel with *yânâh* Ez 18,13. 17 and *²ôšĕk* Ez 22,12) is assumed to mean "usury". But since this *nešek* is permitted in Deut 23,20, very probably its more generic sense "rigor" is to be applied in both places. "You may exact your debts according to the letter of the law, in justice; but where blood-relationship intervenes, be merciful, in charity."[16]

The biblical attitude toward taking interest or increase may generally be characterized as acceptable behavior with non-Israelite debtors but forbidden with kinsmen, illustrated by the following texts:

> If you lend (*talweh*) my people silver, the poor with you, you shall not be to him as a creditor (*nōšeh*), you shall not set interest (*nešek*) on him. (Exod 22:24[25])

---

[16]Robert North, *Sociology of the Biblical Jubilee* (AnBib 4; Rome: Pontifical Biblical Institute, 1954), 177–78.

You shall not charge interest to your brother: interest (*nešek*) on silver, interest on food, interest on anything that was lent at interest. To a foreigner you may charge interest, but to your brother you shall not charge interest, so that YHWH your God may bless you in all you put your hand to in the land where you are entering to inherit. (Deut 23:20–21 [19–20])

If your brother grows poor and feeble among you, you shall support him; as a resident alien and sojourner he shall live with you. You shall not take from him interest (*nešek*) nor increase (*tarbît*); you shall fear your God; your brother shall live with you. Your silver you shall not give to him in exchange for interest (*nešek*); in exchange for increase (*tarbît*) you shall not give your food. (Lev 25:35–37)

But another deuteronomic text infers that, despite legal restrictions, lending at interest was indeed taking place between Israelites, else a remission of debt would not be necessary.

Now this is the manner of the remission: Every owner of a loan in his hand that he lent at interest to his companion shall not oppress his companion and his brother. (Deut 15:2)

Nehemiah remonstrates against the community elite, who are lending at interest:

Moreover, I and my brothers and my assistants are lending silver and grain to them at interest. Let us forsake this interest (*maššā'*). Return to them today their fields, their vineyards, their orchards, and their houses and the hundredth of the silver and the grain and the new wine and the oil that you are lending at interest to them. (Neh 5:10–11)

The "hundredth" amounts to 1% interest, a reasonable return only if charged monthly, since the prevailing per annum interest rates in Mesopotamia were 20% on silver and 33% on grain. Commenting on Neh 5:11, Halligan says, "Frankly, this solution to the economic crisis defies reality. If the economy had deteriorated to the point described in 5.1–5, it could not have been restored instantly by forgiving all debt and returning all forms of security as well as a 1 per cent bonus."[17] Perhaps the word translated "hundredth" (*mĕ'at*) should read "loan" (*maššā't*). One scholar cautions that the complete prohibition of lending excludes the lower classes from access to capital, a "cruel restriction."[18] But another believes that the issue of whether interest is "socially helpful or socially harmful is mainly, though not entirely,

---

[17]John M. Halligan, "Nehemiah 5: By Way of Response to Hoglund and Smith," in *Second Temple Studies: 1. Persian Period* (ed. Philip R. Davies; JSOTSup 117; Sheffield: Sheffield Academic Press, 1991), 152.

[18]North, *Sociology,* 178–79.

a question of the supply of capital."[19] Even if interest per se was not tolerated, some form of economic compensation was appropriate in order to facilitate lending in the economy.

Lending for Collateral. The second general type of compensation available to the Israelite creditor was collateral. If the debtor was unable to repay the loan, the creditor had legal recourse to the underlying collateral. Collateral assets, therefore, were more valuable if they were easily and profitably sold in the market place. If the creditor considered the debtor a good risk, the loan was secured by the debtor's pledge of appropriate assets. The creditor, then, had a first lien on the asset, known as a "hypothecary" pledge since the transfer of assets is hypothetical, i.e., only in contractual agreement, not in reality. This arrangement left the use of the collateral under the authority of the debtor, the collateral serving to compensate the lender only in the event of the default of principal. In some circumstances, the loan was secured by physical transfer of the pledged assets into the possession of the creditor. This is known as "pawn" credit or a "possessory" pledge. This arrangement could either afford the creditor the use of the collateral for the term of the loan, to be returned intact upon full repayment by the borrower, or could restrict the use of the asset by the creditor. The possessory pledge was usually antichretic, i.e., the income from the pledge belonged to the creditor for the duration of the loan. The biblical texts know various types of assets used as collateral, including garments, tools, animals, personal signets, real estate, and even one's own life.

> If a person is poor, you shall not sleep in his pawned collateral. You shall surely return to him the pawned collateral at sunset so he may sleep in his cloak and bless you. (Deut 24:12–13 = Exod 22:25–26 [26–27])

> You shall not turn aside justice from the resident alien or the orphan; you shall not take as pawned collateral the garment of a widow. (Deut 24:17)

> He shall not take as pawned collateral a mill or an upper millstone, for that is a life as pawned collateral. (Deut 24:6)

> The donkey of orphans they drive off, they take as pawned collateral the ox of a widow. (Job 24:3)

> He (Judah) said (to Tamar), "(For payment) I will send a kid from the flock." And she said, "Only if you give pawned collateral until you send it." And he said, "What pawn shall I give you?" And she said, "Your signet and your cord and your staff in your hand." (Gen 38:17–18)

---

[19]John A. Ryan, *Economic Justice* (Library of Theological Ethics; Louisville: Westminster John Knox, 1996), 54.

Our fields and our vineyards and our houses we are pledging as collateral so we may get grain in the famine. (Neh 5:3)

(Judah said to Joseph in Egypt) For your servant gave pawned collateral for the lad for my father saying, "If I do not return him to you, then I will sin against my father forever." So now, let your servant remain here instead of the lad as a servant to my master so the lad may go up with his brothers. (Gen 44:32–33)

The exact procedures related to pawn credit or encumbered lien credit remain unknown. The biblical texts seek to regulate collateral practices by forbidding seizure of property inside a borrower's house (Deut 24:10–11), limiting the time the property may be held (Deut 24:12–13), and proscribing illegal search and seizure (Job 22:6). Among the various legal collateral arrangements is the gage,

an object deposited as security not for money to be repaid but for some *act* which is to be performed . . . (and the) *antichresis,* a form of mortgage in which the creditor has the *usufruct* as well as the custody and hypothetical ownership of the pledge, *until* the debt is paid. This usufruct not merely supplies the place of interest-payments, but constitutes also a gradual amortization of the principal.[20]

The biblical texts may understand the legal arrangements relating to pawned collateral not primarily as a guarantee against default and the consequent loss of principal. Rather, the gage collateral, which mandates labor services, may amortize the loan principal. The term "mortgage," literally "dead pledge," arose because the creditor took over the yield from the property without applying it to reduce the principal amount of the debt, thereby making the property dead, i.e., useless, to the borrower.

Lending by the Temple. As we have seen, texts dealing with lending and borrowing are distributed among legal material, narratives, the prophets, and the wisdom corpus. Even discounting the tendentious nature of some texts, the widespread distribution doubtless reflects the pervasiveness of credit among the populace and the remedies available to lenders. A question of particular interest is whether the Jerusalem temple engaged in lending as did the temples of Mesopotamia (see below). Since lending arose as a mechanism to manage surpluses and shortages, we should not be surprised to find temples using it. The divine sanctions inherent in temple loans would have encouraged prompt and full repayment by the borrower. A few texts may be mentioned in support of lending activity by the Jerusalem temple.

---

[20]North, *Sociology,* 179 (original emphasis).

Amos includes the following behavior in the transgressions of Israel deserving of punishment:

> On garments pawned as collateral they stretch out beside every altar, and wine of those fined they drink (in) the house of their God. (Amos 2:8)

Presumably, the ones with access to the altar and the house of God were the temple personnel. These cultic personnel, therefore, were the ones making loans on behalf of the temple and accumulating pawned garments and fines.

In another text, some of the people of the postexilic community in Jerusalem came to (governor) Nehemiah about a serious situation: "Our fields, vineyards, and houses we are pledging as collateral for loans so that we may receive grain in the famine" (Neh 5:3). Others complain, "We borrowed (*lawînû*) silver for the tax of the king on our fields and vineyards" (v. 4), with the result that "our fields and our vineyards belong to others" (v. 5b). Nehemiah says, "I brought charges against the nobles and officials; I said to them, 'You are charging interest to your brother'" (v. 7). Nehemiah then exhorts them,

> I, my brothers, and my attendants are lending at interest (*nōšîm*) to them silver and grain. Let us forsake this interest (*maššāʾ*). Return to them today their fields, vineyards, olive orchards, and houses, and the hundredth of the silver, grain, new wine, and oil that you are lending at interest to them. They said, "We will return (them) and we will not seek (anything else) from them. Thus we will do as you are saying." So I summoned the priests and I made them swear to do this thing. (vv. 10–12)

Who were the "nobles and officials" engaged in these lending practices? Obviously they were persons with wealth (at least enough to lend) and esteemed in the community, judging by the etymology of the nouns.

Who were the ones made to swear to return the peasants' property? Were the priests summoned by Nehemiah in verse 12 the referent of the pronoun "them," or were the priests called to be witnesses for the nobles and officials who were made to swear? Perhaps the "nobles and officials" were political rivals of Nehemiah, who hoped to gain some favor in the eyes of the populace by curtailing loans with interest. There is no way to resolve the question definitively. It is sufficient to note that temple personnel could be involved in lending practices reversed by Nehemiah in light of the economic crisis faced by the peasants.

We cannot definitively conclude that the Jerusalem temple engaged in making loans, but to the extent that the broader ANE culture influenced the economic environment of Israel/Judah, it seems reasonable to expect that the temple did make loans of its surplus commodities, especially silver and grain. We now turn to the extensive evidence of lending in the surrounding cultures of Mesopotamia and Greece.

Mesopotamia

Large-scale agriculture in Mesopotamia allowed the landowners—temple and state—to prosper from surplus production. Mesopotamian texts excavated to date generally used the word *hubuttatu* to designate a non-interest bearing loan. The assets lent were common items in the ancient economy: silver, barley, dates, wheat, bricks, calves, lambs, or oxen. The interest-bearing loan was termed *hubullu* until the Middle Assyrian period when the same word came to mean the interest on the debt. The "man of debt" was the debtor; the "master of debt" was the creditor. The general term for interest was *ṣibtu,* literally "increase," allowing the term to refer also to the tax on the increase of flocks and herds (see chapter four). The commodity was *ina pāni,* "at the disposal of," or, more commonly, *ina muḫḫi,* "charged against," the debtor. We noted in chapters two and three the use of *ina pāni* as a term related to the accountability of craftsmen for precious commodities.

The typical structure of a sixth century Neo-Babylonian loan document included the amount of debt, the creditor, the debtor, and the time when the debt is to be paid. Temple officials, as custodians of the property of the temple's god, were often listed as creditors without specific mention of the god. As Harris succinctly points out, "In these instances the debtor certainly knew to whom he owed his debt, namely to the temple."[21] In some cases, the creditor was specifically listed as the god. The god Šamaš was thus the notional creditor in over 80% of temple loans from the Old Babylonian period (mid-second millennium). Gods also appeared in the documents as witnesses, although the same god did not generally serve as creditor and witness. In other cases, both the god and the temple officials were listed.

In her seminal study of Old Babylonian temple loans, Harris demonstrated, "More than 90% of the barley loans consist of small loans, 5 GUR of barley or less. About the same percentage of silver loans involve loans of three shekels or less." She concluded, "Most loans were undoubtedly taken by poverty-striken [*sic*] people to tide them over until harvest time."[22] Since the temples lent their accumulated surpluses of grain or silver, they contributed to the economic development of the region, often by lending to high-risk persons.

---

[21]Harris, "Temple Loans," 129.
[22]Ibid., 130–31.

Lending for Interest. The laws of Hammurabi (ca.1700 B.C.E.) regulated loans of both silver and grain, secured and unsecured, and prescribed a maximum interest rate of 33% annually on grain and 20% on silver. Grain presumably carried a higher rate because the risks associated with agriculture were higher than those associated with silver.

> If a merchant gives grain or silver as an interest-bearing loan, he shall take 100 silas of grain per kur as interest (=33%); if he gives silver as an interest-bearing loan, he shall take 36 barleycorns per shekel of silver as interest (=20%).[23]

> If a man who has an interest-bearing loan does not have silver with which to repay it, he (the merchant) shall take grain and silver in accordance with the royal edict and the interest on it at the annual rate of 60 silas per 1 kur (=20%); if the merchant should attempt to increase and collect the interest on the (silver) loan [up to the grain interest rate of 100 silas of grain] per 1 kur (=33%), [or in any other way beyond] 36 barleycorns [per shekel (=20%) of silver], he shall forfeit whatever he had given.[24]

Over a millennium later, around 600 B.C.E., the maximum interest rate on grain loans was lowered to 20%, the same as silver loans, perhaps in response to the increasing role of private banking in the economy. By the fifth century, the prevailing interest rate on loans of both grain and silver was 40%, reflecting the inflationary trend of those centuries. Interest rates apparently went through cycles, just as in more recent times.

The temple often charged interest at below-market rates, as little as one-half the prevailing rate.[25] Perhaps the temple charged reduced rates as a way of offsetting the desire of the creditor to collect as much as possible, or perhaps the temple undercut other creditors in an attempt to capture the market. In many of the temple loan documents, no repayment date was specified, so that the borrower could pay back the loan whenever possible, surely a more advantageous arrangement than private creditors allowed.

Similar to the Old Babylonian loans studied by Harris, loans for silver, copper, or corn from the Neo-Babylonian temple archive of Eanna in Uruk are also considered property of a deity. A debt of silver is regularly called "belonging to (the deities) Ištar and Nanâ for tithe (*ša Ištar u Nanâ ešrû*)." Sometimes, a loan document provided for repayment of principal in a commodity other than the one borrowed: barley or wool instead of borrowed silver; silver instead of borrowed barley and dates. One loan document stipulates that if silver can-

---

[23]Roth, *Law Collections,* 97 gap ¶t.

[24]Ibid., gap ¶u.

[25]Sidney Homer and Richard Sylla, *A History of Interest Rates* (3d ed.; New Brunswick: Rutgers University Press, 1996), 27.

not be repaid, twice as much value in barley must be repaid.[26] There are several possible reasons for the seemingly excessive barley in relation to the silver. Perhaps there was an especially abundant barley harvest that year, depressing the price of barley, or perhaps lending the silver at that particular time created a hardship on the temple, or it may be that the temple was trying to encourage repayment of principal in silver and penalizing the debtor for repayment in a different commodity. If the "excess" barley were construed as interest, the imputed rate of interest on this loan would be nearly 100%.

When interest was specifically stated in debt instruments, the most common was as additional specie to be paid along with the original debt amount. An ancient Akkadian proverb was "To give (a loan) is like making love, to return a loan with interest like the birth of a son" (CAD H̬:217). A promissory note from the ninth year of Nebuchadnezzar (597 B.C.E.) is typical:

> 1/2 mina of silver, the possession of Nabû-ušabši, the son of Nergal-ušallim, son of Nûr-Sin, is owed by Nabû-šar-aḫêšu, the son of Nabû-uṭirra. Yearly, upon one mina, ten shekels of silver shall accumulate.[27]

Note there was no specified repayment date and the annual interest rate was 16.67% as compared to the prevailing interest rate of 20% per annum. There are also examples of recapitalized interest, i.e., the principal amount of the loan was renegotiated to include the unpaid interest accumulated to date. In one text, interest was specifically charged on the principal plus the unpaid interest accumulated to date: "we shall charge you interest and compound interest" (CAD Ṣ:159). In some cases, the interest could be remitted in a different commodity from the principal debt; in one text the interest on a loan of silver is specified as "four grown cows and the young" (NBAD, #139). One debtor pleaded, "Send me fifty excellent lambs so that I may give them or give silver to my creditor" (CAD R:208). Although it is unclear whether the debtor was paying off principal or interest or some combination thereof, the text does demonstrate that payments could be made in different specie from the original debt. Harris describes "a special way of paying interest to the temple for loans which may be considered as a means to help the debtor. There existed the custom of offering food to the god from whom the loan was taken (and thus to his priests) in lieu of paying interest." The interest clause in this arrangement consisted of two words, máš, "interest," and mākalu, "food offering," and is found in loans of two shekels of silver or less.[28]

---

[26]Dougherty, Neo-Babylonian and Persian, #344.

[27]Henry L. F. Lutz, "A Neo-Babylonian Debenture," University of California Publications in Semitic Philology 10/9 (1940): 253.

[28]Harris, "Temple Loans," 132.

The provisions for paying interest may have been as varied as the lenders and borrowers. Some debts were interest-free; some started bearing interest after an initial interest-free period; some set a fixed rate in advance; some set the rate at the prevailing rate at the due date; some left the rate unspecified; some required payment of interest immediately; some deferred any interest payments until the due date of the principal; and some specified payment of interest on demand. As in modern times, repayment terms for principal could include regular installment payments, balloon payments at a specified date, or any combination agreed to by the parties to the loan. One text from the temple archives in Telloh records how oxen and asses work off interest owed on a loan.[29] Perhaps terms were renegotiated (in judicial settings?), as implied in the following:

> Every month PN will lower (the balance of his debt) with PN2 by one shekel of silver for the claim against him until PN2 is paid in full. (*CAD* R:214)

Lending for Collateral. In addition to interest, the other common compensation for the creditor's risk was collateral, assets pledged or transferred to the creditor to secure a loan. Assets used as collateral were varied: real estate, in which case the loan was a mortgage; moveable property, in which case the loan was a chattel mortgage; persons owned or controlled by the debtor; and future anticipated income of the debtor, such as temple prebends or the yield of future harvests. When the debtor owned the real estate free and clear, there would be no problem in the creditor taking title to it in case of default. In the typical Neo-Babylonian promissory note for silver mentioned above, the note concludes, "All his property in town and country, all that there is, [shall be] a pledge for Nabû-ušabši. Another creditor has no right of disposal over it until Nabû-ušabši gets his money, fully repaid."[30] In the following texts, however, the debtor and other parties hold the pledged asset jointly: "One PI of planted ground is held in common in equal shares by PN, PN2 and PN3"; "half of his house, the share (of the house) which (he owns) with PN, is pledged"; "the entire ninth part of his parcel of land, a field with planted (palm trees), his fief land, which he holds with his partners, is pledged" (*CAD* Z:144–45). According to one text, the permission of the other partners was needed to make any change in the sharing arrangement: "PN3 and PN4 will not make monthly payments (to anybody) of the silver (received as) toll from the bridge owned by PN and (half) by PN2 as co-owners, without the permission of PN" (*CAD* Z:149). In cases where the transfer of title was

---

[29]Barton, *Temple Archives of Telloh*, #156.
[30]Lutz, "Neo-Babylonian Debenture," 253.

not feasible or possible, the creditor may have demanded the transfer of replacement assets of equal value.

Lending with Penalties. Another protection available to the creditor was to stipulate a penalty or additional interest if the loan was not fully repaid on time. The temple of Ištar in Calah loaned 5 1/2 *minas* of silver, reimbursable on demand with no stated interest rate. Upon nonpayment, however, interest began accruing at the prevailing rates.[31] A creditor could also decrease his risk by requiring the debtor to involve a partner or through suretyship, an obligation for the debt undertaken by a third-party guarantor.

Factoring Accounts Receivable. The economy of Mesopotamia was predicated on annuities, series of payments over time, including rents, tithes, taxes of all kinds (see chapter four), tribute, prebends, rations, and wages. We have already seen (see chapter five) how the owner of a prebend annuity could convert it into cash in hand by selling to a "performer" (*ēpišānūtu*). The owner of the prebend annuity benefited by receiving silver (or other assets) now; the performer benefited by being entitled to an income stream in the future. The modern term for selling the right to future income is "factoring accounts receivable." By employing this sophisticated cash flow management technique, the owner of the future income stream, the "accounts receivable," sells to another party, the "factor," the right to collect the receivable. The debtor makes future payments directly to the factor, who has no recourse to the original owner of the receivable should the debtor default. The owner, therefore, shifts the credit risk to the factor.

A Simple Example of Factoring. Suppose the local grocer buys a certain amount of grain on credit from a local farmer for 100 shekels. The farmer records an "accounts receivable" (rather than actual "income," since he doesn't have the actual money yet, having to wait until the next year to collect it) of 100 shekels from the grocery. Then, the farmer decides to sell the receivable to a "factor," who pays the farmer for the right to collect the debt from the grocer. In the future, the grocer is obligated to pay the factor; the farmer has his money and is no longer a part of the process. But a shekel to be collected in the future is not worth as much as a shekel in hand today, so the payment of interest by the farmer compensates the factor for this discrepancy. By considering the prevailing interest rate, called the "cost of capital," the amount of shekels to be collected in the future is discounted to the "present value." For example, 83 shekels today would grow to 100 shekels in a year if the sum earned 20% per annum. Inversely, 100 shekels due in a year would be worth 83 shekels today, assuming a 20% interest rate. The owner of the accounts

[31]R. Bogaert, *Les Origines Antiques de la Banque de Depot* (Leiden: Brill, 1966), 61.

receivable (in this case the farmer) who sells the right to a future income stream is paid by the factor the discounted "present value," the value of which is further reduced by collection costs and other risks including the factor's estimate of uncollectability. The factor also discounts what he gives the farmer further to allow for a profit margin for the factor. In our example, our farmer may receive 75 shekels today in exchange for the factor's right to collect 100 shekels from the reliable grocer in one year.

A Modern Use of Factoring. The financial corollary of factoring accounts receivable is selling mortgage loans, with or without retaining the servicing rights, a modern business widely practiced by financial institutions as a risk-management technique. Mortgage banking companies originate loans (sell their money) to consumers (the purchaser of their money, the homeowner who must pay the mortgage) based on the pre-agreed underwriting criteria of the loan purchaser (the factor). The originating bank thus transfers all the risks of collection and default to the loan-purchaser (the factor), and retains as its income the fee charged the homeowner.

Returning to the ancient world, in the following two texts, accounts receivable for the agricultural *sūtu* tax are factored by the palace:

> Two and one-half minas worth of salt-water fish, dates, garlic, and wool, the *s.*-tax of PN (and others), PN2 has purchased (from the palace) for five-sixths mina of silver—he will receive the wool (from the taxpayer) at the time of the wool plucking, and he will then pay the palace five-sixths mina of silver under seal. (*CAD* S:424)

> x silver, the value of salt-water fish, x silver, the value of forty gur of dates, (being) the *s.*-tax of PN for the 25th year of Hammurapi, which PN (hereby undertakes to) give to PN2 (the man to whom the palace has sold the proceeds of the tax). (*CAD* S:424)

If the palace was sufficiently sophisticated to employ factoring as a cash flow management strategy, the temple would have been equally savvy in financial techniques. McEwan discusses a Hellenistic temple text in which someone offered to pay silver for the income of the offering box of the Day One temple for the period of one year. Although this seems to conform to what we have said about factoring accounts receivable, McEwan claims the price paid by the factor is too low to be a sale, and, therefore, must be considered a short-term lease of collection rights.[32] He may be correct in his assessment of the relative value of the cash compared to the future income stream. On the other hand, the daily offerings at the Day One temple may have been less than the "minimum of one half shekel per day" from other temples. Fur-

---

[32]McEwan, *Priest and Temple*, 128.

thermore, caution is always warranted when evaluating the merit of business decisions of two millennia ago. Regardless, the text demonstrates the payment of immediate monies for the rights to future income. Halligan claims that promissory notes were traded among brokers and that speculation in commodity futures "is not beyond the realm of possibility, given the sophistication of the Persian network of commerce."[33] This would be the ancient equivalent of modern-day trading of commodity futures and options.

Use of Money. In the mid-first millennium, credit instruments for commodities and silver facilitated economic life in an agricultural economy by managing surpluses and shortages of commodities. But widespread credit in Mesopotamia could not flourish prior to the extensive use of money in the economy. Despite the frequent use in some English translations of the word "money" for the underlying Hebrew word for "silver," the use of money in the modern sense was rare in the era of the Old Testament. Most modern economists would agree that money is something that can be (1) a means of exchange, something that people use when they want to acquire something else; (2) a mode of payment, something that people give to settle debts or tax obligations that might not involve the receipt of anything else; (3) a standard of value, something to which people may compare other things when they are seeking to explain hierarchies of value and to render accounts in a uniform way so that loss can be minimized; and, according to some economists, (4) a way of storing wealth.[34]

The province of Lydia in Asia Minor generally receives credit for the invention of coinage around 540 B.C.E., but antecedents can be seen in various money-like objects in Mesopotamia. Stamped metal from Ur is known from very early times. Ingots of bronze with fixed, government certified weights are known from Neo-Assyrian texts, although their heavy weight and rarity probably indicate they were not used as currency per se. A text from King Sennacherib (704–681 B.C.E.) mentions standardized half-shekel pieces, probably used at this time as weights rather than circulating coinage: "I executed with superior artistry cast bronze-work (for the figures of large animals), (and) upon an inspiration from the god (Ea), I built clay molds, poured bronze into each, and made their features as perfect as in casting half-shekel pieces" (*CAD* Z:87).

Silver was by far the preferred metal for exchange due to its abundance relative to gold, circulating in the form of rings, coils, and other pieces. Grain was also widely used in exchange because, like silver, it was easily weighed

---

[33]Halligan, "Nehemiah 5," 150.

[34]Daniel C. Snell, "Methods of Exchange and Coinage in Ancient Western Asia," *CANE* 3:1487.

and divided into even parts, exactly replaceable with other grain, and could be stored for years. In contrast to the weighed-out metal bars or grain of wider Mesopotamia, areas of the western Mediterranean basin developed "metal tool money," pieces of copper, iron, lead, gold, or silver shaped as familiar tools (basins, tripods, utensils, etc.) and accepted without reluctance if they had the right traditional form and appearance. "Axe money was popular in various forms also as we know from Homer and with more or less certainty from Cyprus, Tenedos, Crete, Paphos, and Israel. Furthermore, in Cyprus the anchor was used as money."[35] For centuries, exchange in kind and exchange in precious metals occurred side by side. Documents from Persepolis show salaries paid in a mixture of goods and silver until around 490 B.C.E., when silver becomes the dominant means of payment. The idea of silver as currency was slow to catch on outside of Greece because of the long tradition of weighing and because of the well-placed distrust of shaving and counterfeiting. Although subjects of Persia and later empires paid taxes in precious metal, the silver was generally hoarded by the royal administration and not reintroduced into circulation, thereby retarding the development of a "money" economy. Darius I introduced coinage to the Persian Empire by 500 B.C.E. with the gold daric. Minted exclusively by the king, the Persian coins were used to pay mercenaries and some royal functionaries and were not circulated widely in the economy. Strabo reports about the Persians, ". . . most of the gold and silver is used in articles of equipment, but not much in money; and that they consider those metals as better adapted for presents and for depositing in storehouses . . ." (Strabo, *Geogr.* 15.3.21).

Rise of Private Credit Sources. Contemporaneous with the emergence of coinage and increasingly complicated financial transactions, individuals undertook arrangements for managing land and credit. By the fifth century B.C.E., the temple as primary creditor in the Mesopotamian community was supplemented by professional family firms engaged in various financial activities. These private enterprises developed new credit instruments and more complex strategies of land management in response to the economic needs of the communities in southern Mesopotamia. If the temples were to maintain their active economic role in trade and credit, they needed to implement competitive financing arrangements.

The best-documented private firm is the Murašu family of Nippur from the fifth century B.C.E., whose archives have been excavated and published. The texts indicate that, with land as collateral, the Murašu family extended short-term credit to managers of crown estates, temple estates, and owners of land who were in service to the monarchy. Demonstrating keen business acumen,

---

[35]Heichelheim, *Economic History,* 1:213.

the family positioned themselves to take economic advantage of the local situation in Mesopotamia. First, they acquired land rights by pledge, by grant, by purchase, or by lease. Next, they acquired irrigation rights from the state for a fee and supplied the movable resources necessary to farm the land to a tenant, including seed, tools, animals, and possibly labor. In many cases, the Murašu family guaranteed the tenant a stipend and guaranteed the state the predetermined amount of taxes. In this way, they positioned themselves to benefit from any increased agricultural production that led to increased profits. Since the amounts to be paid out to the tenant and to the state were fixed, the Murašu family members were able to use their expertise in land management and their economies of scale to increase the agricultural production of the land.

In the short term, everyone seemed to benefit—the tenant was guaranteed a stipend on which to live; the landowner converted a fixed asset into a liquid asset; the government was guaranteed a fixed amount of taxes; and the Murašu family made a profit. But in the long term, this arrangement of land management weakened the wider economy by concentrating the incentive for agricultural efficiencies in the hands of a few and by determining land use based primarily on economic factors. More concentrated land management, a weaker general economy, the cost of wars with Egypt and the Greek city states, and prolonged political unrest combined over time to cause economic inflation: the interest rate in the Babylonian period (early sixth century) was approximately 10%; in the early Persian period (late sixth century) it rose to 20%; by the end of the fifth century it was 50% in the Murašu documents.

Activity in the Murašu documents increased significantly in the last decades of the fifth century. When Darius II came to power in 423 B.C.E., he increased the amount of silver tribute required of the general populace to support the military apparatus needed to quell insurrections. Apparently, many were unable to comply and turned to the Murašu family (or temples) for an economic solution. By the dawn of the fourth century, significantly more land was in the hands of the Murašu family, and the power of the Persian Empire would soon be eclipsed by the glory of Greece.

Egypt and Greece

A noticeable difference between Egyptian temples and Mesopotamian temples was the apparent lack of deposits and loans in the economy of the former. There appear to have been no loans by temples to individuals until after Alexander's conquest in the fourth century B.C.E. Written evidence of lending by individuals is scant before the demotic papyri of the seventh century B.C.E., although informal lending arrangements secured by personal reputation and oaths taken in the name of the local deity could have occurred in the Egyptian economy for centuries. In demotic texts from the Persian period, legal instruments termed "document of claim" established a legal contract for the creditor. As in Mesopotamia, loans are attested in silver and in commodities, principally in grain. Loans in written contracts were secured by charging interest, pledging or conveying property, or guaranteeing the terms of the contract by a third party. Interest was specified using terms derived from "to add" or "to give birth." Third-party guarantors were said to "accept the hand" of the debtor. Where interest is specified in the early demotic texts, the rates are quite high (500%). Reforms in the late eighth century capped the maximum amount collectable at twice the amount borrowed, an effective interest rate of 100%. Further Ptolemaic reforms in the third century reduced the maximum interest rate to 24%, according to the New Kingdom texts from Deir el-Medina.[36] As the Egyptian economy became increasingly monetized in the final centuries of the first millennium B.C.E., lending activity became increasingly widespread and concentrated in silver. Business contracts of small amounts and individual loans among soldiers and civilians were commonplace in the pre-Roman period, although not necessarily connected with the temples. The lack of information on temple deposits and loans may not indicate reality on the ground, but, more likely, the evidence points to the degree of state involvement in the temple economy and the primary connection of temples with the Pharaoh's afterlife.

In Greece, there is evidence for the use of temple assets for loans to states and individuals as early as the sixth century. Lending is attested for the temple of Apollo at Delos, of Zeus at Olympus, of Artemis at Sardis, of Athena at Ilion, and of Apollo, Athena, and Artemis at Halicarnasse. Only three temples (Ephesus, Delphi, and Priene) document deposits and loans, but a century separates the attestations of deposits and loans.[37] Repayment was not always assured; the temple on Delos executed a promissory note for funds lent to the Athenian city-state and never received repayment of eighty percent of the loan.[38]

The oldest Greek terms for interest are found for loans of cattle, seed, and weighed-out metal money. The temple on the island of Delos consistently made loans at 10% interest despite the current prevailing market rate. Initially below the prevailing rate of 20% in the fifth century, by the end of the second century the market rate had declined to the point that the temple

[36]Joseph Manning, "Demotic Papyri (664–30 BCE)," in *Security for Debt in Ancient Near Eastern Law* (ed. by Raymond Westbrook and Richard Jasnow; Leiden: Brill, 2001), 312.

[37]Bogaert, *Origines Antiques,* 131.

[38]Homer and Sylla, *History of Interest Rates,* 43.

could no longer compete in the credit market. As in Mesopotamia, the lender sometimes hedged the risk by requiring collateral equal to or greater than the amount of the loan. The term generally used for real estate collateral is *hypothēkē,* a hypothecary pledge, indicating that the property remained under the control of the debtor and was only transferred to the creditor upon default. A marking stone called a *horos* was used to indicate the limit or boundary of the real estate, with severe penalties imposed for tampering. Notice of encumbrance of the land, and sometimes the name of the creditor and terms of the loan, were engraved on the *horos.* Since the debtor retained possession of the property, his name did not appear on the *horos.* One part of Solon's economic reforms in 594 B.C.E. was to pull up every *horos,* thus freeing the land from encumbrance. Other economic reforms under Solon included canceling all existing debts and prohibiting future pledging of persons as debt security, redeeming all debt slaves from abroad, limiting the amount of land owned by one person, and forbidding the export of agricultural products except olive oil. Almost 150 years later, temple officials demanded real estate collateral for outstanding temple loans, and the *horos* stone was again set up on encumbered property. As in Mesopotamia, late payment fees could be charged as a way of increasing the overall return on the loan. Since a large proportion of the economy in Greece was devoted to trade, sea loans were popular, sometimes called "bottomry loans," using the cargo and/or the ship itself as collateral. The rates of return for such risky ventures were very high, commonly ranging from 20% to 30% per voyage (40% to 60% per season). It was not uncommon for the creditor to accompany his collateral on the voyage. The temples of Delphi and Olympia made interest bearing loans to meet the expenses of bringing the league's navy into seaworthy condition.

With the improvement of tools and engraving techniques, the earliest currency was made of electrum, a blend of gold and silver ore occurring naturally in Asia Minor. But the first "coins" were in fact large bars, not useful for the everyday buying and selling of the marketplace, but serviceable for mercenary wages and offerings to temples. In the final decades of the seventh century and the first decades of the sixth century, Corinth and Athens used the less-expensive silver rather than electrum to make coins, with the innovation of small denominations.

Although deposit and lending functions originated in Greek temples, during the fifth century B.C.E. private individuals began to participate as moneychangers in those areas where many different currencies were circulated. By charging a commission, *agio,* that varied according to market conditions, the moneychangers provided a necessary service and collected a tidy profit. Private lending encompassed the full range of secured and unsecured loans. In areas where debt slavery upon default became illegal, pawn credit or possessory pledge became the norm. Banking activities in Athens included currency exchange, pawn brokers, *giro* transfers from one depositor's account to another, and letters of credit for travelers.

As the center of a Mediterranean trading network, Delos naturally attracted persons to facilitate money changing, depositing, and lending, particularly maritime lending. But the high volume and relatively high risk of maritime lending could not be entirely undertaken by the professional moneylenders. To generate enough capital to engage in maritime trade at acceptable levels of risk, the merchants of Delos organized themselves into religious brotherhood associations called *collegia sodalicia*. These religious fraternal groups facilitated commerce by making "loans to members, vouching for creditworthiness, combining efforts to find warehouse or cargo space, making maritime loans, and forming commercial partnerships" known as *koinōniai* or *societates*.[39]

One type of religious brotherhood association, the *eranos* association, seems to have been specifically organized to facilitate personal unsecured credit on Delos. Though perhaps originally organized for its social benefits, the group evolved into a mutual lending society. Based on friendship and reciprocity, the terms of *eranos* loans assumed no interest or collateral and extended repayment dates. In the unlikely event of default, the penalty was 150% of the loan amount. Over time, *eranos* lending was extended to those outside the membership of the association, to friends, and to politicians. Evidence indicates that business used *eranos* loans alongside traditional commercial debt instruments.

Vows

As we explained above, Mesopotamian temple loan documents typically include the amount of debt, the creditor, the debtor, and the time when the debt is to be paid. In many cases, the god of the temple appears in the loan document as the creditor; in other cases, the temple officials are listed. The temple loan document with the god as the creditor provided a ready vehicle for a vow to a god for future benevolence, with the god as creditor and the votary as creditor. Conditions are given, which when fulfilled, will result in the fulfillment of the vow. The most common Mesopotamian texts record a vow by an ill person to give a sun disk to the sun god Šamaš upon restoration to health.[40]

---

[39]Rauh, *Sacred Bonds of Commerce,* 251.
[40]Harris, "Temple Loans," 133–36.

The following biblical texts understand the vow to be an obligation not unlike the loan.

> If you vow a vow to YHWH your God, you shall not delay to repay it, for YHWH your God will surely seek it from you and it would be a sin against you. . . . You must be careful to do whatever comes out of your lips, just as you vowed to YHWH your God voluntarily what you said by your mouth. (Deut 23:22, 24 [21, 23])

> Now Jephthah vowed a vow to YHWH and said, "If you make sure to give the Ammonites into my hand, then the one who comes out of the doors of my house to meet me when I return in safety from the Ammonites, that one will be for YHWH, and I will offer him up as a burnt offering." (Judg 11:30–31)

> (Hannah) vowed a vow, "if you (YHWH) will give your maidservant a male child, then I will give him to YHWH all the days of his life" . . . For this lad I prayed, and YHWH gave to me my request that I asked of him. Moreover, I give him over on request to YHWH. (1 Sam 1:11, 27–28)

> Just as you vow a vow to God, do not delay to repay it, for there is no delight in fools; what you vow, repay. (Eccl 5:3 [4])

In the biblical material, the verb root *šālam* (Piel stem) describes the fulfillment of a vow to the Lord. This is the same verb for repaying a loan! The fulfillment of the vow is considered to be "payment" or "repayment." In both cases, the debtor has made a promise and is under obligation to meet that commitment. Likewise in Mesopotamia, the same verbs for "repay" are used in loan contracts involving barley or silver and in vows to the deity.

If we compare the typical ANE loan contract with the vow to a deity, we can see the striking similarities in structure. Consider the typical loan made by the temple to a farmer who needs seed grain and promises to repay after the next harvest.

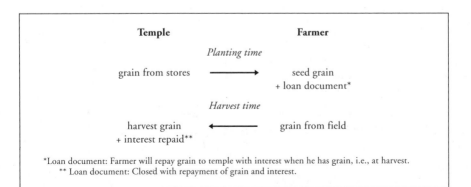

Temple		Farmer
	Planting time	
grain from stores	⟶	seed grain + loan document*
	Harvest time	
harvest grain + interest repaid**	⟵	grain from field

*Loan document: Farmer will repay grain to temple with interest when he has grain, i.e., at harvest.
** Loan document: Closed with repayment of grain and interest.

Now consider the vow to the deity of the temple by a person who is in need of healing. On the left side is the typical loan of grain described above. On the right side is the vow.

Temple	Farmer	God Shamash	Sick person
Planting time		*Time of need/illness*	
grain from stores ➡	seed grain + loan document	healing power ➡	need for health + vow to repay
Harvest time		*Time of renewed health*	
harvest grain + interest repaid	⬅ grain from field	repayment with equivilancy*	⬅ health

*Because the recipient of healing cannot repay in kind, the vow to repay is fulfilled with something of equivalent value.

The structural similarities are striking, and the loan document serves contractually to bind the parties in a conventional loan or in a vow. Both loans and vows must be "repaid."

Excursus—Birth Narrative of Samuel

Three particular verses from the birth narrative of Samuel offer tantalizing connections between credit instruments executed by the temple and vows made to the Lord. The opening chapters of First Samuel are vigorously debated by scholars who see editorial layers in the text: the narrative of Hannah, Elkanah, and Samuel; the narrative of Eli's sons; and psalmody. Scholars have also noticed that Hannah's explanation of the name Samuel in 1:20 as "I asked (*šā'al*) him of YHWH" seems to explain the name Saul (*šā'ûl*) better than the name Samuel (*šĕmû'ēl*). Whatever positions are taken on these and other critical issues, all who study the Hebrew text can agree that the verb *šā'al* dominates the birth narrative of Samuel as it is now presented. In its basic stem, *šā'al* is the common verb for "ask, inquire." Sometimes, beyond the common meaning "ask," the verb is a technical term for "borrow," as the following texts illustrate: "If a person borrows (*yiš'al*) anything from his neighbor and it is broken or dies, he will repay in full (*šallēm yĕšallēm*)" (Exod 22:13 [14]); a man felling a tree cried out, "Alas, my axe head was borrowed (*šā'ûl*)" (2 Kgs 6:5); A creditor comes to seize a woman's two children to satisfy an unpaid debt, so the woman is told to borrow (*ša'ălî*) vessels from her neighbors (2 Kgs 4:3). The borrowed vessels fill with oil, which she then sells to satisfy the debt and rescue her children. So we see that *šāʾal* is a technical term for "borrow," and in the causative (Hiphil) stem, it means "lend," (lit. cause to borrow). An important feature of Samuel's birth narrative is its setting at the shrine in Shiloh, twice referred to as the house (*bêt*) of YHWH and once as the temple (*hêkāl*) of YHWH.

So, to review the important events in the narrative recounted in First Samuel:

1:11   At the doorpost of the temple in Shiloh, Hannah vows a vow: "YHWH, if you will give your maidservant a son, I will give him to YHWH."

1:17   Eli questions Hannah and blesses her: "May the God of Israel grant your request which you asked (*šāʾalt*)."

1:20   Hannah bears a son and names him Samuel (*šěmûʾēl*) because "from YHWH I asked him (*šěʾiltîu*)."

1:28   After Samuel is weaned, Hannah brings him to Shiloh. "Therefore, I lend him (*hišʾiltihû*) to YHWH all the days that he is, he was borrowed (*šāʾûl*) from YHWH."

2:20   One year when Hannah brings a robe to Samuel, Eli blesses Elkanah and Hannah:

> "May YHWH repay* (*yěšillēm*) you with offspring in exchange for the loan (*haš-šěʾēlâ*) that she lent* (*hišʾilâ*) to YHWH." (*emending Hebrew text to follow Dead Sea Scrolls [4QSamᵃ] and Septuagint)

2:21   So Hannah bore three sons and two daughters.

This narrative sequence appears to follow the pattern of making and re-paying vows at the temple that we see in the Mesopotamian temple archives. But there is an interesting twist in the sequence of the story. The diagram on the following page illustrates this unusual arrangement. On the left is the typical vow to the deity, which, as we have seen, is structurally similar to the loan contract for grain or silver. On the right is Hannah's vow.

Rather than repaying her vow and ending the transaction, Hannah essentially exacts a vow from YHWH. Instead of using Samuel as *repayment* for her vow as she initially promised, she uses Samuel as a *loan*. She lends Samuel to YHWH and then receives additional children as repayment plus interest for her loan. Hannah turns out to be a pretty shrewd financier.

An ancient Akkadian proverb says, "To give (a loan) is like making love, to return a loan with interest like the birth of a son" (*CAD* H:217). In the same way that interest is the fruit of making a loan, children are the fruit of

God Shamash	Sick person		YHWH	Hannah

Expected outcome

Time of need/illness   *Time of infertility*

stores of → need for health   stores of → need for fertility
healing power   + vow to repay   fertility power   + vow to repay

Time of renewed health   *Time of fertility*

repayment ← health   repayment ← fertility, i.e., a son
with equivilancy*   with equivilancy**

Actual outcome (1 Sam 1:28)

                                             Time of fertility

                      need for Samuel ← fertility, i.e., a son
                      + vow to repay***

                                             Time of infertility

                      Stores of fertility ← repayment with
                                             equivalency
                                             (2 sons, 2 daughters)

* Because the recipient of healing cannot repay in kind (healing), the vow to repay is fulfilled with
   something of equivalent value, usually silver or gold.
** Because Hannah cannot repay in kind (fertility), the vow to repay is fulfilled with something of
   equivalent value, her son Samuel.
*** God repays the loan of Samuel with another son to take his place plus two more sons and two
   daughters as "interest" on the loan.

lovemaking. This proverb seems to be applicable to Hannah's situation, lending her son Samuel to YHWH and receiving additional children as interest on her loan. "I will pay my vow to the Lord" is more than a pious prayer—it is a contractual agreement between debtor and creditor.

Concluding Matters

This book has highlighted the economic role of temples as significant economic institutions in their respective societies in Jerusalem and Mesopotamia, and, to a lesser extent, in Egypt and Greece. By carefully reading biblical texts and by synthesizing the administrative and economic information excavated and published from major temple archives of Mesopotamia, we can now suggest a synthetic composite picture of an ancient temple of the mid-first millennium B.C.E. As stated in the introductory chapter, I intend to present a synchronic view, commingling information from different time periods to develop a composite picture of how the ancient temple as an institution functioned in the economies of the first millennium B.C.E. I am *not* claiming that, were we able to be transported back to a particular decade, any one temple actually functioned according to all aspects of my composite, synchronic paradigm. I *am* claiming that the Jerusalem temple functioned in ancient Israelite society in ways remarkably similar to other ANE temples, especially those in Mesopotamia of the seventh to fifth centuries B.C.E.

An Economic Model of the Temple in the ANE

The "house of the god"—the cultic shrine—necessitated the "household of the god," that is, the resources essential to the care and feeding of the gods. The temple complex, with its fields and flocks, storehouses and stables, and production facilities and personnel, constituted a self-sustaining household functioning as an economic unit in itself. Within this autonomous economic unit, temple assets (land, herds, facilities, stores, and personnel) were put to productive use to generate the food, clothing, tools, furnishings, and ritual items, which the deity and the deity's household then consumed. The movement of resources within the economic unit of the temple is what I call the "internal" temple economy. Although the shrine and altar may have been the central focus of the temple complex from a religious perspective since the deity was present there, the temple storehouses were the central focus economically. Thousands of cuneiform texts document the receipt and disbursement of commodities into and out of the storehouses and workshops, recording the precise quantities as well as the individuals responsible for the goods. Figure 1 depicts the internal temple economy.

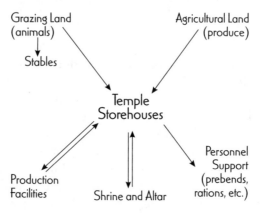

Figure 1. Internal Temple Economy

The flow of resources within the internal temple economy, however, was not as insular as this figure depicts. Agricultural lands produced a bounty of one crop and insufficient amounts of another; grazing herds decreased from low birth rates and disease outbreaks or increased from superior animal husbandry techniques; temple personnel were unable to keep up with the workload at harvest and birthing times, yet were idle in other seasons.

That is to say, the resources of temples did not always exactly match the needs of the gods and their households. To compensate for the natural excesses and deficits of an agricultural economy, the internal temple economy expanded into the local and regional economies. Creative land-leasing arrangements and various hiring strategies allowed the temple to cultivate arable land, manage flocks and herds, and run production workshops at full capacity. The temple traded excess stores for needed commodities. As a divinely-protected area, the temple was ideally suited to witness oaths and to safeguard the wealth of others by accepting deposits into its treasuries. With its stores of commodities, the temple functioned as a creditor for the community, utilizing a variety of methods to be compensated for risk and minimize loss. The "expanded temple economy" is the label I apply to the wider range of the temple's economic influence as it made productive use of its own assets and judiciously employed the community's assets, as depicted in Figure 2.

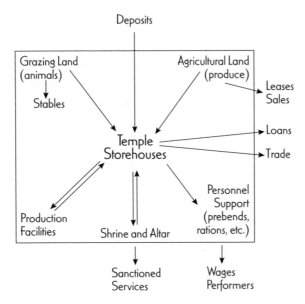

Figure 2. Expanded Temple Economy

Further, the temple was entitled to a share of the produce from nontemple assets—lands, herds, and other forms of wealth owned by the state and private individuals. From ancient times, individuals and communities have contributed, voluntarily or not, to the temple in support of its mission of caring for the god. Obligatory inflows in the form of tithes and taxes entered the temple economy; nonobligatory inflows were voluntary contributions in the form of land, produce, personnel, and cultic items. Likewise, goods exited the temple economy to persons outside the temple's purview. Obligatory outflows included provisioning the royal table and paying taxes; also obligatory, from the temple's point of view, was the expropriation of temple treasures by local and foreign rulers. Finally, temple resources were used to care for the needy of the community. In most cases, the contributions to the temple were commingled with the temple's own assets, perhaps even manipulated for economic gain, before being disbursed to the eventual consumer. In some cases, the temple served as a collection point and pass-through agent for income destined for the state.

The external inflows and outflows of the temple economy often lead scholars to conclude that temples functioned as "banks" in antiquity. I contend that this description is inaccurate. Strictly speaking, a bank accepts deposits and then permits others the right to access those deposits through negotiable instruments. Temple archives demonstrate that deposits by individuals were held under strict accountability for that particular individual. Loans made by temples were from their own surpluses and not from individuals' deposits. So temples were not "banks" in antiquity. Rather, the more precise designation for the role of the temple in antiquity would be "financial intermediary." As collector, user, and disburser of goods and financial services, the temple transferred value from contributor to consumer. Figure 3 is a synthetic, composite, economic model of the temple in the ANE as a financial intermediary.

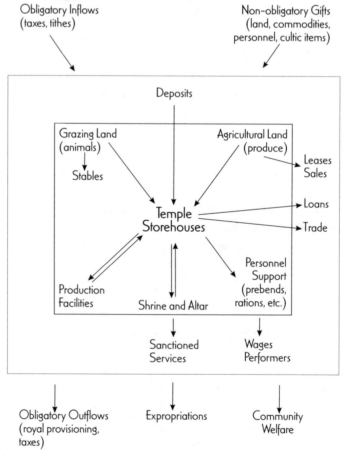

Figure 3. External Temple Economy

Throughout the ANE, the temple's most basic economic contribution was providing employment for a number of citizens, and furnishing housing, food, and clothing. Temple personnel expended goods distributed to them in excess of their personal consumption in the local economy, creating jobs for more local citizens, or they invested surpluses in trading ventures with traveling merchants, again influencing the wider economy. Wages paid to temporary personnel, in commodities or silver, had the same effect. Leasing arrangements of temple land or animals stimulated the local economy, as did the need for particular items for cultic rituals. The prices paid by the temple for these goods and services influenced the general level of prices and wages in the economy.

As central collection site and storage facility for commodities native to the region, the temple managed its perishable stocks by distributing commodities as rations or prebends to temple personnel, and as food supplies to the political authorities. Distribution of surpluses of nonperishable commodities stimulated trade and commercial ventures throughout the region and beyond. Credit instruments developed as a way of managing surpluses through lending to persons in the community, whether the peasant farmer in need of seed grain or the merchant seeking a profitable investment opportunity. Interest rates set by the temple relative to the market rate contributed to or dampened inflationary tendencies in the economy. Weights and measures became standardized as farmers and herders fulfilled leasing contracts, repaid loans, and paid their tithes and taxes.

With literate administrative staff in place to account for the temple's tithes and stores, the temple was a logical choice as the central register even for transactions not involving the temple: land sales or leasing contracts between individuals, judicial decisions of all kinds, and oaths related to commercial contracts. Finally, the temple was in a position to serve as emergency supplier of food to the community and to demonstrate a commitment to the marginalized of society.

Specific Findings regarding the Jerusalem Temple

This book has argued that the Jerusalem temple functioned as an economic institution in ancient Israel/Judah in ways similar to other ANE temples, specifically Mesopotamian temples in the seventh to fifth centuries B.C.E. In its role as collector, user, and disburser of goods and financial services, the Jerusalem temple functioned as a financial intermediary. Biblical texts, our primary source for the operations of the Jerusalem temple, demonstrate an economic dimension to temple operations. The collection site of tithes and taxes, the Jerusalem temple stored commodities and precious metals for use in the internal temple economy in the cultic rituals associated with the "house of YHWH" and in the housing, feeding, and clothing of the "household of YHWH," the temple personnel. Collection methods, specifically baskets at the gates and at the altar, mirror those of Mesopotamian temples.

Likewise, Jerusalem temple personnel were counterparts to temple personnel in Mesopotamia. In particular, we note the work of the *šōʿēr*, the person I have called the "gater." Stationed at the gates, the "gaters" were charged with, at a minimum, safeguarding the contents of the baskets placed at the thresholds, and perhaps, assaying the items deposited, assigning value, and crediting the account of the depositor. The traditional translation of *šōʿēr* as "gatekeeper" does not communicate the full range of activities and responsibilities of this position. A translation of "gate clerk" or "gate accountant" comes closer to capturing the role. Likewise, the *sōpēr*, connected with the storehouses, did more than is indicated in the traditional translation "scribe." He was a counter, a recorder, a ledger-keeper, and an enumerator. Both officials counted, tallied, and recorded receipts, the former at the thresholds of the temple gates, and the latter for the temple storehouses.

Biblical texts address the accountability of temple personnel with systems strikingly similar to systems of accountability used in Mesopotamia to safeguard materials from misuse or theft, termed *iškaru* and *ina pāni*. Precious commodities are put "in the hand of" (*bĕyad*) the responsible party, who must then account for the items later, usually by returning a finished product. The structure of the Exodus account of the wilderness tabernacle conforms to the Mesopotamian *iškaru* system. The plan of the tabernacle revealed to Moses in Exod 25–31 functions as the record of raw materials dispensed by the ruler of a temple, in this case YHWH, to the chief administrator, Moses. The record of the construction of the tabernacle in Exod 35–40 is the return of the finished product to the chief administrator, who double-checks the accounting inventory and accepts the work.

Tantalizing hints in the biblical texts suggest that the Jerusalem temple engaged in regional trade, assumed fiduciary responsibility for deposits, made loans of surpluses, and was concerned for the welfare of the needy in ways similar to Mesopotamian temples. The birth narrative of Samuel is a vow patterned after the ancient loan document, although Hannah shrewdly manages the situation to her advantage. Instead of using Samuel as repayment for her vow as she initially promised, she uses him as a loan, later receiving additional children as repayment of principal plus interest.

Contribution

In the introductory chapter I outlined my twofold purpose for writing this book. First, I wanted to raise the consciousness of pastors and laity that the temple in ancient Israel was not *just* for worship. I don't imagine that this work will cause anyone who plays a game of word association to hear "temple" and then shout out "economic institution." But I do hope that increased awareness of the economic dimensions of the Jerusalem temple in society will influence our reading of biblical texts. Second, I wanted to demonstrate that, since the temple is the central socioeconomic-religious institution in ancient Israel, worship was not disconnected from politics, economics, or sociology. The modern corollary is that the life of discipleship is not bifurcated into sacred and secular, but is part of a holistic response to a gracious God. I hope that this book contributes to recapturing something of the integrative character of life that our ancestors in the faith experienced and that the Holy One desires for all creation.

Selected Bibliography

Ackerman, Susan. *Under Every Green Tree: Popular Religion in Sixth-Century Judah.* HSM 46. Atlanta: Scholars Press, 1992.

Ackroyd, Peter. *Archaeology, Politics and Religion: The Persian Period.* Denver: Criterion, 1982.

———. *Exile and Restoration: A Study of Hebrew Thought of the Sixth Century BC.* OTL. London: SCM Press, 1968.

———. *Israel Under Babylon and Persia.* The New Clarendon Bible: Old Testament 4. Oxford: Oxford University Press, 1970.

———. "The Jewish Community in Palestine in the Persian Period." Pages 130–61 in *Cambridge History of Judaism,* vol. 1: *Introduction, The Persian Period.* Edited by W. D. Davies and Louis Finkelstein. Cambridge: Cambridge University Press, 1984.

———. "The Temple Vessels—A Continuity Theme." Pages 166–81 in *Studies in the Religion of Ancient Israel.* Edited by G. W. Anderson et al. VTSup 23. Leiden: Brill, 1972.

Adams, Robert M. *Heartland of Cities: Surveys of Ancient Settlements and Land Use on the Central Floodplain of the Euphrates.* Chicago: University of Chicago Press, 1981.

Aharoni, Yohanan. *Arad Inscriptions.* Jerusalem: Israel Exploration Society, 1981.

Ahlström, Gösta W. "Administration of the State in Canaan and Ancient Israel." Pages 587–603 in vol. 1 of *CANE.* 4 vols. Edited by Jack Sasson. New York: Scribner's, 1995.

Amusin, J. D., and Michael Heltzer. "The Inscription from Mesad Hashavyahu: Complaint of a Reaper of the Seventh Century BC." *IEJ* 14 (1964): 148–57.

Anderson, Gary A. *Sacrifices and Offerings in Ancient Israel: Studies in Their Social and Political Importance.* HSM 41. Atlanta: Scholars Press, 1987.

Anderson, Gary A., and Saul M. Olyan, eds. *Priesthood and Cult in Ancient Israel.* JSOTSup. Sheffield: Sheffield Academic Press, 1991.

Applebaum, Shimon. "Economic Life in Palestine." Pages 631–700 in *The Jewish People in the First Century: Historical Geography, Political History, Social, Cultural and Religious Life and Institutions.* Edited by Shmuel Safrai and M. Stern. Philadelphia: Fortress, 1976.

———. "The Social and Economic Status of the Jews in the Diaspora." Pages 700–92 in *The Jewish People in the First Century: Historical Geography, Political History, Social, Cultural and Religious Life and Institutions.* Edited by Shmuel Safrai. Philadelphia: Fortress, 1976.

Arnold, Dieter. "Royal Cult Complexes of the Old and Middle Kingdoms." Pages 31–85 in *Temples of Ancient Egypt.* Edited by Byron E. Shafer. Ithaca, N.Y.: Cornell University Press, 1997.

Avalos, Hector. "Legal and Social Institutions in Canaan and Ancient Israel." Pages 615–31 in vol. 1 of *CANE.* Edited by Jack Sasson. 4 vols. New York: Scribner's, 1995.

Avigad, N. *Bullae and Seals from a Post-Exilic Judaean Archive.* Jerusalem: Hebrew University of Jerusalem, 1976.

———. "A New Class of Yehud Stamps." *IEJ* 7 (1957): 146–53.

Balcer, Jack M. "Ionia and Sparda Under the Achaemenid Empire the Sixth and Fifth Centuries BC: Tribute, Taxation and Assessment." Pages 1–27 in *Le Tribut dans l'Empire Perse: Actes de la Table Ronde de Paris 12–13 Décembre 1986.* Edited by Pierre Briant and Clarisse Herrenschmidt. Travaux de l'Institut d'Études Iraniennes de l'Université de la Sorbonne Nouvelle 13. Paris-Louvain: Peeters, 1989.

Baron, Salo W. *To the Beginning of the Christian Era.* Vol. 1 of *A Social and Religious History of the Jews.* Philadelphia: Jewish Publication Society, 1952.

Baron, Salo W., and Arcadius Kahan. *Economic History of the Jews.* New York: Schocken Books, 1975.

Barton, George A. *Haverford Library Collection of Cuneiform Tablets or Documents from the Temple Archives of Telloh.* Philadelphia: Winston, 1904–1914.

Beaulieu, Paul-Alain. "An Episode in the Fall of Babylon to the Persians." *JNES* 52 (1993): 241–61.

———. *Late Babylonian Texts in the Nies Babylonian Collection.* Bethesda: CDL Press, 1994.

———. *Legal and Administrative Texts from the Reign of Nabonidus.* YOS 19. New Haven: Yale University Press, 2000.

Becking, Bob, and Marjo C. A. Korpel, eds. *The Crisis of Israelite Religion: Transformation of Religious Tradition in Exilic and Post-Exilic Times.* Leiden: Brill, 1999.

Bedford, Peter. "On Models and Texts: A Response to Blenkinsopp and Petersen." Pages 154–62 in *Second Temple Studies: 1. Persian Period.* Edited by Philip R. Davies. JSOTSup 117. Sheffield: Sheffield Academic Press, 1991.

Bell, John Fred. *A History of Economic Thought.* New York: Ronald Press, 1953.

Bengtson, H. *The Greeks and the Persians from the Sixth to the Fourth Centuries.* New York: Delacorte, 1968.

Berquist, Jon L. *Judaism in Persia's Shadow: A Social and Historical Approach.* Minneapolis: Fortress, 1995.

Betlyon, John W. "The Provincial Government of Persian Period Judea and the Yehud Coins." *JBL* 105 (1986): 633–42.

Bickerman, Elias J. "The Diaspora: The Babylonian Captivity." Pages 342–57 in *Cambridge History of Judaism,* vol. 1: *Introduction, The Persian Period.* Edited by W. D. Davies and Louis Finkelstein. Cambridge: Cambridge University Press, 1984.

———. "The Edict of Cyrus in Ezra 1." *JBL* 65 (1946): 249–75.

Binder, Donald D. *Into the Temple Courts: The Place of the Synagogues in the Second Temple Period.* SBLDS 169. Atlanta: SBL, 1999.

Birch, Bruce C. et al. *A Theological Introduction to the Old Testament.* Nashville: Abingdon, 1999.

Blenkinsopp, Joseph. *Ezra-Nehemiah: A Commentary.* OTL. Philadelphia: Westminster, 1988.

———. "The Mission of Udjahorresnet and Those of Ezra and Nehemiah." *JBL* 106 (1987): 409–21.

———. "Temple and Society in Achaemenid Judah." Pages 22–53 in *Second Temple Studies: 1. Persian Period.* Edited by Philip R. Davies. JSOTSup 117. Sheffield: Sheffield Academic Press, 1991.

Blomquist, Tina H. *Gates and Gods: Cults in the City Gates of Iron Age Palestine.* ConBOT 46. Stockholm: Almqvist & Wiksell, 1999.

Bogaert, R. *Les Origines Antiques de la Banque de Depot.* Leiden: Brill, 1966.

Bongenaar, A. C. V. M. "Money in the Neo-Babylonian Institutions." Pages 159–74 in *Trade and Finance in Ancient Mesopotamia.* Edited by J. G. Dercksen. Leiden: Nederlands Instituut voor het Nabije Oosten, 1999.

———. *The Neo-Babylonian Ebabbar Temple at Sippar: Its Administration and Its Prosopography.* Uitgaven Van Het Nederlands Historisch-Archaeologisch Instituut te Istanbul 80. Istanbul: Nederlands Historisch-Archaeologisch Instituut te Istanbul, 1997.

Bourguet, Émile. *L'administration Financiére Du Sanctuaire Pythique Au IVe Siécle Avant J.-C.* Paris: Fontemoing, 1905.

Bowman, Raymond A. *Aramaic Ritual Texts from Persepolis.* The University of Chicago Oriental Institute Publications 91. Chicago: University of Chicago Press, 1970.

Bresciani, Edda. "The Diaspora: Egypt, Persian Satrapy." Pages 358–71 in *Cambridge History of Judaism,* vol. 1: *Introduction, The Persian Period.* Edited by W. D. Davies and Louis Finkelstein. Cambridge: Cambridge University Press, 1984.

———. "Osservazioni Sul Sistema Tributario Dell' Egitto Durante la Dominazione Persiana." Pages 29–34 in *Le Tribut dans l'Empire Perse: Actes de la Table Ronde de Paris 12–13 Décembre 1986.* Edited by Pierre Briant and Clarisse Herrenschmidt. Travaux de l'Institut d'Études Iraniennes de l'Université de la Sorbonne Nouvelle 13. Paris-Louvain: Peeters, 1989.

Brettler, Marc Zvi. "The Many Faces of God in Exodus 19." Pages 353–67 in *Jews, Christians, and the Theology of the Hebrew Scriptures.* Edited by Alice Ogden Bellis and Joel S. Kaminsky. SBLSymS 8. Atlanta: SBL, 2000.

Briant, Pierre. "Social and Legal Institutions in Achaemenid Iran." Pages 517–28 in vol. 1 of *CANE.* 4 vols. Edited by Jack Sasson. New York: Charles Scribner's Sons, 1995.

———. "Table Du Roi, Tribut et Redistribution Chez les Achéménides." Pages 35–44 in *Le Tribut dans l'Empire Perse: Actes de la Table Ronde de Paris 12–13 Décembre 1986.* Edited by Pierre Briant and Clarisse Herrenschmidt. Travaux de l'Institut d'Études Iraniennes de l'Université de la Sorbonne Nouvelle 13. Paris-Louvain: Peeters, 1989.

Bright, John. *A History of Israel.* 4th ed. Louisville: Westminster John Knox, 2000.

Broshi, Magen. "The Role of the Temple in the Herodian Economy." *JJS* 38 (1987): 31–37.

Browne, Laurence E. "A Jewish Sanctuary in Babylonia." *JTS* 17 (1916): 400–01.

Buchholz, Todd C. "Biblical Laws and the Economic Growth of Ancient Israel." *Journal of Law and Religion* 6 (1988): 389–427.

Campbell, Edward F., Jr. "Jewish Shrines of the Hellenistic and Persian Periods." Pages 159–67 in *Symposia: Celebrating the Seventy-Fifth Anniversary of the Founding of the American Schools of Oriental Research (1900–1975).* Edited by Frank Moore Cross. Cambridge, Mass.: American Schools of Oriental Research, 1979.

Carroll, Robert P. "So What Do We *Know* About the Temple? The Temple in the Prophets." Pages 34–51 in *Second Temple Studies 2: Temple and Community in the Persian Period.* Edited by Tamara C. Eskenazi and Kent H. Richards. JSOTSup 175. Sheffield: Sheffield Academic Press, 1994.

————. "Textual Strategies and Ideology in the Second Temple Period." Pages 108–24 in *Second Temple Studies: 1. Persian Period.* Edited by Philip R. Davies. JSOTSup 117. Sheffield: Sheffield Academic Press, 1991.

Carter, Charles E. *The Emergence of Yehud in the Persian Period: A Social and Demographic Study.* JSOTSup 294. Sheffield: Sheffield Academic Press, 1999.

————. "The Province of Yehud in the Post-Exilic Period: Soundings in Site Distribution and Demography." Pages 106–45 in *Second Temple Studies 2: Temple and Community in the Persian Period.* Edited by Tamara C. Eskenazi and Kent H. Richards. JSOTSup 175. Sheffield: Sheffield Academic Press, 1994.

Chaney, Marvin L. "Debt Easement in Israelite History and Tradition." Pages 127–39 in *The Bible and the Politics of Exegesis: Essays in Honor of Norman K. Gottwald on His Sixty-Fifth Birthday.* Edited by David Jobling, Peggy L. Day, and Gerald T. Sheppard. Cleveland: Pilgrim, 1991.

Chirichigno, Gregory C. *Debt-Slavery in Israel and the Ancient Near East.* JSOTSup 141. Sheffield: Sheffield Academic Press, 1993.

Claburn, W. Eugene. "The Fiscal Basis of Josiah's Reforms." *JBL* 92 (1973): 11–22.

Claessen, Henri J. M. "Tribute and Taxation or How to Finance Early States and Empires." Pages 45–59 in *Le Tribut dans l'Empire Perse: Actes de la Table Ronde de Paris 12–13 Décembre 1986.* Edited by Pierre Briant and Clarisse Herrenschmidt. Travaux de l'Institut d'Études Iraniennes de l'Université de la Sorbonne Nouvelle 13. Paris and Louvain: Peeters, 1989.

Clarysse, W. "Egyptian Estate-Holders in the Ptolemaic Period." Pages 731–43 in *State and Temple Economy in the Ancient Near East.* Edited by Edward Lipinski. OLA 5. Leuven: Departement Orientalistiek, 1979.

Clay, Albert T. *Neo-Babylonian Letters from Erech.* YOS 3. New Haven: Yale University Press, 1919.

Clines, David J. A. "Haggai's Temple, Constructed, Deconstructed and Reconstructed." Pages 60–87 in *Second Temple Studies 2: Temple and Community in the Persian Period.* Edited by Tamara C. Eskenazi and Kent H. Richards. JSOTSup 175. Sheffield: Sheffield Academic Press, 1994.

Cocquerillat, Denise. *Palmeraies et Cultures de l'Eanna d'Uruk (559–520).* Ausgrabungen der Deutschen Forschungsgemeinschaft in Uruk-Warka 8. Berlin: Mann, 1968.

Cogan, Morton. *Imperialism and Religion: Assyria, Judah and Israel in the Eighth and Seventh Centuries B.C.E.* SBLMS 19. Missoula: Scholars Press, 1974.

Cohen, Edward E. *Athenian Economy and Society: A Banking Perspective.* Princeton: Princeton University Press, 1992.

Cole, Steven W. *Nippur IV: The Early Neo-Babylonian Governor's Archive from Nippur.* Chicago: University of Chicago Press, 1996.

Cole, Susan G. "Temples and Sanctuaries, Greco-Roman." Pages 380–82 in vol. 6 of the *Anchor Bible Dictionary.* Edited by David Noel Freedman. 6 vols. New York: Doubleday, 1992.

Coogan, Michael D. *West Semitic Personal Names in the Murašu Documents.* HSM 7. Missoula: Scholars Press, 1976.

Cook, J. M. *The Persian Empire.* London: Dent & Sons, 1983.

Cooke, G. A. *A Text-Book of North-Semitic Inscriptions.* Oxford: Clarendon, 1903.

Corsaro, Mauro. "Autonomia Cittadina e Fiscalità Regia: Le Città Greche d'Asia Nel Sistma Tributario Achemenide." Pages 61–75 in *Le Tribut dans l'Empire Perse: Actes de la Table Ronde de Paris 12–13 Décembre 1986.* Edited by Pierre Briant and Clarisse Herrenschmidt. Travaux de l'Institut d'Études Iraniennes de l'Université de la Sorbonne Nouvelle 13. Paris-Louvain: Peeters, 1989.

Cowley, A. *Aramaic Papyri of the Fifth Century B.C.* Oxford: Clarendon, 1923.

Creach, Jerome F. D. *Yahweh as Refuge and the Editing of the Hebrew Psalter.* JSOTSup 217. Sheffield: Sheffield Academic Press, 1996.

Cross, Frank Moore. *Canaanite Myth and Hebrew Epic: Essays in the History of the Religion of Israel.* Cambridge, Mass.: Harvard University Press, 1973.

———. "A Fragment of a Monumental Inscription from the City of David." *IEJ* 51 (2001): 44–47.

———. *From Epic to Canon: History and Literature in Ancient Israel.* Baltimore: Johns Hopkins University Press, 1998.

———. "A Reconstruction of the Judean Restoration." *JBL* 94 (1975): 4–18.

Dandamaev, Muhammed A. "Achaemenid Babylonia." Pages 296–311 in *Ancient Mesopotamia: Socio-Economic History.* Edited by I. M. Diakonoff. Moscow: Nauka, 1969.

———. "The Diaspora: Babylonia in the Persian Age." Pages 326–41 in *Cambridge History of Judaism,* vol. 1: *Introduction, The Persian Period.* Edited by W. D. Davies and Louis Finkelstein. Cambridge: Cambridge University Press, 1984.

———. *A Political History of the Achaemenid Empire.* Leiden: Brill, 1989.

———. "Slavery and the Structure of Society." Pages 152–77 in *The Culture and Social Institutions of Ancient Iran.* Edited by Muhammed A.

Dandamaev and V. G. Lukonin. Cambridge: Cambridge University Press, 1989.

———. "State and Temple in Babylonia in the First Millenium B.C." Pages 589–96 in *State and Temple Economy in the Ancient Near East.* Edited by Edward Lipinski. OLA 6. Leuven: Departement Orientalistiek, 1979.

Dandamaev, Muhammed A., and V. G. Lukonin. *The Culture and Social Institutions of Ancient Iran.* Cambridge: Cambridge University Press, 1989.

Davies, Philip R. "Sociology and the Second Temple." Pages 11–19 in *Second Temple Studies 1: Persian Period.* Edited by Philip R. Davies. JSOTSup 117. Sheffield: Sheffield Academic Press, 1991.

Davies, Philip R., ed. *Second Temple Studies: 1. Persian Period.* JSOTSup 117. Sheffield: Sheffield Academic Press, 1991.

Dearman, John A. *Property Rights in the Eighth-Century Prophets.* SBLDS 106. Atlanta: Scholars Press, 1988.

Delcor, M. "Le Trésor de la Maison de Yahweh Des Origines a l'Exil." *VT* 12 (1962): 353–77.

Descat, Raymond. "Notes sur la Politique Tributaire de Darius Ier." Pages 77–93 in *Le Tribut dans l'Empire Perse: Actes de la Table Ronde de Paris 12–13 Décembre 1986.* Edited by Pierre Briant and Clarisse Herrenschmidt. Travaux de l'Institut d'Études Iraniennes de l'Université de la Sorbonne Nouvelle 13. Paris-Louvain: Peeters, 1989.

Dever, William G. "Asherah, Consort of Yahweh? New Evidence from Kuntillet 'Ajrûd." *BASOR* 255 (1984): 21–37.

———. "Palaces and Temples in Canaan and Ancient Israel." Pages 605–14 in vol. 1 of *CANE.* Edited by Jack Sasson. 4 vols. New York: Scribner's, 1995.

———. "Temples and Sanctuaries, Syria-Palestine." In *ABD [CD Rom],* 1997.

Dougherty, Raymond P. "Cuneiform Parallels to Solomon's Provisioning System." *AASOR* 5 (1923–4): 23–65.

———. *Neo-Babylonian and Persian Periods.* Vol. 2 of *Archives from Erech.* New Haven: Yale University Press, 1933.

———. *Records from Erech: Time of Nabonidus (555–538 B.C.).* YOS 6. New York: AMS Press, 1920.

———. *The Shirkutu of Babylonian Deities.* New York: AMS Press, 1923.

———. *Time of Nebuchadrezzar and Nabonidus.* Vol. 1 of *Archives from Erech.* New Haven: Yale University Press, 1923.

Driel, G. van. "Capital Formation and Investment in an Institutional Context in Ancient Mesopotamia." Pages 25–42 in *Trade and Finance in Ancient Mesopotamia.* Edited by J. G. Dercksen. Leiden: Nederlands Instituut voor het Nabije Oosten, 1999.

Driver, G. R. *Aramaic Documents of the Fifth Century B.C.* Oxford: Clarendon, 1957.

Dubberstein, Waldo H. "The Chronology of Cyrus and Cambyses." *AJSL* 55 (1930): 417–19.

———. "Comparative Prices in Later Babylonia (625–400 B.C.)." *AJSL* 56 (1939): 20–43.

Edwards, George W. "Maladjustment of Palestinian Economy Under Herod." *JBR* 17 (1949): 116–19.

Elat, Moshe. "The Monarchy and the Development of Trade in Ancient Israel." Pages 527–46 in *State and Temple Economy in the Ancient Near East.* Edited by Edward Lipinski. OLA 5. Leuven: Departement Orientalistiek, 1979.

Elayi, Josette, and Jean Sapin. *Beyond the River: New Perspectives on Transeuphrate'ne.* JSOTSup 250. Sheffield: Sheffield Academic Press, 1998.

Ellis, Maria DeJong. *Agriculture and the State in Ancient Mesopotamia: An Introduction to the Problems of Land Tenure.* Philadelphia: Occasional Publications of the Babylonian Fund, 1976.

———. "Taxation in Ancient Mesopotamia: The History of the Term Miksu." *JCS* 26 (1974): 211–50.

Elon, Menachem. "Taxation." Pages 837–73 in vol. 15 of *Encyclopaedia Judaica.* Jerusalem: Keter, 1972.

Epstein, I., trans. *The Babylonian Talmud: Seder Mo'ed.* London: Soncino, 1938.

Eskenazi, Tamara C., and Kent H. Richards, eds. *Second Temple Studies: 2. Temple and Community in the Persian Period.* JSOTSup 175. Sheffield: Sheffield Academic Press, 1994.

Fager, Jeffrey A. *Land Tenure and the Biblical Jubilee: Uncovering Hebrew Ethics through the Sociology of Knowledge.* JSOTSup 155. Sheffield: Sheffield Academic Press, 1993.

Falkenstein, Adam. *The Sumerian Temple City.* Los Angeles: Undena Publications, 1974.

Farmer, William R. "Economic Basis of the Qumran Community." *TZ* 11 (1955): 295–308.

Fennely, James M. "The Persepolis Ritual." *BA* 43 (1980): 135–62.

Filson, Floyd V. "Temple, Synagogue, and Church." *BA* 7 (1944): 77–88.

Finley, M. I. *The Ancient Economy.* 2d ed. Berkeley: University of California Press, 1985.

Fleming, Daniel E. "Mari's Large Public Tent and the Priestly Tent Sanctuary," *VT* 50 (2000): 484–98.

Fox, Michael V., ed. *Temple in Society.* Winona Lake, Ind.: Eisenbrauns, 1988.

Frame, Grant. "Neo-Babylonian and Achaemenid Economic Texts from the Sippar Collection of the British Museum." *JAOS* 104 (1984): 745–52.

Frey, Jörg. "Temple and Rival Temple—The Cases of Elephantine, Mt. Gerizim, and Leontopolis." Pages 171–203 in *Gemeinde Ohne Tempel; Community Without Temple.* Edited by Beate Ego, Armin Lange and Peter Pilhofer. WUNT 118. Tübingen: Mohr Siebeck, 1999.

Frymer-Kensky, Tikva. "Israel." Pages 251–63 in *Security for Debt in Ancient Near Eastern Law.* Edited by Raymond Westbrook and Richard Jasnow. Leiden: Brill, 2001.

Galán, José M. "The Ancient Egyptian *Sed* Festival and the Exemption from Corvée." *JNES* 59 (2000): 255–64.

Garnsey, Peter, Keith Hopkins, and C. R. Whittaker. *Trade in the Ancient Economy.* Berkeley: University of California Press, 1983.

Gelb, Ignace J. "The Ancient Mesopotamian Ration System." *JNES* 24 (1965): 230–43.

———. "On the Alleged Temple and State Economics in Ancient Mesopotamia." Pages 137–54 in *Studi in Onore Di E. Volterra, 6.* Edited by J. Schacht et al. Milan: Giuffrè, 1969.

Gelston, A. "The Foundations of the Second Temple." *VT* 16 (1966): 232–35.

Ginzberg, Eli. "Studies in the Economics of the Bible." *JQR* 22 (1932): 343–47.

Giovinazzo, Grazia. "The Tithe Eshrû in Neo-Babylonian and Achaemenid Period." Pages 95–106 in *Le Tribut dans l'Empire Perse: Actes de la Table Ronde de Paris 12–13 Décembre 1986.* Edited by Pierre Briant and Clarisse Herrenschmidt. Travaux de l'Institut d'Études Iraniennes de l'Université de la Sorbonne Nouvelle 13. Paris and Louvain: Peeters, 1989.

Glotz, Gustave. *The Aegean Civilization.* Translated by M. R. Dovie and E. M. Riley. New York: Knopf, 1925.

Gottwald, Norman K. *The Hebrew Bible in Its Social World and in Ours.* Atlanta: Scholars Press, 1993.

Grabbe, Lester L. *Judaism from Cyrus to Hadrian: Sources, History, Synthesis.* Minneapolis: Fortress, 1991.

———. "Reconstructing History from the Book of Ezra." Pages 98–106 in *Second Temple Studies: 1. Persian Period.* Edited by Philip R. Davies. JSOTSup 117. Sheffield: Sheffield Academic Press, 1991.

———. "Sup-Urbs or Only Hyp-Urbs? Prophets and Populations in Ancient Israel and Socio-Historical Method." Pages 95–123 in *"Every City Shall Be Forsaken": Urbanism and Prophecy in Ancient Israel and the Near East.* Edited by Lester L. Grabbe and Robert D. Haak. JSOTSup 330. Sheffield: Sheffield Academic Press, 2001.

————. "What Was Ezra's Mission?" Pages 286–99 in *Second Temple Studies: 2. Temple and Community in the Persian Period.* Edited by Tamara C. Eskenazi and Kent H. Richards. JSOTSup 175. Sheffield: Sheffield Academic Press, 1994.

Grant, Michael, and Rachael Kitzinger, eds. *Civilization of the Ancient Mediterranean: Greece and Rome.* 3 Vols. New York: Scribner's, 1988.

Grayson, A. K. *Assyrian and Babylonian Chronicles.* Locust Valley, N.Y.: Augustin, 1975.

Grintz, Yehoshua M., Bezalel Porten, and Shmuel Safrai. "Temple." Pages 942–84 in vol. 15 of *Encyclopaedia Judaica.* Jerusalem: Keter, 1972.

Gruber, Mayer I. "Private Life in Ancient Israel." Pages 633–48 in vol. 1 of *CANE.* Edited by Jack Sasson. 4 vols. New York: Scribner's, 1995.

Halligan, John M. "Nehemiah 5: By Way of Response to Hoglund and Smith." Pages 146–53 in *Second Temple Studies: 1. Persian Period.* Edited by Philip R. Davies. JSOTSup 117. Sheffield: Sheffield Academic Press, 1991.

Hallock, R. *Persepolis Fortification Tablets.* OIP 92. Chicago: University of Chicago Press, 1969.

Haney, Lewis H. *History of Economic Thought.* New York: Macmillan, 1949.

Haran, Menahem. *Temples and Temple Service in Ancient Israel.* Oxford: Clarendon, 1985.

Harris, Rivkah. "Old Babylonian Temple Loans." *JCS* 14 (1960): 126–37.

Heichelheim, Fritz M. *An Ancient Economic History.* Leiden: Sijthoff's, 1958.

Heltzer, Michael. "On Tithe Paid in Grain in Ugarit." *IEJ* 25 (1975): 124–28.

————. "Some Questions Concerning the Economic Policies of Josiah, King of Judah." *IEJ* 50 (2000): 105–8.

Herman, Menahem. *Tithe as Gift: The Institution in the Pentateuch and in Light of Mauss's Prestation Theory.* San Francisco: Mellen Research University Press, 1991.

Herodotus. *Histories.* LCL. Translated by A. D. Godley. Cambridge: Harvard University Press, 1938.

Herrenschmidt, Clarisse. "Le Tribut dans les Inscriptions en Vieux-Perse et dans les Tablettes Élamites." Pages 107–20 in *Le Tribut dans l'Empire Perse: Actes de la Table Ronde de Paris 12–13 Décembre 1986.* Edited by Pierre Briant and Clarisse Herrenschmidt. Travaux de l'Institut d'Études Iraniennes de l'Université de la Sorbonne Nouvelle 13. Paris and Louvain: Peeters, 1989.

Hoglund, Kenneth G. "The Achaemenid Context." Pages 54–72 in *Second Temple Studies: 1. Persian Period.* Edited by Philip R. Davies, 54–72. JSOTSup 117. Sheffield: Sheffield Academic Press, 1991.

———. *Achaemenid Imperial Administration in Syria-Palestine and the Missions of Ezra and Nehemiah*. SBLDS 125. Atlanta: Scholars Press, 1992.

Holladay, John S., Jr. "The Kingdoms of Israel and Judah: Political and Economic Centralization in the Iron IIA-B (Ca. 1000–750 BCE)." Pages 368–98 in *The Archaeology of Society in the Holy Land*. Edited by Thomas E. Levy. New York: Facts on File, 1995.

———. "Religion in Israel and Judah Under the Monarchy: An Explicitly Archaeological Approach." Pages 249–99 in *Ancient Israelite Religion: Essays in Honor of Frank Moore Cross*. Edited by Patrick D. Miller, Paul D. Hanson, and S. Dean McBride Jr. Philadelphia: Fortress, 1987.

Holland, Thomas A. "A Study of Palestinian Iron Age Baked Clay Figurines, with Special Reference to Jerusalem: Cave 1." *Levant* 9 (1977): 121–55.

Homer, Sidney, and Richard Sylla. *A History of Interest Rates*. 3d ed. New Brunswick: Rutgers University Press, 1996.

Hopkins, Keith. "Taxes and Trade in the Roman Empire (200 B.C.–A.D. 400)." *JRS* 70 (1980): 101–25.

Horsley, Richard. "Empire, Temple and Community—but No Bourgeoisie!" Pages 163–74 in *Second Temple Studies: 1. Persian Period*. Edited by Philip R. Davies. JSOTSup 117. Sheffield: Sheffield Academic Press, 1991.

Huehnergard, John. *A Grammar of Akkadian*. HSS 45. Atlanta: Scholars Press, 1997.

Hurowitz, Victor A. "Another Fiscal Practice in the Ancient Near East: 2 Kings 12:5–17 and a Letter to Esarhaddon (LAS 277)." *JNES* 45 (1986): 289–94.

Isaac, Benjamin. "A Donation for Herod's Temple in Jerusalem." *IEJ* 33 (1983): 86–92.

Jakobson, V. A. "The Social Structure of the Neo-Assyrian Empire." Pages 277–95 in *Ancient Mesopotamia: Socio-Economic History*. Edited by I. M. Diakonoff. Moscow: Nauka, 1969.

Jankowska, N. B. "Some Problems of the Economy of the Assyrian Empire." Pages 235–76 in *Ancient Mesopotamia: Socio-Economic History*. Edited by I. M. Diakonoff. Moscow: Nauka, 1969.

Janssen, Jac J. "The Role of the Temple in the Egyptian Economy during the New Kingdom." Pages 505–15 in *State and Temple Economy in the Ancient Near East*. Edited by Edward Lipinski. OLA 6. Leuven: Departement Orientalistiek, 1979.

Janzen, David. "The 'Mission' of Ezra and the Persian-Period Temple Community." *JBL* 119 (2000): 619–43.

———. "Politics, Settlement, and Temple Community in Persian-Period Yehud." *CBQ* 64 (2002): 490–510.

Japhet, Sara. *I & II Chronicles*. OTL. Louisville: Westminster John Knox, 1993.

―――. "Composition and Chronology in the Book of Ezra-Nehemiah." Pages 189–216 in *Second Temple Studies 2: Temple and Community in the Persian Period*. Edited by Tamara C. Eskenazi and Kent H. Richards. JSOTSup 175. Sheffield: Sheffield Academic Press, 1994.

―――. "Sheshbazzar and Zerubbabel—Against the Background of the Historical and Religious Tendencies of Ezra-Nehemiah (I)." *ZAW* 94 (1982): 66–98.

―――. "Sheshbazzar and Zerubbabel—Against the Background of the Historical and Religious Tendencies of Ezra-Nehemiah (II)." *ZAW* 95 (1983): 218–30.

―――. "The Temple in the Restoration Period: Reality and Ideology." *USQR* 44 (1991): 195–251.

Jasnow, Richard. "Pre-Demotic Pharaonic Sources." Pages 35–45 in *Security for Debt in Ancient Near Eastern Law*. Edited by Raymond Westbrook and Richard Jasnow. Leiden: Brill, 2001.

Joannès, Francis. "Private Commerce and Banking in Achaemenid Babylon." Pages 1475–85 in vol. 3 of *CANE*. Edited by Jack Sasson. 4 vols. New York: Scribner's, 1995.

―――. *Textes Economiques de la Babylonie Recente*. Paris: Editions A. D. P. F., 1982.

Josephus. *Jewish Antiquities*. LCL. Translated by Ralph Marcus. Cambridge: Harvard University Press, 1938.

―――. *Jewish War*. LCL. Translated by H. St. J. Thackeray. Cambridge: Harvard University Press, 1938.

Kapelrud, Arvid S. *Central Ideas in Amos*. Oslo: Oslo University Press, 1961.

Kautzsch, E. *Gesenius' Hebrew Grammar*. 2d ed. Translated by A. E. Cowley. Oxford: Clarendon, 1910.

Keel, Othmar, and Christoph Uehlinger. *Gods, Goddesses, and Images of God in Ancient Israel*. Translated by Thomas H. Trapp. Minneapolis: Fortress, 1998.

Keiser, Clarence E. *Letters and Contracts from Erech Written in the Neo-Babylonian Period*. Babylonian Inscriptions in the Collection of James B. Nies 1. New Haven: Yale University Press, 1917.

Kemp, Barry J. "Temple and Town in Ancient Egypt." Pages 657–80 in *Man, Settlement and Urbanism*. Edited by Peter J. Ucko, Ruth Tringham, and G. W. Dimbleby. Cambridge, Mass.: Schenkman, 1972.

Kent, John Harvey. "The Temple Estates of Delos, Rheneia and Mykonos." *Hesperia* 17 (1948).

Kessler, John. "Reconstructing Haggai's Jerusalem: Demographic and Socio-logical Considerations and the Search for an Adequate Methodological Point of Departure." Pages 137–58 in *"Every City Shall Be Forsaken": Urbanism and Prophecy in Ancient Israel and the Near East.* Edited by Lester L. Grabbe and Robert D. Haak. JSOTSup 330. Sheffield: Sheffield Academic Press, 2001.

Kletter, Raz. *Economic Keystones: The Weight System of the Kingdom of Judah.* JSOTSup 276. Sheffield: Sheffield Academic Press, 1998.

Kraeling, Emil G. *The Brooklyn Museum Aramaic Papyri: New Documents of the Fifth Century B.C. from the Jewish Colony at Elephantine.* New Haven: Yale University Press, 1953.

Kuhrt, Amélie. "Babylonia from Cyrus to Xerxes." Pages 112–38 in *Cambridge Ancient History,* vol. 4: *Persia, Greece and the Western Mediterranean, c.525 to 479 BC.* 2d ed. Edited by John Boardman, N. G. L. Hammond, D. M. Lewis, and M. Ostwald. Cambridge: Cambridge University Press, 1988.

———. "Conclusions." Pages 217–22 in *Le Tribut dans l'Empire Perse: Actes de la Table Ronde de Paris 12–13 Décembre 1986.* Edited by Pierre Briant and Clarisse Herrenschmidt. Travaux de l'Institut d'Études Iraniennes de l'Université de la Sorbonne Nouvelle 13. Paris and Louvain: Peeters, 1989.

———. "The Cyrus Cylinder and Achaemenid Imperial Policy." *JSOT* 25 (1983): 83–97.

———. "Nabonidus and the Babylonian Priesthood." Pages 119–55 in *Pagan Priests.* Edited by Mary Beard and John North. Ithaca: Cornell University Press, 1990.

———. "Usurpation, Conquest and Ceremonial: From Babylon to Persia." Pages 20–55 in *Rituals of Royalty: Power and Ceremonial in Traditional Societies.* Edited by David Cannadine and Simon Price. Cambridge: Cambridge University Press, 1987.

Kuhrt, Amélie, and S. White. "Xerxes' Destruction of Babylonian Temples." Pages 69–78 in *The Greek Sources.* Vol. 2 of *Achaemenid History.* Edited by Amélie Kuhrt and Heleen Sancisi-Weerdenburg. Leiden: Nederlands Instituut voor het Nabije Oosten, 1987.

Lambert, Wilfred G. *Babylonian Wisdom Literature.* Oxford: Clarendon, 1960.

Lemche, Niels Peter. "The History of Ancient Syria and Palestine: An Overview." Pages 1195–1218 in vol. 2 of *CANE.* 4 vols. Edited by Jack Sasson. New York: Charles Scribner's Sons, 1995. Repr., 4 volumes in 2; Peabody, Mass.: Hendrickson, 2000.

Levy, Jean-Philippe. *The Economic Life of the Ancient World.* Translated by John G. Biram. Chicago: University of Chicago Press, 1967.

Lipinski, Edward. "Les Temples Neo-Assyriens et les Origines Du Monnayage." Pages 565–88 in *State and Temple Economy in the Ancient Near East.* Edited by Edward Lipinski. OLA 6. Leuven: Departement Orientalistiek, 1979.

Lundquist, John M. "The Legitimizing Role of the Temple in the Origin of the State." Pages 271–97 in the *SBL Seminar Papers, 1982.* Society of Biblical Literature Seminar Papers 21. Chico, Calif.: Scholars Press, 1982.

———. "What is a Temple? A Preliminary Typology." Pages 205–19 in *The Quest for the Kingdom of God: Studies in Honor of George E. Mendenhall.* Edited by H. B. Huffmon, F. A. Spina, and A. R. W. Green. Winona Lake, Ind.: Eisenbrauns, 1982.

Lutz, Henry L. F. "A Neo-Babylonian Debenture." *University of California Publications in Semitic Philology* 10/9 (1940): 251–56.

———. "A Recorded Deposition Concerning Presentment for Tax Payment." *University of California Publications in Semitic Philology* 10/10 (1940): 257–64.

———. "An Uruk Document of the Time of Cambyses." *University of California Publications in Semitic Philology* 10/8 (1937): 243–50.

MacGinnis, John D. A. *Letters and Orders from Sippar and the Administration of the Ebabbara in the Late Babylonian Period.* Grudnia, Poland: Bonami, 1995.

Manning, Joseph. "Demotic Papyri (664–30 BCE)." Pages 307–26 in *Security for Debt in Ancient Near Eastern Law.* Edited by Raymond Westbrook and Richard Jasnow. Leiden: Brill, 2001.

Margalith, Othniel. "The Political Role of Ezra as Persian Governor." *ZAW* 98 (1986): 110–12.

Marinkovic, Peter. "What Does Zechariah 1–8 Tell Us about the Second Temple?" Pages 88–103 in *Second Temple Studies 2: Temple and Community in the Persian Period.* Edited by Tamara C. Eskenazi and Kent H. Richards. JSOTSup 175. Sheffield: Sheffield Academic Press, 1994.

McBride, S. Dean, Jr. "The Deuteronomic Name Theology." Ph.D. diss. Harvard University, 1969.

McEvenue, Sean E. "The Political Structure of Judah from Cyrus to Nehemiah." *CBQ* 43 (1981): 353–64.

McEwan, Gilbert J. P. *Priest and Temple in Hellenistic Babylonia.* Wiesbaden: Steiner, 1981.

Meigs, Walter B. et al. *Intermediate Accounting.* 2d ed. New York: McGraw-Hill, 1968.

Mendelsohn, I. "Guilds in Ancient Palestine." *BASOR* 80 (1940): 17–21.

———. "Guilds in Babylon and Assyria." *JAOS* 60 (1940): 68–72.

Menzel, Brigitte. *Assyrische Tempel.* 2 vols. Studia Pohl: Series Maior 10/1. Rome: Biblical Institute, 1981.

Mettinger, Tryggve N. D. *The Dethronement of Sabaoth: Studies in the Shem and Kabod Theologies.* ConBOT 18. Lund: Gleerup, 1982.

———. "Israelite Aniconism: Developments and Origins." Pages 173–204 in *The Image and The Book.* Edited by Karel van der Toorn. Leuven: Peeters, 1997.

———. *No Graven Image? Israelite Aniconism in Its Ancient Near Eastern Context.* ConBOT 42. Stockholm: Almqvist & Wiksell, 1995.

Meyers, Carol L. "Temple, Jerusalem." Pages 350–69 in vol. 6 of *Anchor Bible Dictionary.* Edited by David Noel Freedman. New York: Doubleday, 1992.

Meyers, Carol L., and Eric M. Meyers. *Haggai-Zechariah 1–8.* AB 25B. Garden City, N.Y.: Doubleday, 1987.

Meyers, Eric M., ed. *The Oxford Encyclopedia of Archaeology in the Near East.* 5 vols. Oxford: Oxford University Press, 1997.

Milgrom, Jacob. *Studies in Levitical Terminology I: The Encroacher and the Levite, the Term 'Aboda.* University of California Publications Near Eastern Studies 14. Berkeley: University of California Press, 1970.

Miller, J. Maxwell, and John H. Hayes. *A History of Ancient Israel and Judah.* Philadelphia: Westminster, 1986.

Miller, Patrick D. *The Religion of Ancient Israel.* Louisville: Westminster John Knox, 2000.

Miller, Patrick D., Paul D. Hanson, and S. Dean McBride Jr. *Ancient Israelite Religion: Essays in Honor of Frank Moore Cross.* Philadelphia: Fortress, 1987.

Moore, Ellen W. *Neo-Babylonian Business and Administrative Documents.* Ann Arbor: University of Michigan Press, 1935.

———. *Neo-Babylonian Documents in the University of Michigan Collection.* Ann Arbor: University of Michigan Press, 1939.

Morgenstern, Julian. "Jerusalem—486 BC." *HUCA* 27 (1956): 101–79; 28 (1957): 15–47; (1960) 1–29.

Myers, Jacob M. *I & II Chronicles.* AB. Garden City, N.Y.: Doubleday, 1965.

———. *Ezra, Nehemiah.* AB. Garden City, N.Y.: Doubleday, 1965.

Na'aman, Nadav. "No Anthropomorphic Graven Image: Notes on the Assumed Anthropomorphic Cult Statues in the Temples of YHWH in the Pre-Exilic Period." *UF* 31 (1999): 391–415.

Nelson, Harold H. "The Egyptian Temple." *BA* 7 (1944): 44–53.

Neumann, Hans. "Ur-Dumuzida and Ur-DUN: Reflections on the Relationship Between State-Initiated Foreign Trade and Private Economic Activity in Mesopotamia Towards the End of the Third Millennium BC." Pages 43–53 in *Trade and Finance in Ancient Mesopotamia*. Edited by J. G. Dercksen. Leiden: Nederlands Instituut voor het Nabije Oosten, 1999.

Nissen, Hans J., Peter Damerow, and Robert K. Englund. *Archaic Bookkeeping: Early Writing and Techniques of Economic Administration in the Ancient Near East*. Translated by Paul Larsen. Chicago: The University of Chicago Press, 1993.

Nissinen, Martti. "City as Lofty as Heaven: Arbela and Other Cities in Neo-Assyrian Prophecy." Pages 172–209 in *"Every City Shall Be Forsaken": Urbanism and Prophecy in Ancient Israel and the Near East*. Edited by Lester L. Grabbe and Robert D. Haak. JSOTSup 330. Sheffield: Sheffield Academic Press, 2001.

North, Douglass C. *Structure and Change in Economic History*. New York: Norton, 1981.

North, Robert. *Sociology of the Biblical Jubilee*. AnBib 4. Rome: Pontifical Biblical Institute, 1954.

O'Connor, David. "The Social and Economic Organization of Ancient Egyptian Temples." Pages 319–29 in vol. 1 of *CANE*. Edited by Jack Sasson. 4 vols. New York: Scribner's, 1995.

Oded, Bustenay. *Mass Deportations and Deportees in the Neo-Assyrian Empire*. Wiesbaden: Harrassowitz, 1979.

Olmstead, A. T. *History of the Persian Empire*. Chicago: Chicago University Press, 1948.

Oppenheim, A. Leo. *Ancient Mesopotamia: Portrait of a Dead Civilization*. Chicago: University of Chicago Press, 1964.

————. "A Bird's Eye View of Mesopotamian Economic History." Pages 27–37 in *Trade and Markets in the Early Empires*. Edited by Karl Polányi, Conrad M. Arensberg, and Harry W. Pearson. Glencoe, N.Y.: Free Press, 1957.

————. "A Fiscal Practice of the Ancient Near East." *JNES* 6 (1947): 116–20.

————. *Letters from Mesopotamia: Official Business and Private Letters on Clay Tablets from Two Millennia*. Chicago: University of Chicago Press, 1967.

————. "The Mesopotamian Temple." *BA* 7 (1944): 54–63.

————. "On an Operational Device in Mesopotamian Bureaucracy." *JNES* 18 (1959): 121–28.

Paul, Shalom M. *Amos*. Hermeneia. Minneapolis: Fortress, 1991.

Pearce, Laurie E. "The Scribes and Scholars of Ancient Mesopotamia." Pages 2265–78 in vol. 4 of *CANE*. Edited by Jack Sasson. 4 vols. New York: Scribner's, 1995.

Perry, Kenneth W. *Accounting: An Introduction.* New York: McGraw-Hill, 1971.

Petersen, David L. *Haggai and Zechariah 1–8: A Commentary.* OTL. Philadelphia: Westminster, 1984.

———. *Late Israelite Prophecy: Studies in Deutero-Prophetic Literature and in Chronicles.* SBLMS 23. Missoula: Scholars Press, 1977.

———. "The Temple in Persian Period Prophetic Texts." Pages 125–45 in *Second Temple Studies: 1. Persian Period.* Edited by Philip R. Davies. JSOTSup 117. Sheffield: Sheffield Academic Press, 1991.

———. "Zerubbabel and Jerusalem Temple Reconstruction." *CBQ* 36 (1974): 366–72.

Philo. *On the Special Laws.* LCL. Translated by F. H. Colson. Cambridge: Harvard University Press, 1938.

Polányi, Karl. "The Economy as Instituted Process." Pages 243–70 in *Trade and Markets in the Early Empires.* Edited by Karl Polányi, Conrad M. Arensberg, and Harry W. Pearson. Glencoe, N.Y.: Free Press, 1957.

Porten, Bezalel. *Archives from Elephantine: The Life of an Ancient Jewish Military Colony.* Berkeley: University of California Press, 1968.

———. "The Diaspora: The Jews in Egypt." Pages 372–400 in *Cambridge History of Judaism,* vol. 1: *Introduction, The Persian Period.* Edited by W. D. Davies and Louis Finkelstein. Cambridge: Cambridge University Press, 1984.

———. *Jews of Elephantine and Arameans of Syene (Fifth Century B.C.E.): Fifty Aramaic Texts.* Jerusalem: Hebrew University, 1976.

Porten, Bezalel, and Ada Yardeni. *Textbook of Aramaic Documents from Ancient Egypt.* 4 vols. Jerusalem: Hebrew University, 1986.

Postgate, J. N. "The Economic Structure of the Assyrian Empire." Pages 193–221 in *Power and Propoganda: A Symposium on Ancient Empires.* Edited by Mogens Trolle Larsen. Copenhagen Studies in Assyriology: Mesopotamia 7. Copenhagen: Akademisk Forlag, 1979.

———. "Review of *Assyrische Tempel* by Brigitte Menzel." *JSS* 28 (1983): 155–59.

———. "The Role of the Temple in the Mesopotamian Secular Community." Pages 811–25 in *Man, Settlement and Urbanism.* Edited by Peter J. Ucko, Ruth Tringham, and G. W. Dimbleby. Cambridge, Mass.: Schenkman, 1972.

———. *Taxation and Conscription in the Assyrian Empire.* Rome: Biblical Institute, 1974.

Powell, Marvin A. "Wir Müssen Unsere Nische Nutzen: Monies, Motives, and Methods." Pages 5–23 in *Trade and Finance in Ancient Mesopotamia*. Edited by J. G. Dercksen. Leiden: Nederlands Instituut voor het Nabije Oosten, 1999.

Quaegebeur, Jan. "Role Economique Du Clerge en Egypte Hellenistique." Pages 707–29 in *State and Temple Economy in the Ancient Near East*. Edited by Edward Lipinski. OLA 6. Leuven: Departement Orientalistiek, 1979.

Rabinowitz, Isaac. "Aramaic Inscriptions of the Fifth Century B.C.E. from a North-Arab Shrine in Egypt." *JNES* 15 (1956): 1–9.

Rauh, Nicholas K. *The Sacred Bonds of Commerce: Religion, Economy, and Trade Society at Hellenistic Roman Delos, 166–87 B.C.* Amsterdam: Gieben, 1993.

Reger, Gary. *Regionalism and Change in the Economy of Independent Delos, 314–167 B.C.* Berkeley: University of California Press, 1994.

Renger, Johannes. "Interaction of Temple, Palace, and 'Private Enterprise' in the Old Babylonian Economy." Pages 249–56 in *State and Temple Economy in the Ancient Near East*. Edited by Edward Lipinski. OLA 5. Leuven: Departement Orientalistiek, 1979.

———. "Notes on the Goldsmiths, Jewelers and Carpenters of Neobabylonian Eanna." *JAOS* 91 (1971): 494–503.

Robertson, John F. "On Profit-Seeking, Market Orientations, and Mentality in the 'Ancient Near East'." *JAOS* 113 (1993): 437–43.

———. "The Social and Economic Organization of Ancient Mesopotamian Temples." Pages 443–54 in vol. 1 of *CANE*. Edited by Jack Sasson. 4 vols. New York: Scribner's, 1995.

———. "Temples and Sanctuaries, Mesopotamia." Pages 372–76 in vol. 6 of *Anchor Bible Dictionary*. Edited by David Noel Freedman. New York: Doubleday, 1992.

Rostovtzeff, M. *The Social and Economic History of the Hellenistic World*. Oxford: Oxford University Press, 1941.

Roth, Martha T. *Law Collections from Mesopotamia and Asia Minor*. 2d ed. SBLWAW 6. Atlanta: Scholars Press, 1997.

Ryan, John A. *Economic Justice*. Library of Theological Ethics. Louisville: Westminster John Knox, 1996.

Sack, Ronald H. *Cuneiform Documents from the Chaldean and Persian Periods*. London and Toronto: Associated University Presses, 1994.

———. "Review of *Textes Economiques de la Babylonie Recente* by Francis Joannès." *JNES* 45 (1986): 81–82.

Sancisi-Weerdenburg, Heleen. "Gifts in the Persian Empire." Pages 129–46 in *Le Tribut dans l'Empire Perse: Actes de la Table Ronde de Paris 12–13*

Décembre 1986. Edited by Pierre Briant and Clarisse Herrenschmidt. Travaux de l'Institut d'Études Iraniennes de l'Université de la Sorbonne Nouvelle 13. Paris and Louvain: Peeters, 1989.

Sass, Benjamin, and Christoph Uehlinger, eds. *Studies in the Iconography of Northwest Semitic Inscribed Seals: Proceedings of a Symposium Held in Fribourg on April 17–20, 1991.* OBO 125. Fribourg: University Press, 1993.

Schaper, Joachim. "The Jerusalem Temple as an Instrument of the Achaemenid Fiscal Administration." *VT* 45 (1995): 528–39.

———. "The Temple Treasury Committee in the Times of Nehemiah and Ezra." *VT* 47 (1997): 200–6.

Schmandt-Besserat, Denise. "Record Keeping Before Writing." Pages 2097–106 in vol. 4 of *CANE.* Edited by Jack Sasson. 4 vols. New York: Scribner's, 1995.

Schmidt, E. F. *The Treasury of Persepolis.* Chicago: University of Chicago, 1939.

Shanks, Herschel. "Three Shekels for the Lord: Ancient Inscription Records Gift to Solomon's Temple." *BAR* 23/6 (1997): 28–32.

Silver, Morris. *Economic Structures of the Ancient Near East.* Beckenham, England: Croom Helm, 1985.

———. "Karl Polányi and Markets in the Ancient Near East: The Challenge of the Evidence." *Journal of Economic History* 43 (1983): 795–829.

———. *Prophets and Markets: The Political Economy of Ancient Israel.* Boston: Kluwer-Nijhoff, 1983.

Smelser, Neil J. *The Sociology of Economic Life.* Englewood Cliffs, N.J.: Prentice-Hall, 1976.

Smith, Daniel L. "The Politics of Ezra: Sociological Indicators of Postexilic Judaean Society." Pages 73–97 in *Second Temple Studies: 1. Persian Period.* Edited by Philip R. Davies. JSOTSup 117. Sheffield: Sheffield Academic Press, 1991.

Smith, Morton. "Jewish Religious Life in the Persian Period." Pages 219–78 in *Cambridge History of Judaism,* vol. 1: *Introduction, The Persian Period.* Edited by W. D. Davies and Louis Finkelstein. Cambridge: Cambridge University Press, 1984.

Smith, Sidney. *Babylonian Historical Texts Relating to the Capture and Downfall of Babylon.* London: Meuthen, 1924.

Snell, Daniel C. "Ancient Israelite and Neo-Assyrian Societies and Economies: A Comparative Approach." Pages 221–24 in *The Tablet and the Scroll: Near Eastern Studies in Honor of William W. Hallo.* Edited by Mark E. Cohen, Daniel C. Snell, and David B. Weisberg. Bethesda, Md.: CDL Press, 1993.

————. "Methods of Exchange and Coinage in Ancient Western Asia." Pages 1487–97 in vol. 3 of *CANE*. Edited by Jack Sasson. 4 vols. New York: Scribner's, 1995.

Sollberger, Edmond. "The Temple in Babylonia." Pages 31–34 in *Le Temple et le Culte*. Uitgaven Van Het Nederlands Historisch-Archaeologisch Instituut te Istanbul 37. Leiden: Nederlands Historisch-Archaeologisch Instituut te Istambul, 1975.

Sperber, Daniel. "Tax Gatherers." Pages 873–74 in vol. 15 of *Encyclopaedia Judaica*. Jerusalem: Keter, 1972.

Spiro, S. J. "Who Was the Haber? A New Approach to an Ancient Institution." *JSJ* 11 (1980): 186–216.

Stager, Lawrence E., and Samuel Wolff. "Production and Commerce in Temple Courtyards: An Olive Press in the Sacred Precinct at Tel Dan." *BASOR* 243 (1981): 95–102.

Starr, Chester G. *The Economic and Social Growth of Early Greece, 800–500 B.C.* New York: Oxford University Press, 1977.

Stern, Ephraim. "The Archaeology of Persian Palestine." Pages 88–114 in *Cambridge History of Judaism*, vol. 1: *Introduction, The Persian Period*. Edited by W. D. Davies and Louis Finkelstein. Cambridge: Cambridge University Press, 1984.

————. *Material Culture of the Land of the Bible in the Persian Period 538–332 BC*. Warminster: Aris & Phillips, 1982.

————. "The Persian Empire and the Political and Social History of Palestine in the Persian Period." Pages 70–87 in *Cambridge History of Judaism*, vol. 1: *Introduction, The Persian Period*. Edited by W. D. Davies and Louis Finkelstein. Cambridge: Cambridge University Press, 1984.

Stolper, Matthew W. *Entrepreneurs and Empire: The Murašu Archive, the Murašu Firm and Persian Rule in Babylon*. Istanbul: Nederlands Historisch-Archaeologisch Instituut te Istanbul, 1985.

————. "On Interpreting Tributary Relationships in Achaemenid Babylonia." Pages 147–56 in *Le Tribut dans l'Empire Perse: Actes de la Table Ronde de Paris 12–13 Décembre 1986*. Edited by Pierre Briant and Clarisse Herrenschmidt. Travaux de l'Institut d'Études Iraniennes de l'Université de la Sorbonne Nouvelle 13. Paris-Louvain: Peeters, 1989.

————. *Late Achaemenid, Early Macedonian and Early Seleucid Records of Deposit and Related Texts*. Supplemento Agli Annali 77. Naples: Istituto Universitario Orientale, 1993.

————. "Mesopotamia, 482–330 B.C." Pages 234–60 in *Cambridge Ancient History*, vol. 6: *The Fourth Century B.C.* 2d ed. Edited by D. M. Lewis, John Boardman, Simon Hornblower, and M. Ostwald. Cambridge: Cambridge University Press, 1994.

Strabo. *Geography.* LCL. Translated by Horace L. Jones. Cambridge, Mass.: Harvard University Press, 1938.

Sweeney, Marvin A. "Reconceiving the Paradigms of Old Testament Theology in the Post-Shoah Period." Pages 155–72 in *Jews, Christians, and the Theology of the Hebrew Scriptures.* Edited by Alice Ogden Bellis and Joel S. Kaminsky. SBLSymS 8. Atlanta: Society of Biblical Literature, 2000.

Tod, Marcus N. *A Selection of Greek Historical Inscriptions to the End of the Fifth Century B.C.* Oxford: Clarendon, 1933.

Torrey, C. C. "The Evolution of a Financier in the Ancient Near East." *JNES* 2 (1943): 295–301.

———. "The Foundry of the Second Temple at Jerusalem." *JBL* 55 (1936): 247–60.

Tremayne, Archibald. *Records from Erech: Time of Cyrus and Cambyses (538–521 B.C.).* New York: AMS, 1925.

Tuell, Steven S. *The Law of the Temple in Ezekiel 40–48.* HSM 49. Atlanta: Scholars Press, 1992.

Uehlinger, Christoph. "Anthropomorphic Cult Statuary in Iron Age Palestine and the Search for Yahweh's Cult Images." Pages 97–155 in *The Image and The Book.* Edited by Karel van der Toorn. Leuven: Uitgeverij Peeters, 1997.

Vaughn, Andrew G. *Theology, History, and Archaeology in the Chronicler's Account of Hezekiah.* Atlanta: Scholar's Press, 1999.

Vaux, Roland de. *Ancient Israel: Its Life and Institutions.* Translated by John McHugh. Grand Rapids: William B. Eerdmans, 1997.

———. *The Bible and the Ancient Near East.* Translated by Damian McHugh. Garden City, New York: Doubleday, 1971.

Veenhof, Klaas R. "Silver and Credit in Old Assyrian Trade." Pages 55–83 in *Trade and Finance in Ancient Mesopotamia.* Edited by J. G. Dercksen. Leiden: Nederlands Instituut voor het Nabije Oosten, 1999.

Vogelsang, Willem. "Gold from Dardistan: Some Comparative Remarks on the Tribute System in the Extreme Northwest of the Indian Subcontinent." Pages 157–71 in *Le Tribut dans l'Empire Perse: Actes de la Table Ronde de Paris 12–13 Décembre 1986.* Edited by Pierre Briant and Clarisse Herrenschmidt. Travaux de l'Institut d'Études Iraniennes de l'Université de la Sorbonne Nouvelle 13. Paris and Louvain: Peeters, 1989.

Wallinga, Herman T. "Persian Tribute and Delian Tribute." Pages 173–81 in *Le Tribut dans l'Empire Perse: Actes de la Table Ronde de Paris 12–13 Décembre 1986.* Edited by Pierre Briant and Clarisse Herrenschmidt. Travaux de l'Institut d'Études Iraniennes de l'Université de la Sorbonne Nouvelle 13. Paris and Louvain: Peeters, 1989.

Ward, William A. "Temples and Sanctuaries, Egypt." Pages 369–72 in vol. 6 of *Anchor Bible Dictionary*. Edited by David Noel Freedman. 6 vols. New York: Doubleday, 1992.

Waterman, Leroy. *Royal Correspondence of the Assyrian Empire*. Ann Arbor: University of Michigan Press, 1930–36.

Weinberg, Joel P. *The Citizen-Temple Community*. Translated by Daniel Smith-Christopher. JSOTSup 151. Sheffield: Sheffield Academic Press, 1992.

Weinfeld, Moshe. *Social Justice in Ancient Israel and in the Ancient Near East*. Minneapolis: Fortress, 1995.

Weisberg, David B. *Guild Structure and Political Allegiance in Early Achaemenid Mesopotamia*. New Haven: Yale University Press, 1967.

———. "A Neo-Babylonian Temple Report." *JAOS* 87 (1967): 8–12.

———. *Texts from the Time of Nebuchadnezzar*. YOS 17. New Haven: Yale University Press, 1980.

Westbrook, Raymond. "Conclusions." Pages 327–40 in *Security for Debt in Ancient Near Eastern Law*. Edited by Raymond Westbrook and Richard Jasnow. Leiden: Brill, 2001.

———. "The Old Babylonian Period." Pages 63–92 in *Security for Debt in Ancient Near Eastern Law*. Edited by Raymond Westbrook and Richard Jasnow. Leiden: Brill, 2001.

Westermann, William Linn. "Warehouses and Trapezite Banking in Antiquity." *Journal of Economic and Business History* 3/1 (November 1930): 30–54.

Weston, J. Fred, and Eugene F. Brigham. *Essentials of Managerial Finance*. New York: Holt, Rinehart and Winston, 1971.

Wiesehöfer, Josef. "Tauta Gar en Atelea: Beobachtungen Zur Abgabenfreiheit Im Achaimenidenreich." Pages 183–91 in *Le Tribut dans l'Empire Perse: Actes de la Table Ronde de Paris 12–13 Décembre 1986*. Edited by Pierre Briant and Clarisse Herrenschmidt. Travaux de l'Institut d'Études Iraniennes de l'Université de la Sorbonne Nouvelle 13. Paris and Louvain: Peeters, 1989.

Willi, Thomas. "Late Persian Judaism and Its Conception of an Integral Israel According to Chronicles: Some Observations on Form and Function of the Genealogy of Judah in 1 Chronicles 2.3–4.23." Pages 146–62 in *Second Temple Studies 2: Temple and Community in the Persian Period*. Edited by Tamara C. Eskenazi and Kent H. Richards. JSOTSup 175. Sheffield: Sheffield Academic Press, 1994.

Williamson, H. G. M. "Review of *The Citizen-Temple Community* by Joel P. Weinberg." *VT* 45 (1995): 574.

Willi-Plein, Ina. "Warum Musste der Zweite Tempel Gebaut Werden?" Pages 57–73 in *Gemeinde Ohne Tempel: Community Without Temple*. Edited by Beate Ego, Armin Lange, and Peter Pilhofer. WUNT 118. Tübingen: Mohr/Siebeck, 1999.

Wischnitzer, Mark. "Tithe." Pages 1156–62 in vol. 15 of *Encyclopaedia Judaica*. Jerusalem: Keter, 1972.

Wiseman, D.J. *Chronicles of Chaldaean Kings*. London: British Museum, 1956.

Woolley, L., and M. E. L. Mallowan. *Ur Excavations IX: The Neo-Babylonian and Persian Periods*. London: Skilton, 1962.

Wright, G. Ernest. "The Temple in Palestine-Syria." *BA* 7 (1944): 65–77.

Wright, John W. "Guarding the Gates: 1 Chronicles 26.1–19 and the Roles of Gatekeepers in Chronicles." *JSOT* 48 (1990): 69–81.

Yoffee, Norman. *The Economic Role of the Crown in the Old Babylonian Period*. Malibu: Undena, 1977.

Zaccagnini, Carlo. "Patterns of Mobility among Ancient Near Eastern Craftsmen." *JNES* 42 (1983): 245–64.

———. "Prehistory of the Achaemenid Tributary System." Pages 193–215 in *Le Tribut dans l'Empire Perse: Actes de la Table Ronde de Paris 12–13 Décembre 1986*. Edited by Pierre Briant and Clarisse Herrenschmidt. Travaux de l'Institut d'Études Iraniennes de l'Université de la Sorbonne Nouvelle 13. Paris and Louvain: Peeters, 1989.

Zevit, Ziony. "The Khirbet el-Qôm Inscription Mentioning a Goddess." *BASOR* 255 (1984): 39–47.

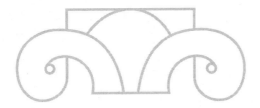

Index of Names and Subjects

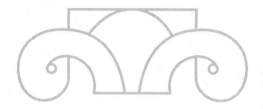

Index of Foreign Words

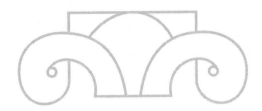

Index of Ancient Sources